TRANSNATIONAL STUDIES IN EAST-WEST RELATIONS

General Editor: W. E. Butler

Studies on Socialist Legal Systems
Faculty of Laws
University College London

ANGLO-POLISH LEGAL ESSAYS

Edited by

W. E. BUTLER

Professor of Comparative Law in the University of London

Transnational Publishers, Inc.
Dobbs Ferry, New York

Library of Congress Cataloging in Publication Data
Main entry under title:

Anglo-Polish legal essays.

(Studies on socialist legal systems) (Transnational studies in East-West relations)
Includes index.
1. Law—Poland—Addresses, essays, lectures.
2. Law—Great Britain—Addresses, essays, lectures.
I. Butler, William Elliott, 1939- . II. Series.
III. Series: Transnational studies in East-West relations.

LAW	349.41	81-16259
ISBN 0-941320-00-6	344.1	AACR2

Manufactured in the United States of America

CONTENTS

INTERNATIONAL LAW AND COMMERCE

ACKNOWLEDGEMENTS

The 1981 London-Warsaw Legal Colloquium was an extension of an exchange agreement dating from 1977, when the Institute of State and Law of the Polish Academy of Sciences acceded to my request that my Field Course for "Introduction to Socialist Legal Systems," offered as an option in the LL.B. degree, visit Poland in order to see something of Polish legal institutions firsthand. During our 1977 visit, so efficiently and memorably arranged by Professor L. Bar of the Institute, the then Vice-Dean of the Faculty of Law and Administration of Warsaw University, Professor J. Rajski, expressed a willingness on behalf of his institution to enter into a reciprocal annual exchange of field courses. Under an inter-faculty agreement these exchanges have given students and staff from both universities an unparalleled opportunity to visit legal institutions and interview officials as an integral part of their comparative legal studies.

In Poland our groups have been privileged to visit the Supreme Court, the Sejm, the State Economic Arbitrazh, the Warsaw Bar Association, the Procuracy, the Ministry of Justice, the editorial board of *Państwo i prawo*, a Warsaw district headquarters of *Solidarność*, the Warsaw City Hall, several units of local government, and the universities of Torun and Lublin, and we are grateful to the countless individuals who have given so generously of their time on our behalf. Our own programmes in England have included visits to the Royal Courts of Justice, Old Bailey, industrial tribunals, Parliament, Messrs. Baker & McKenzie, the Honourable Society of Gray's Inn, the Mary Ward Legal Centre, and Oxford University. To Dr. Bernard Rudden, Professor of Comparative Law at Oxford University, Mr. David Winter, OBE, and Mr. D. Montagu-Scott special thanks are due for extending hospitality to our Polish guests.

I also wish to express my personal appreciation to Lord Lloyd of Hampstead, Quain Professor of Jurisprudence in the University of London and Head of the Department of Laws, to Dean Resich of the Warsaw University Faculty of Law and Administration, and to my colleagues at University College London whose support, both moral and tangible, has been indispensable to the success of the exchange.

For grants to assist with the Field Course and the Legal Colloquium, we are indebted to University College London and to The British Council. Miss Lorely Teulon has typed the volume with her usual unparalleled skill.

W.E.B.

London
September 1981

CONTRIBUTORS

AUSTIN, R.C., LLB (Auckland), Lecturer in Laws, University College London

BUTLER, W.E., AB (American Univ.), JD (Harvard), MA, PhD (Johns Hopkins), LLD (London), Professor of Comparative Law in the University of London

FRANKOWSKI, S., doc. dr hab., Faculty of Law and Administration, Warsaw University

GARLICKI, L., doc. dr hab., Faculty of Law and Administration, Warsaw University

GUEST, S.F.D., BA, LLB (Otago), BLitt (Oxon.), Lecturer in Laws and Sub-Dean, University College London

JAKUBOWSKI, J., prof. dr., Faculty of Law and Administration, Warsaw University

LACEY, Nicola, LLB (London), BCL (Oxon.), Lecturer in Laws, University College London

LEWIS, A.D.E., MA, LLB (Camb.), Lecturer in Laws, University College London

OKOLSKI, J., doc. dr hab., Faculty of Law and Administration, Warsaw University

OLIVER, A. Dawn H., MA (Camb.), Lecturer in Laws, University College London

PIONTEK, E., doc. dr hab., Faculty of Law and Administration, Warsaw University

RIDEOUT, R.W., LLM, PhD (London), Professor of Labour Law in the University of London

SUCHECKI, W., doc. dr hab., Faculty of Law and Administration, Warsaw University

WOŁODKIEWICZ, W., prof. dr., Faculty of Law and Administration, Warsaw University

INTRODUCTION

W. E. Butler

The onset of the 1980s finds the British and Polish legal systems endeavouring to grapple with or respond to economic, social, and political developments of considerable moment in their respective histories. Recent and incipient reforms in Poland have affected the equation of power among the political parties and the State, the legal status and nature of trade unions, the role of the Sejm and its constituent organs, the relationship between Church and State, the functions of the media, among others, and promise to bring fundamental transformations to the role of law in the management of the national economy. The United Kingdom too finds itself reassessing the role of the State vis-à-vis the economy, the relationship of trade unions both to the bargaining relationship between employer and employee and to the party political process at large, the interaction between the courts and matters of public policy, and the subtle but nonetheless very real changes that occur in the distribution of governmental power within a Parliamentary system operating under an unwritten Constitution.

In February-March 1981 a Colloquium was held reciprocally at the Faculty of Law and Administration of Warsaw University (February) and at the Faculty of Laws, University College London (March). Seven members from each Faculty delivered papers on matters of current concern in their respective legal systems in the realm of legal theory, civil law, public law, and international law and commerce. The first inter-university colloquium of its kind in the field of Law between Poland and the United Kingdom, it produced essays of considerable interest and importance which disclosed both startling symmetries between these two very different social orders and regrettable gaps in our respective knowledge of each other's legal system.

Legal theory was perhaps the realm of greatest respective ignorance. Mr. Guest and Mrs. Lacey, each products of Oxford, presented papers discussing some of the finer points of contention among contemporary English legal philosophers. This is a body of literature not available in Eastern European languages, so that both the issues and the contenders are largely unfamiliar to Marxian specialists on the theory of state and law. Professor Suchecki contributed in turn an essay demarcating some of the major developments in twentieth-century Polish legal philosophy with particular reference to recent trends. Although the major premises of the Marxist philosophy of law are now standard fare in most English university jurisprudence courses, the distinctive application and development of these in the Polish context will be new and of great interest to Western students of the subject.

English and Polish law share in considerable measure either the principle or the fiction (depending on one's point of view) that the courts in their respective jurisdictions either do not and/or should not "make" law. Dr. Frankowski treats an element of this perennial issue which will be novel to most common lawyers. Judicial systems employ various techniques to encourage consistency and uniformity in the substance of court decisions; socialist legal systems widely use binding "explanations" or "directives" of various appellations issued by supreme courts to inferior courts as a means of clarifying areas of the law where uncertainty or ambiguity is believed to exist. In the Polish instance, Frankowski argues that the Supreme Court has found itself arrogating the legislator's function by "making" or "altering" law in the guise of explaining or interpreting it. Around the institution of guiding explanations or directives in recent years there has emerged a considerable literature in the socialist legal systems as to whether these are "enactments" which can be considered to be proper "sources of law."

"Civil law' means many things to many people.

Continental jurists are often startled when they ask who teaches "civil law" in an English law faculty to learn that there is no such subject, or if there be such, it treats a foreign legal system. It is refreshing, therefore, that representatives of two families of legal systems which see themselves as distinct from the "civil law" systems of Western continental Europe should explore, in the case of England, an oft-forgotten, and in the instance of Poland, a never-forgotten, link respectively with the civilian Romanist legacy of earlier times.

The classical realm of civil law as a branch of law has come under searching re-examination in Poland as traditional civil law concepts are found wanting conceptually and in practice in a society where national economic planning must be integrated into horizontal contractual relationships in the state sector. Dr. Okolski illuminates the dilemma for Polish draftsmen in the realm of economic contracts, and Professor Jakubowski, for many of the same reasons as well as some peculiar to international commerce, explains the thinking which may see Poland join the handful of socialist legal systems having a separate Code of International Trade Law.

Although the United Kingdom and Poland have profoundly differing legal philosophies and politico-economic orders, in the realm of public law there are recent developments which superficially at least share elements in common.

Mrs. Oliver traces what she deems to be rather basic alterations in the locus of power in Parliament and government, changes accomplished without benefit of constitutional "amendment" or "revision," but nonetheless of a nature which ought to be a matter of genuine concern in a representative democracy. Professor Rideout echoes some of the same concerns in his assessment of the manner in which British governments during the 1970s sought to limit or redirect the capacities of trade unions to exercise their considerable political and economic influence. The emergence in Poland of the *Solidarność* trade union movement has confronted the Polish authorities and public with many similar considerations, albeit in a wholly different context. Dr. Garlicki relates the very considerable impact of these developments, some seemingly extra-constitutional, on Polish constitutional law. Garlicki also touches upon a reform enacted early in 1980 introducing judicial review of the legality of administrative decisions. The Polish system of administrative tribunals is just getting underway and hence it would be premature to evaluate its achievements and failures; inevitably, no doubt, Polish judges will find themselves preoccupied with some of the considerations which exercise the wits of English courts in delimiting the scope of judicial review over "policy" being pursued by government bodies. Mr. Austin examines the current state of the art in his essay on the judicial role in policy review.

The trend internationally toward greater harmonisation, unification, and even integration in economic relations has disposed Polish jurists, as we have noted, to fashion a Code of International Trade Law. On the institutional level, within the framework of the Council of Mutual Economic Assistance (COMECON), there are emerging new types of organisations possessing qualities of both classical inter-state international institutions and of multinational corporations. Their legal status and personality is much debated by jurists in socialist countries; of particular interest to the common lawyer will be the fact that these new types of organisation may be empowered, and in some cases are, to open branches in western countries for the purpose of purchasing or selling goods and services. Dr. Piontek outlines the features of these entities, which he sees as quite unique to COMECON.

TWO THEORIES OF ADJUDICATION

S. F. D. Guest

Two theories of adjudication, both currently debated in the United Kingdom and the United States, are the object of concern here. Each theory has two aspects. Each purports to be descriptive of the way lawyers think, that is, descriptive of the framework in which conceptions of the law operate, although the second theory does not claim that its descriptive aspect represents legal thought in the United Kingdom as accurately as it does legal thought in the United States. Each also purports to be prescriptive in that, if legal thought is not in accordance with the respective descriptions, it *ought* so to be in accordance. The second theory thus regards United Kingdom legal thought as poorer for not accurately matching its descriptive aspect.

This distinction between the descriptive and prescriptive aspects of legal theory is particularly crucial for understanding the first theory. The first theory relies both in its descriptive and prescriptive aspects upon the concept of a legal fact. Law is identified exclusively by reference to fact, in particular that certain members of a community act in a characteristic way. If the members of a community do so act, then the theory is correct descriptively and if the moral reasons offered by the theory justify their acting in this way then the theory is prescriptive as well. (I ignore the sceptic who claims that there are no reasons which, independently of facts, can justify moral conclusions.)

It is important, therefore, to see that the first theory is not to be denied the moral status of being a prescriptive theory merely because it insists that we *ought* to view law as a fact (a paradigm subject for description), for there may be moral reasons for viewing law as fact, and independent, therefore, of morality. For example, Hart justifies his theory, which I have taken as typical of the first theory, on the ground that it serves clarity by distinguishing questions of what it is morally right to do and questions of what is legally valid.[1] If we see these questions as distinct, the moral argument goes, we view the equation with greater clarity and are more likely to come to a morally better conclusion.

Ultimately, of course, this argument rests on the view that our legal obligation to the state is to be determined by factual means. But it should be clear that this does not preclude there being prescriptive moral grounds for the first theory.

To set the two theories in context, another distinction must be drawn between questions arising generally about law, wherever the phenomenon occurs, and those that arise about what, in any particular community, is the law on a particular point as it applies to a particular group of persons. Loosely, the distinction is between the nature of law, as opposed say to custom or morality, and the professional questions within a particular community about law. These questions are not wholly distinct, however, because any theory about the nature of law must include, perhaps implicitly, some theory of adjudication. For example, it seems reasonable to suppose that in distinguishing a theory between law and custom, there must be implicit some account of how particular propositions of law are to be distinguished from particular propositions of custom.

The converse proposition is, however, not so clear. It is not evident that any theory of adjudication, or of the way particular laws apply to particular people, entails a general theory of the nature of law. The ambiguity arises for the following reason: any social theory, that is, a theory about man and the way he acts within a community, will represent a certain tension between

---

1 Paradoxically: what it would be right to do if we did not have obligations to the state and what obligations we have to the state independently of what it is right for us to do.

what happens causally and regularly and what is an adequate explanation of what actually happens. Unlike inanimate objects acting in accordance with the "laws" of science, men make their own choices. Indeed, the possibility of divergent behaviour is logically tied to the concept of laws governing men. Consequently, a theory that explains events is to be preferred to a mere record of events (a causal explanation) because the latter - if it is possible at all - will lack explanatory power. Explanation requires that some things which actually happen will have to be discounted or enhanced in terms of a theory that explains what *significantly* happens.

That significance is a criterion for legal theory is true both for theories about the nature of law and for theories about professional questions. For example, in the former case, international or primitive law, or Nazi law, may be relegated to secondary positions with the prevalent municipal legal systems taking a primary place. In the latter instance, for example, United Kingdom judicial decisions, in which judges are said to have performed a legislative role by deciding on the grounds of policy, might be discounted in terms of a full explanation of what judges generally and significantly do.

However, a special ambiguity arises in regard to the professional question. Because this question is very closely tied to the complex and different practices of each community, it is virtually impossible to give sufficient weight to the requirement of describing what mostly or significantly happens. To generalise from certain instances, for example, adjudication in the United Kingdom and the United States, to a theory about all adjudicative practices would be to abandon the requirement of tension between a record of existing practices and an explanation or interpretation of that record.

On the other hand, there is no reason for us to suppose that a theory of adjudication in particular societies would not be successful merely because it is not a part of general jurisprudence. Indeed, there is no reason to suppose that such a theory of adjudication, while in accordance with the requirement of significance in respect of the United Kingdom and the United States, should not be advanced as a matter of prescription. For example, say that a theory of adjudicative practices in the United Kingdom and the United States centrally employs the idea of a right. The adjudicative practices of other legal systems might not centrally, if at all, employ the idea but, according to the prescriptive aspect of this U.K./ U.S. theory of adjudication, such adjudicative practices should (morally) include that idea. And this might mean not just the inclusion of that idea but a complete readjustment of the adjudicative practices altogether. This prescriptive aspect of such a theory would not purport to interpret or explain non-U.K./U.S. adjudicative practices; on the contrary, it would declare them to be bad, on moral grounds, and for this reason prescribe alternative ways of behaving.

Positivism. Both theories are theories of positivism. The issue is complicated, since often, but wrongly, the second theory is regarded as not a positivist theory merely because it attacks the first theory, which is more widely regarded as a positivist theory. The problem dissolves once it is appreciated that each theory represents a different form of positivism. The salient feature of positivism, in all forms in which it is discussed in contemporary legal philosophy, is that it postulates that questions of legal validity are conceptually distinct from questions of what it is morally right or wrong to do. This, for example, is clearly what Hart views the theory as, both in his seminal *Harvard Law Review* article[2] and later in *The Concept of Law*.[3] This simple and general form of the theory could be called P_1.

---

2 H.L.A. Hart, "Positivism and the Separation of Law and Morals," *Harvard Law Review*, LXXI, (1958), pp. 593-629.

3 Hart, *The Concept of Law* (Oxford, 1961), pp. 181-182.

Another more particular form of positivism exists in Hart's *The Concept of Law*. This form (P_2) separates questions of value (moral or otherwise) from law and, for example, Hart achieves a conceptual distinction between morality and law by declaring that questions of legal validity are to be settled by reference either to the fact of official acceptance that certain propositions are valid rules or by means of a comparison of these propositions with criteria of validity in fact accepted by the officials.

The two forms of positivism are therefore related by logical entailment. The second form of the theory entails the first, given that propositions of morality cannot be identified either by fact or by formal procedures identified ultimately by fact. The reverse entailment does not, however, occur. That is, P_1 does not entail P_2, because it is possible both for P_1 to be true and for P_2 to be false. There is nothing in logic which says that there cannot be legal value judgments, in which case it is possible for a theory of law to claim that it separates questions of legal validity from what is morally right or wrong to do and yet not be bound in logic to claim that that separation is achieved by a distinction between fact and value.

Hart has not explored this logical possibility in *The Concept of Law*. At times, in particular in Chapter VII, he talks as though legal value propositions existed, but he then reiterates in Chapter IX that positivism is the theory that separates legal questions from moral questions. The reason Hart has not explored the possibility is simply that his conception of positivism is supported by largely implicit, but at times explicit, references to the moral preference he has for clarity. The force of the argument is: for clarity in dealing with matters of morality, distinguish between law and morality, and this is best achieved (that is, achieves the most clarity) by locating legal matters in the realm of fact or factually determined procedures. Hart's primary interest is therefore to achieve a separation between law and morality and the fact that his theory is a P_2 theory as well is only a means to this end.

Two points arise. First, I am not here concerned to raise the question of what constitutes a "fact" or "formal identification" in the law, for I regard that question as too sceptical. I just accept that there are, in the law, facts, or to put in several of its guises, objectively verifiable legal truths, legally demonstrable truths, or non-controversial legal propositions. Solicitors deal with such facts constantly, and the concept of fact with which legal theory must deal is just this one. There are rules, such as, for example, those contained in s. 9 of the Wills Act, 1837, which are accepted as uncontroversial rules of the United Kingdom legal system (*e.g.*, in clearly specified circumstances, two witnesses are required for a will).

The second point is that I assume that "fact" and "value" exist in different categories of thought. Again, I need refer only to the fact that lawyers distinguish such categories, but the sceptic who is not willing to make the assumption must turn his efforts away from legal philosophy and first address the general and famous philosophical proposition that you cannot derive an "ought" from an "is".

The First Theory: P_1 and P_2 (Hart). This is the theory generally accepted by lawyers in the United Kingdom, and to some extent by lawyers in the United States. It is simply that law and morality are distinguished because law can only be identified by fact. Austin, for example, had such a theory. Law, he said, consisted of the sovereign's commands (supplying, of course, extended definitions of both sovereignty and command):

$$L \equiv SC$$

Employing the distinction, to which I earlier referred, between professional questions and questions about nature, the answer to the professional question of "what is the law (on A) in a particular country (X) ?" in Austin's terms is, simply, that you look for the sovereign of X and find out what he has commanded.

$$L_{AX} \equiv S_X C_A$$

Hart's theory is more sophisticated because of his analysis of legal rules into two main types; the primary rules (like Austin's commands) which impose duties, and the secondary rules which confer powers, the most relevant one here being the power (or capacity) of identifying law by means of a rule of recognition. Thus, Hart's answer to the question of the nature of law is:

$$L \equiv P/S$$ (the union of primary and secondary rules)

and his answer to the professional question is

$$L_{AX} \equiv A^{R/R_X}$$ (A is recognised by a rule of recognition in X)

A full understanding of the P_1P_2 theory of adjudication requires a consideration of the concept of a controversial - or, as it is called by Dworkin - a hard, case. This is a situation where it is uncertain what the law is or ought to be. For example, is a skateboard a vehicle for the purpose of a regulation denying vehicles access to the park ? Is duress a defence to murder in the first degree ? Is foresight of a probability of death, as opposed to foresight of a high probability, sufficient malice for murder ? These sorts of questions have always been regarded by lawyers as controversial legal questions inasmuch as sensible and rational arguments may be put up on either side for or against the truth of the propositions.

Because Hart's theory is a P_2 theory as well, since what the true proposition of law is in these cases cannot be identified factually (or demonstrably or objectively), there *is* no true or false proposition of law nor indeed any proposition of law at all. The P_1P_2's answer in such circumstances is that in hard cases there is no law at all. And to say that there is no law in these cases is not to say that the action is permitted, because that itself is a proposition of law; rather, it is to say that the action is neither permitted nor prohibited.

Symbolically, the law on A in X is that which has been posited factually (or demonstrably, or objectively) in X:

$$\text{(i)} \quad L_{AX} \equiv F_{AX}$$

$$\text{and} \quad \text{(ii)} \quad \sim F_{AX} \equiv \sim L_{AX}$$

$$\text{and} \quad \text{(iii)} \quad \sim F_{AX} \not\equiv L_{\sim AX}$$

Point (iii) is an essential part of the P_1P_2 theory because law is identified by fact. If $\sim F_{AX}$ were logically equivalent to $L_{\sim AX}$, then the proposition of law, $\sim A$, would have been identified by a non-fact, and this contradicts the theory.

Here a slight modification to the P_1P_2 theory could be achieved. One might say that under the theory there *is* law in hard cases but that it lacks a standard truth value (truth or falsity) or possesses a third value. This would lead to difficulties in practical reasoning (what would the consequences be of such a decision ?). Logical difficulties also would arise with the concept of adjudication where a decision with a clearly defined consequence is required. We need not pursue the point, since no positivist to my knowledge has claimed the third value as an inherent part of his theory.

Certain consequences flow from the P_1P_2 theory. The first is that judges do not "find" the law in hard cases, because it is not there to be found, but rather create new law. The second, following from this, is that when a judge makes a decision about what the law ought to be and applies that decision to the parties before him, as is the virtually universal practice, the law is being applied retrospectively. A third is that, in legal systems where there is official acceptance of the doctrine of the separation of powers, deriving from Montesquieu, and under which judges are not supposed to create law, there is an inconsistency if judges are, as the P_1P_2 theory entails, creating law.

The first and second consequences are consequences that the P_1P_2 theory has for general jurisprudence, but the third only applies to particular systems.

The Second Theory. P_1 and non-P_2 (Dworkin). Dworkin's theory attacks and supplants the P_1P_2 theory. His is a P_1 theory only, and therefore one which allows for non-moral legal value propositions of law. There are, he says, value legal propositions, for example, principles, within legal systems. There is talk of rights and duties in the law within legal systems even though such rights and duties cannot be identified factually. In the United Kingdom and United States legal systems lawyers use a concept of fairness that is inconsistent with retrospective legislation and a concept of a division of legislative and adjudicative powers that is inconsistent with judges creating new law.

Apart from this, an argument has to be produced to deny truth and falsity as predicable of value propositions. The argument generally can be asserted as the demonstrability thesis:

> Propositions are true or false *iff* they can be demonstrated to be true or false.

We could perhaps assert this as being true for propositions of morality since there are no demonstrably true propositions of morality. But the case is less strong for law, where there are demonstrably true propositions, for example, that in specified circumstances, two witnesses are required for a will. Indeed, it is of practical importance for legal thought that there be demonstrably true and false propositions of law. In law there is, so to speak, something to go from. In arguing about whether duress extends to first degree murder, we have the demonstrably true propositions that Privy Council decisions on the matter do not bind English courts, that duress extends to second degree murder, that first degree and second degree murder are distinguished on the ground that the first degree murderer brings about the immediate cause of death, and so on. Looking at the structure of legal argument it seems incorrect - and unnecessary - to say that the proposition that duress extends to first degree is neither true nor false.

Seeming incorrect might not be enough; it may be an embedded mistake which must be extracted. But it is unclear why it would be a mistake since it is not clear what would count as a mistake in this context. Would, for example, some practical purpose be served by not talking of the truth and falsity of non-demonstrably true or false propositions of law ? Certainly, in capturing and even prescribing the logic of adjudication there seems good reason for assuming the demonstrability thesis to be false.

The P_1 theory requires a connexion between demonstrably true propositions of law and non-demonstrably true propositions of law. This is achieved by reference to the justification of the demonstrably true propositions and using these as justifications for the non-demonstrably true propositions. Simply, a non-demonstrable proposition of law is a true proposition of law if it is consistent with the justification of the demonstrable propositions of law. We can use the rule of recognition thesis to make the link clearer: the true proposition of law is the one consistent with the theory justifying the rule of recognition.

Symbolically,

(iv) $L_{AX} \equiv A^{R/R_X}$ *or* A is consistent with the theory justifying the R/R_X

or, more generally,

(v) $L_{AX} \equiv F_{AX}$ *or* A is consistent with the theory justifying the facts of professional practice in X.

This aspect of the P_1 theory improves, in my view, on the P_1P_2 theory because it gives general sense to the concept of adjudication in any legal system. This aspect of the P_1 theory also is part of general jurisprudence. Dworkin's theory improves on Hart's theory by giving sense to the question "what is the law in particular legal systems ?". It makes the reasonable assertion that all legal systems are informed by some theory that justifies the settled practices of the system.

The Rights Thesis. But Dworkin's theory is also a theory of rights. Such a theory appears also to be part of his general claim and, as argued above, it fails as a theory of general jurisprudence because it is descriptively particular to some Western legal systems.

The rights theory is connected to claim (iv) in the following way: the theory justifying the R/R in, say, the United Kingdom/United States legal system is a theory of democracy which, in turn, is based on respect for an individual's views about his own life (or, crudely, his dignity).

Sometimes decisions have to be justified in terms of the good of society as a whole, itself a requirement of democracy, without reference to particular individuals (for example, increasing the money supply, or raising the gross national product). Sometimes, on the other hand, decisions have to be justified in terms of the good of individuals themselves (for example, protecting an individual against the advance of another). Sometimes these two sorts of justification conflict, and there are, of course, classic examples.

Resolution of such conflicts, under Dworkin's rights theory, must always be in terms of the justifications that allow these conflicts to arise. The conflicts arise precisely because weight is placed on the justification in terms of the good of the individual himself; consequently, weight must be given to this justification and can not be ignored. Thus, an unindividuated justification in the public good may be paramount when it is consistent with respect for individual dignity. For example, a policy of reverse discrimination may be paramount,[4] or it may be a paramount unindividuated justification to run a motorway through A's land where A's land has been singled out for no other reason than that was the best place and A has been compensated. And there may be a paramount individuated justification for a decision to prevent planners from running a motorway through A's land if the only unindividuated justification that could be provided was that it would be economically more efficient to do so because A was less likely through financial reasons to protest. Or, an unindividuated justification for decreasing the level of violence by executing hostages may not be paramount because it means treating individuals randomly, although the execution of the perpetrators may be a paramount unindividuated justification. (We can, therefore, use the distinctions themselves to reconcile deterrence and retribution as justifications.)

All this, of course, is not to say that any of the decisions are justified in absolute moral terms; it is to say, rather, that given the distinction between individuated and unindividuated justifications, certain logical consequences follow which may be paramount without logical contradiction. Someone who accepts that the distinction holds must accept in consistency that unindividuated justifications are restrained by respect for individual dignity. If he does not, he merely views individuated justifications as a sub-class of unindividuated justifications.

Unindividuated justifications Dworkin calls policy arguments, and individuated justifications are called arguments of principle. There is no doubt in my view that lawyers in the United Kingdom and the United States employ these two sorts of argument. Further, Dworkin asserts, policy arguments are about goals, and arguments of principle are about rights. The democratic theory,

---

4 See Dworkin, *Taking Rights Seriously* (London, 1977), Ch. 9.

based on the dignity of the individual, informs the UK/US legal system. It requires that new decisions about goals and rights be made by an elected and responsible body. However, decisions about existing rights must be protected from the elected body just because that body may make decisions about goals and the temptation may be to ignore individuated justifications altogether. Since the theory of democracy requires such a distinction, it is consistent, and indeed in practice necessary, for there to be a politically insulated institution to determine existing rights. Since decisions about existing rights arise just because they concern individuals, it is consistent with democratic theory that such institutions (the courts) be politically insulated and ignore unindividuated justifications (although certain individuated decisions such as respecting Parliamentary enactments may appear to be unindividuated because the enactment itself was justified on an unindividuated basis).

All this holds whether or not one accepts the central moral idea of the dignity of the individual. The arguments that are therefore relevant to a criticism of Dworkin's P_1 theory should be directed toward the following propositions:

(1) that it does not follow from the central moral idea of the dignity of the individual that there are some unjustifiable unindividuated decisions that enhance the public good and, consequently, that there is no important distinction to be drawn between arguments about rights and arguments about goals;

or (2) even if there were such a distinction, it is not reflected in the democratic theory outlined above,

or (3) even if it were reflected in the theory outlined, that theory does not inform the United Kingdom/United States legal system.

Apart from this, one could accept both that the P_1 theory (that law and morality are conceptually distinct) *and* morally approve of the democratic theory that informs the United Kingdom/ United States legal system. This is what Dworkin does. So it would be wrong to say that because he morally approves of a legal system which requires justification in terms of rights, he does not have a P_1 theory (or that he has a "natural law" theory as some of his critics claim by virtue of the *non sequitur* that $\sim P_1$ is equivalent to a natural law theory). It is simply that Dworkin approves of the theory that he claims informs the United Kingdom/United States legal system and that he wants to see it continue to work because he holds the idea of a right as centrally important.

However, as has been pointed out, the particular theory that informs the United Kingdom/ United States legal system, whether or not any particular person morally accepts it, is particular to that system (and several others) and it is insufficient, at any rate descriptively, to be regarded as a part of general jurisprudence. For example, it is clear that such a theory does not inform the socialist legal system, although that is not, of course, to say that it should not.

Conclusion

It is my contention that Hart's theory is a universal descriptive and prescriptive P_1P_2 theory and that Dworkin's theory is a particular descriptive and universal prescriptive $P_1{\sim}P_2$ theory.

THE PLACE OF THE DESTINCTION BETWEEN MOMENTARY AND NON-MOMENTARY LEGAL SYSTEMS IN LEGAL ANALYSIS

N. Lacey

The present paper explores a suggestion made by J.W. Harris in his recent book *Law and Legal Science*,[1] to the effect that the widely debated distinction between rules and principles, drawn by Professor R.M. Dworkin,[2] derives not "from a difference in logical type between the sentences expressing them, but from a difference in logical type between the systems of which they are members".[3] Currently valid rules, Harris asserts, belong to momentary systems: principles, policies, and other weight-bearing devices belong to non-momentary systems. We concentrate here upon the distinction between momentary and non-momentary legal systems and their place in legal theory.

Momentary and Non-Momentary Legal Systems

The distinction between momentary and non-momentary legal systems was first drawn by J. Raz in *The Concept of a Legal System*,[4] and has since been used not only by Harris but also by J.M. Finnis.[5] A momentary system, according to Raz, is the set of all the laws of one system valid at any

1 J.H. Harris, *Law and Legal Science* (Oxford, 1979).

2 R.M. Dworkin, "Is Law a System of Rules ?," reprinted as "The Model of Rules 1," in *id., Taking Rights Seriously* (London, 1977). The distinction is used and further developed during the course of his book, notably in chapters 3 and 4.

3 Harris, note 1 above, pp. 66-67.

4 J. Raz, *The Concept of a Legal System* (Oxford, 1970); see, for example, pp. 34-35, 186-189.

5 J.M. Finnis, "Revolutions and Continuity of Law," in A.W.B. Simpson (ed.), *Oxford Essays in Jurisprudence* (2d series; Oxford, 1973).

particular moment: each momentary system belongs to a non-momentary system, and different momentary systems can overlap in content, be identical or be entirely different, yet still be members of the same non-momentary system. Here we might drawn an analogy between this distinction and one familiar to all of us in the course of our everyday lives. We might liken the non-momentary system to a cinema film, and the momentary system to each individual frame of the film. As we watch the film, we can only fully understand and appreciate it when we are aware of elements which run through the entire film, such as character development and plot: but nevertheless, at any one moment, all that exists of the film show is any one individual frame, clearly identifiable and vital to the continuity of the film.

The momentary/non-momentary distinction was used by Raz to illustrate the limitations of the accounts of law given by Austin and Kelsen.[6] In his representation of law as the commands of a sovereign, a political superior whom his subjects habitually obey, Austin only explains the existence of a series of momentary systems, and not the continuity of a legal system, that is, the existence of a non-momentary system, despite changes in the sovereign. Austin's theory might account for an intermediate, periodic system, continuous through the life of one sovereign, but this does not undermine Raz's criticism. For, as we shall see below, such a periodic system is not equivalent to a fully-fledged non-momentary system, nor could Austin's notion of tacit acceptance account satisfactorily for the place of laws of previous sovereigns in the periodic systems of later sovereigns.[7]

Kelsen's theory of the basic norm partially overcomes the problems encountered in Austin's

---

6 Raz, note 4 above, pp. 34-35, 186-189.

7 For detailed criticisms of this aspect of Austin's theory, see Raz, note 4 above, pp. 33-35, and H.L.A. Hart, *The Concept of Law* (Oxford, 1961), chapter 4.

theory by substituting obedience to laws for obedience to a person, but it commits Kelsen to the view that no two momentary systems containing different original laws, or *grundnorms*, can belong to the same non-momentary system. This precludes Kelsen from giving an explanation of the gradual emergence of a new ultimate law-creating force, unauthorised by the basic norm of that system, such as the emergence of precedent in the English non-momentary system, except in terms of discontinuity of that system. It also commits him to the view that the legal systems of colonies granted independence are yet continuous with the systems of their parent states.[8] Kelsen's theory too, then, is shown to be unsatisfactory when scrutinised in the light of the momentary/non-momentary distinction.

In considering the question of the identity of legal systems, Raz himself is primarily concerned with criteria for the identification of momentary systems, and the principle of authoritative recognition which he identifies is that a momentary system contains all, and only all, the laws recognised by the primary law-applying organs which it institutes.[9] He suggests that the criteria for identification of non-momentary systems, that is, those which account for the continuity of law, comprise more than just constitutional continuity and homogeneity of content, but also the "complex forms of social life, such as religion, states, régimes, tribes, etc.".[10] To produce a theory of non-momentary systems of law, jurisprudence alone will not suffice; we must have recourse to other social sciences as well. Raz suggests that the study of only momentary systems may be a compromise,[11] and the true nature of law may only be revealed by a study of the legal system

8 Raz, *The Authority of Law* (Oxford, 1979), pp. 127-129.

9 Raz, note 4 above, p. 192.

10 *Ibid.*, pp. 188-189; also, see Harris, note 1 above, pp. 23, 171.

11 *Ibid.*, p. 189.

"in its fullest sense". Indeed, he has since extended the boundaries of his inquiry, for he has published essays on matters clearly falling outside the strict province of the momentary system, for example, on "The Functions of Law".[12]

The preoccupation of analytical jurists with the momentary system in isolation from its non-momentary system, and hence with theories of discontinuity, is the subject of the paper in which Finnis first used this distinction.[13] Finnis, like Raz, comes to the conclusion that the question of the identity of the non-momentary system can only be analysed in terms of other social sciences as well as jurisprudence, and he points out that these other sciences were long ago identified by Aristotle as history and ethics.[14] Finnis is even more sympathetic to the need for such an integrated analysis than is Raz: he describes questions such as "What is the relevant society to which I owe allegiance ?" and "With whose collective debts am I concerned ?" as "germane to jurisprudence",[15] and as being characterised by the analysis of the "internal attitude" developed by Professor H.L.A. Hart.[16] Finnis's concern to explore the nature of law in "its fullest sense" is clearly illustrated by his recent book,[17] which integrates the study of questions about the nature of law with ones about ethics, theology, history and politics.

For the sake of completeness, we shall refer to two other analyses which might be taken to be using a distinction approximating to the momentary/non-momentary one. First, Kelsen distinguishes

---

12 Raz, note 8 above, chapter 9.

13 Finnis, note 5 above.

14 *Ibid.*, pp. 71-72.

15 *Ibid.*, p. 74.

16 Hart, note 7 above, pp. 55ff., 97ff.

17 Finnis, *Natural Law and Natural Rights* (Oxford, 1980).

between static and dynamic systems.[18] Static systems are represented as those containing norms valid by virtue of their contents: their norms have an inherent appeal because they are derivable from the basic norm and from one another by the intellectual operation of inference from the general to the particular. Morality is therefore, in Kelsen's terms, a static system. Dynamic systems are those containing norms valid by virtue of having been created in accordance with the procedure established, or under authority delegated by, a fundamental norm, and allowing for the creation of further norms in the same way. Thus, according to Kelsen, the legal system is a dynamic one, though it may have static aspects.[19]

However, at one point,[20] Kelsen refers to a static theory of law, one which is concerned with the legal norms already created, applied or obeyed by acts of human behaviour, thus describing the law as a system of valid norms; the law "in a state of rest".[21] Dynamic theories, on the other hand, are concerned with *acts* of creation and application, with the *process* whereby the law is created and applied; "the law in motion".[22] Kelsen's use of the words "static" and "dynamic" to apply both to types of system and types of theory is rather confusing, for there is no correlation between Kelsen's dynamic systems and Raz's non-momentary, or between Kelsen's static and Raz's momentary systems, despite the similarity of terminology. The distinction drawn by Kelsen is not, as Raz's is, about the temporal nature of the two types of system, but about the "mode of existence" (or validity) of the norms they contain, and about the genetic structural relationship between those

---

18 H. Kelsen, *General Theory of Law and State* (Cambridge, Mass., 1946), pp. 112-114.

19 Kelsen, *The Pure Theory of Law* (London, 1967), p. 197.

20 *Ibid.*, p. 70.

21 *Ibid.*, p. 70.

22 *Ibid.*, p. 70.

norms.

The expressions "the law in a state of rest" and "in motion", on the other hand, applied by Kelsen to static and dynamic *theories*, are suggestive of Raz's momentary/non-momentary distinction; but we must now allow ourselves to be misled by too literal a construal of what is clearly intended as a metaphor. In what sense could a rule, for instance, ever be said to be "in motion" or "at rest" ? At this point we should be careful to distinguish inquiries into the content of law, or its operative structure, and inquiries concerned with its creation, or genetic structure.[23] A theory which focuses on the momentary system is indeed concerned with the law "in a state of rest", that is, with the *content* of the present law, rather than with its method of creation, or the extent of or reasons for its endurance through time. But, contrary to the implication of Kelsen's metaphor, both his static *and* dynamic theories are concerned with the *content*, and not the creation, of the *momentary* system. Each momentary system can be represented in a dynamic or a static way: the two types of theory are interchangeable in respect of any one momentary system. This clearly sets Kelsen's distinction apart from Raz's momentary/non-momentary classification, theories in respect of those two systems not being intertranslatable in any sense. As Raz has explained,[24] Kelsen's static and dynamic points of view are representative of two different and alternative principles of individuation of norms: the static principle represents every law as a norm imposing a duty by stipulating a sanction; the dynamic allows for norms conferring legislative powers as well. The two types of theory are different ways of representing the *same*, not different, legal systems. Thus the type of theory on which an account concentrates is a function of the type of theory the theorist intends to produce: dynamic and static theories are merely different recon-

---

23 Raz, note 4 above, pp. 184-185, p. 184, n. 1.

24 *Ibid.*, pp. 110-114.

structions of the same phenomena, engineered to suit the purposes of the theorist.

The correlation between types of theory and types of system is also suggested by our final momentary/non-momentary distinction: that drawn by Professor R.W.M. Dias in two articles written before *The Concept of a Legal System*.[25] Dias distinguished between the present time-frame and a continuing one: the present time-frame is used in identifying rules of law for immediate purposes. It is an instantaneous cross-section, identifying what is law at a given moment by means of formal criteria of validity. However, as Dias observes, rules do not really exist in this artificially momentary way, but endure and have effects over periods of time, and a concept of law which explains its truly systematic, continuous nature must include the factors essential to its birth, continuance and functioning. In order to "do justice" according to a rule,[26] for instance in the interpretation of a present-frame rule contained in a statute, we must keep in mind the values and ideals which inspired its creation and development, and the practicalities which affect its working.

It is clear, however, that Dias's analysis is not equivalent to that of Raz, for his continuum, or non-momentary system, consists not so much of past and present legal standards dating back to a major revolution (see below), as of the ideals, reasons, policies, and doctrines which prompt the creation, development, and continued existence of sequences of rules constituting the present time-frames. However, he does speak of both rules and customs as being "part of" the continuum, and his assertion that the question of legal validity applies only to the present time-frame, "validity" of

---

25 R.W.M. Dias, "Legal Politics: Norms Behind the Grundnorm," *Cambridge Law Journal*, XXVI (1968), 233-259; *id.*, "A Temporal Approach Towards a New Natural Law," *Cambridge Law Journal*, XXVIII (1970), 75-95.

26 *Ibid.*, XXVI, p. 255.

the continuum comprising such questions as "Why was this criterion, and is it still, accepted ?",[27] is consistent with the accounts of the distinction given by Raz and Finnis.

Dias correlated the distinction between the present time-frame and the continuum with that between positivist and natural law theories. He contends that there is no conflict between the two, positivism being concerned only with the formulation of criteria identifying what is valid law at any given moment, natural law, such as that of Professor Fuller,[28] being concerned with "durability", the reasons for the continuity of law, moral goodness being a *sine qua non* of continuance.[29] Where positivist theorists such as Kelsen have dealt with questions about the identity of the continuing time-frame, according to Dias,[30] they have mistaken one factor in the explanation of continuity, that of effectiveness, for the entire explanation. Like Raz and Finnis, Dias sees the continuum as being the point at which jurisprudential questions intersect with social, moral, historical, political, and ethical issues.

Even this brief review suggests that the connection Dias has noted indeed exists: Raz, a positivist theorist, identifies the momentary system as his primary focus of interest, as does Harris, whereas Finnis, a natural law theorist, favours an approach taking in the historic legal system. But this is not to say that there is any conceptual reason why positivism and natural law should be concerned solely with one or the other system, or why they should be concerned with different systems, and indeed neither Raz nor Harris claims that a purely momentary analysis is a comprehensive

---

27 *Ibid.*, XXVIII, p. 84.

28 L. Fuller, *The Morality of Law* (rev. ed.; New Haven, 1969).

29 Dias, note 25 above, XXVIII, pp. 77-78.

30 *Ibid.*, XXVI, p. 256; XXVIII, p. 80.

one.[31] Thus while Dias's observations are accurate in respect of contemporary legal theory, due to the particular areas of interest of the theorists concerned, there is no reason to suppose that some future analysis, whether positivist or natural law, could not account for both these aspects of the phenomenon of law. Indeed, Professor Dworkin might be taken to be claiming that his account achieves just this.

Before turning to Harris's use of this distinction, it will be helpful to clarify the particular temporal point at which a rule becomes part of the momentary system. We may distinguish three significant points of time in the "life" of a rule of law. First, there is the date at which that rule is enacted. A paradigm case is the passing of an Act of Parliament, and there are clearly difficulties in identifying this point in the case of rules which gradually emerge through custom. Second, there is the point at which the temporal sphere of validity of the norm begins, which is not necessarily the same as the date of enactment, as in the case of an Act which states that it will come into effect at some future date. The case of retrospective legislation illuminates the third significant temporal dimension of a rule of law, that relating to the activities which are covered by the rule, which may take place before or after the date of enactment, and before or during the temporal sphere of validity of the rule. When we are describing the content of the momentary system, it is clearly important to know which of these three points we have in mind in attributing membership of that current system to a given standard. In Raz's case (as for Harris) it is the second of the points I have enumerated at which a standard attains that status, though in explaining the reasons for, and in justifying the content of the momentary system, we must look beyond that point to times before and after it.

The accepted practice of retroactive legislation in many jurisdictions poses a problem for the

---

31 Note 4 above, p. 189; note 1 above, pp. 112-115.

description of the content of momentary legal systems (as do overruling decisions of the courts if a declaratory theory of adjudication is accepted),[32] for a description of the present momentary system, though complete, will be rendered useless by later retroactive changes in the law. Although as a matter of logic a later description of that momentary system would still exclude a retroactive law, since the momentary system only focuses on the second temporal period, what would be the point of such a description, either current or later, if it could only give us an incomplete account of the way in which our actions will be classified by the law ? We *could* include the retroactive law in a *later* description of a prior momentary system by conflating the second and third temporal dimensions of legal rules, that is, by saying that the temporal sphere of validity of a law coincides with the period during which all the acts which it covers may take place, but this, it is submitted, would be an unnecessarily artificial account. For it would result in our having to say that the particular act covered was always illegal, that is, that it had that same legal status according to the successive momentary systems current during the third temporal period. If we were to accept this, we could never say with certainty what was the legal status of, for example, my doing X now: this could only be determined at the end of the non-momentary system, for a retroactive law might always be passed applicable to X.[33] A better analysis is that my doing X now *is* legally permitted, but that a future retroactive statute outlawing that act would mean that my past act would be interpreted in a legally different way, that is, it would be understood as illegal,[34] and result in some legal sanction being visited upon me. Thus,

32 S.R. Munzer, "Retroactive Law," *Journal of Legal Studies*, VI (1977), 375.

33 *Ibid.*, p. 378.

34 *Ibid.*, p. 381.

to adopt Munzer's distinction,[35] my second element consists of the time *during* which a law is valid; my third element consists of the period *for* which a law is valid, that is the time during which all the acts which it covers may take place. I wish to keep these two periods conceptually distinct, reserving the term "valid" for the second element, although the two coincide in the case of ordinary, prospective laws. This analysis, keeping the second and third elements separate, leads to the conclusion that where there is the possibility of retroactive legislation (objectionable though that may be on other grounds), the description of the momentary legal system is of limited utility.

Before moving on to Harris's use of the distinction, let us review the position advanced in relation to each of the phenomena:

Momentary Legal System: a timeslice or snapshot of the legal system, comprising all the legal standards valid by reference to the criteria of recognition of the system at any given moment.

Non-momentary Legal System: the complete body of all legal standards, currently valid, obsolete and repealed, reaching back all the way to the last "revolution" (in the sense of an event so serious in terms of its political, legal, religious, social or cultural consequences, or a combination of them, that the legal system after it cannot be said to be the same system as before),[36] its continuous existence being fully explicable only in terms of its historical, political and social context. The non-momentary system is, in one sense, our legal heritage.

The Distinction Drawn by Harris between Momentary and Non-Momentary Legal Systems

According to Harris, the momentary legal system consists of all the currently valid laws of a

35 *Ibid.*, p. 386.

36 Finnis, note 5 above, p. 73.

given community:[37] in this sense, the legal system contains only rules of the pure-norm variety, related to each other by the four principles of exclusion, subsumption, derogation, and non-contradiction.[38] These four structural principles are postulated by legal scientists in their reconstruction of the legal system for the purposes of descriptive legal science. In carrying out its primary task, that of describing existing legal duties, legal science focuses its attention on the momentary system. The four principles, which construct the body of legal rules into a normative field of meaning in which legal science presupposes a determinate number of independent legislative sources, makes hierarchical connections between rules originating in inferior and superior sources, rejects rules which conflict with rules originating in superior sources, and rejects the possibility of describing a legal system in such a way that one could affirm both the existence and the non-existence of a duty covering the same act-situation on the same occasion, are referred to by Harris as "the rule-systematising logic of legal science".[39] The constituents of the momentary system have the normative function of describing existing legal duties, and are valid according to Harris's first or second conceptions of validity, that is, by virtue of conformity to a particular higher rule, or as a consistent part of a legal normative field of meaning.[40]

Harris's non-momentary legal system consists of a set of paper rules and other choice-guidance devices, "a historical congeries of rules, principles, policies, doctrines and maxims, forming part of an official tradition",[41] to which the four structural principles do not apply. The legal

---

37 See Harris, note 1 above, pp. 11, 111.

38 *Ibid.*, p. 10.

39 *Ibid.*, p. 10.

40 *Ibid.*, p. 107.

41 *Ibid.*, p. 12.

system in this sense is the focus of interest of legal science in exercising its critical function, and its various constituents are united by their common normative function: they all have some critical, explanatory or predictive role in relation to the rules of the momentary system at any given time, influencing, explaining, or predicting the developments from one momentary system to another. The constituents of the non-momentary system can only be valid by reference to Harris's third or fourth conceptions of validity, that is, by virtue of their correspondence with social reality, or by some inherent claim to fulfilment.[42] This distinction in terms of the conception of validity involved is a significant one, particularly in the light of Kelsen's view of validity as the specific mode of existence of norms.[43] Members of momentary and non-momentary legal systems are therefore distinguished not only by their normative function but also by their specific existence: the distinction is thus similar to Dworkin's argument distinguishing rules from principles according to their differing modes of existence and functions in legal decision-making.

So Harris, like Raz, identifies the two types, or senses, of legal system as reflecting different areas of scientific interest and inquiry, but he goes further than Raz in specifically designating one as being solely of descriptive, the other of solely critical, significance. This is reminiscent of Dias's assimilation of momentary systems with positivist, descriptive theories, and non-momentary systems with natural law, justificatory theories of law, and the same criticisms offered earlier can be applied here.[44] But we may be able to understand Harris's point more clearly if we consider the possibility that the distinction

---

42 *Ibid.*, p. 107.

43 Kelsen, note 19 above, p. 10.

44 Dias, note 25 above, XXVIII, p. 79. Contrary to the implications of Dias's comments, Fuller's account purports to be both normative *and* descriptive.

which he draws between momentary and non-momentary systems is not the same one as that drawn by Raz. What evidence is there for such an interpretation ? First, Harris's distinction draws very little, if at all, upon the difference in temporal nature between the two types of legal system. Indeed, his conception of the non-momentary system is actually a momentary one: it consists of all the standards which have critical, explanatory, or predictive normative functions in relation to the rules of the momentary system at any given time. To put the point in another way, for Raz, Harris's third conception of validity as applied to members of the non-momentary system would include standards which had corresponded to social reality at some time in the past history of the system, whereas for Harris, that correspondence must be actual. Thus, principles, maxims, and other standards which stretch so far back in time that they now have no further normative function to perform in relation to the current legal rules are no longer members of Harris's non-momentary system. That system is thus in no sense a legal heritage, and in hardly any sense historic; it is merely a collection of second order standards existing in the legal institution at the same moment as any one momentary system.

Second, Harris's momentary system is not a subset of his non-momentary system, whereas Raz's is. In the case of Raz's distinction, it would be accurate to say that each momentary system *belongs* to a non-momentary system, but this is not true for Harris's distinction. For in his case, the rules of the momentary system need not necessarily ever be members of a non-momentary system: the two types of system consist of standards with different types of normative function, and if a rule never has any such critical, predictive, or explanatory function in relation to any *other* rule, it will never join the ranks of the non-momentary order. Similarly, we can invert this argument to show that there may be rules which belong to the non-momentary system, by virtue of their functions in relation to the momentary system, but which never become part of any momentary system since they are never constitutive of any existing legal duties.

Thus it seems that Harris's use of Raz's terminology has been misleading, for the distinction he has in mind is a different one, and depends on the task of legal science in question, as exemplified by the normative functions of and the conception of validity appropriate to the members of the system being referred to. It might be thought that Harris's distinction is closer to Kelsen's distinction between static and dynamic systems than to Raz's. Harris's momentary systems, like Kelsen's dynamic ones, consist of norms valid by virtue of their source and mode of creation; non-momentary systems, like static ones, consist of standards valid by virtue of their content (which gives them a certain role to play in relation to the momentary system). The analogy, however, would be misleading, since Kelsen never claimed that his dynamic systems were governed by all of Harris's four structural principles, and Harris's choice of words so opposed to Kelsen's in their *prima facie* purport (dynamic/momentary, static/non-momentary) suggests that he did not have Kelsen's distinction in mind in framing his own. Nor has Harris's distinction anything to do with Kelsen's distinction between static and dynamic theories of law, principles of individuation forming no part of Harris's distinction. A rule, for Harris, is a norm individuated in the same way whether it belongs to a momentary system, a non-momentary one, or both. As we saw above, both Kelsen's static and dynamic points of view apply to what is in Harris's view a momentary system, and Harris rejects both of these principles of individuation himself.[45]

45 Harris, note 1 above, pp. 20-21, 102-106.

Contribution of Raz's and Harris's Momentary/ Non-Momentary Distinctions to the Theory of Legal System

The utility of each distinction, it is submitted, is considerable, despite the danger of speaking of the momentary system as if it were a real entity with a life of its own independent of its non-momentary system in Raz's sense. Both Harris's and Raz's momentary systems are useful concepts in that they exemplify the area of legal standards which can be clearly identified and applied in the majority of cases, and can be used with a high degree of certainty as guides to action by citizens (although Raz's momentary system is to be preferred to Harris's because of its wider scope, in that it, unlike Harris's, can encompass generalised and provisional legal rules, the results of inadequate or imprecise source-rules).

The momentary system consists, in a sense, of the "central case" of legal standards: these standards allow us and others to ascertain our legal position, in most circumstances, at any given moment. In terms of adjudication, where the judge acts as legal scientist, this descriptive function can be carried out by the judge where the facts before him fall directly under a rule which is part of the current momentary system. Harris's descriptive function thus captures an important aspect of rule-application, to which the word "momentary" is quite appropriate. This is well portrayed by Honoré[46] in a discussion of the rule in *Rylands* v. *Fletcher*.[47] Honoré points out that there are certain limitations on the formulation of even common law rules: the rule in question would never be cited as "all occupiers must take precautions ..." despite the fact that that is the point or purpose of the rule. The rule, once ascertained, is applied in a truly "momentary" way,

---

46 A.M. Honoré, "Real Laws," in P.M. Hacker and J. Raz, *Law, Morality and Society* (Oxford, 1977), p. 101.

47 [1868] L.R. 3 H.L. 330.

without backward-looking reference to its mode of creation or forward-looking reference to its purpose. Harris's analysis of the momentary system also captures the sense in which mistaken decisions are law, despite possibly violating standards which are part of his non-momentary system.

But we must now allow ourselves to be deceived into regarding the true nature of law as being revealed merely by sets of momentary systems, by reason of the ease with which we can identify those systems' content. For, not only can we not explain the identity or continuity of non-momentary systems merely in terms of sets of momentary systems, but such an analysis also fails to capture certain important aspects of law as a social institution. Simply, rules have effects over periods of time, and they are enacted or developed with specific or general purposes in mind. In addition, the legal framework as a whole enables us to plan our actions and form plans of life so as not to contravene legality; it guides our behaviour over periods of time; it creates facilities and an environment in which we can pursue, within certain set limits, our conceptions of the good. These fundamental aspects of the nature of law are lost when we look at it only in its momentary sense: the momentary system is a useful, but an artificial, analytical construct with a specific, limited function.

Harris's conception of the non-momentary system has a role to play in capturing what is peculiarly legal about the reasons given for legal decisions when purely "momentary" law runs out or is uncertain or inconclusive. The tests given by Harris and Dworkin for identifying the materials which constitute this "system", and distinguishing them from other moral and social norms, that is, existence in official tradition or institutional history, are vague and difficult to apply. This may well be inevitable, but the task of improving upon those criteria is a worthwhile one, though beyond the scope of this paper.

Raz's conception of the non-momentary system

captures the sense in which law exists and develops over time, yet maintains its identity, and the sense in which that identity is determined by the social context in which the law itself exists, and of which it is a small part in a complex whole. Raz's non-momentary system is, it is submitted, constitutive of the true *systematic* nature of law, for in its historic sense law forms a cohesive if diverse whole with an identity. It is a system in a sense in which the momentary and Harris's non-momentary systems are not, for they are merely more or less artificial collections of standards grouped together in order to perform some specific legal science function, and not true systems at all. All three conceptions of legal system represent, however, legitimate and useful areas of legal scientific inquiry. They may all serve as useful critical tools in legal theory, so long as we are careful to keep the three-fold distinction in mind, and not to confuse Harris's unfortunately mis-named non-momentary system with that of Raz.

THE QUEST FOR VALUE-ORIENTED JURISPRUDENCE

W. Suchecki

Although Marx's pronouncements on the subject of law are rather scanty and date only from his early works, they enable us, nevertheless, to assess generally his attitude toward the Hegelian philosophy of right and law, the concept of the law of nature, the historical school of law in Germany, and the positivist trend in law. Harking back to the heritage of classical German philosophy, Marx stressed the influence that the thought of Kant, Hegel, Fichte, and Schelling had on shaping his outlook. As for the rationalist traditions of the Enlightenment, he was more inclined to associate himself with the ideas of historicism than with the quest for supratemporal principles and values so characteristic of natural law theory. He could not neglect, however, the revolutionary ideas fostered in the early period by the proponents of the law of nature, who effectively contrasted them with the existing legal order. The trend toward change of the existing system was rooted, however, not in an *a priori* accepted ideal model but in the analysis of the extant social reality. The demand for change could not be dictated by a subjective voluntarist aspiration of progressive social forces; the opportunity for change to materialise depended on the objective process of social development. This was reflected in his assertion that "no social order is ever destroyed before the productive forces for which it is sufficient have been developed, and new superior relations of production never replace older ones before the material conditions for their existence have matured within the framework of the old society."[1]

It is difficult to ascertain whether the

1 "Preface to a Contribution to the Critique of Political Economy," in *Karl Marx Early Writings* (New York, 1975), p. 426.

criticism of the existing system, of the legal order and particular provisions of law, supports the law of nature approach. In his criticism of the views of Savigny, Puchta, and Hugo, that is, of the idea of *Volksgeist*, Marx followed a line of reasoning similar to that of the historical school in Germany. His argument that the legislator does not invent laws but only formulates them, gives verbal expression in positive enactments to the internal laws of customary relationships,[2] cannot be divorced from his views on the correlation between the meaning of law and institutions of law and the material conditions that go into the making of the social existence of man.

Since there is a great deal of misunderstanding on this score, it is worthwhile to recall what Engels had to say on the question of the relationship existing between the economic base and the superstructure in his letter to Starkenburg: "It is not that the economic situation is the only cause, that it alone is the sole active factor, whereas everything else is just a passive effect. To the contrary, an interaction takes place here on the basis of economic necessity which in the last instance always paves the way for itself."[3] It is to be noted that relationships on a macrosociological scale are involved here. It is that scale which determines both the scope of verifiability of objective regularities, as reflected in social consciousness, and the possibility of predicting social phenomena. In this context, the question arises as to how the relative independence of jurisprudence and ideology in general should be understood. Engels' view: "we do not recognise an independent development of various

---

2 K. Marx and F. Engels, *Selected Works* (Warsaw, 1949), I, p. 179. Similarly, in "A Contribution to the Critique of Hegelian Philosophy of Right," note 1 above, p. 314, where he observed: "The legislative authority does not make laws, only discovers and formulates them."

3 *Ibid.*, II, p. 482.

domains"[4] should be understood as meaning that the development of ideology on a macrosociological scale cannot be confined exclusively to the intellectual process, that it is necessary to seek its objective determinants in historically variable conditions of human existence.[5]

Some investigators, while concentrating on the interrelationships between the productive forces and the relations of production, on the one hand, and the superstructure [institutions and ideas], on the other, neglect altogether the interaction between individual elements of the latter, as well as the impact of the conditions of man's material existence with varying intensity on particular domains of social consciousness. Judging by what Marx said about himself,[6] his interest in jurisprudence was a secondary one. Incidentally, at no time did he give priority to this area of knowledge. His dominant interests were philosophy and history, followed by economics.

It would be an oversimplification to perceive in the Marxian conception only economic determinism or an approach based solely on the aspect of causality, leading to complete neglect of the axiological aspect. Prior to 1932, when the "Economic and Philosophical Manuscripts" and other works of the young Marx were published, many authors considered that his conceptions lacked axiological elements, and "ethical socialism" frequently was being contraposed to his ideas. Among those taking

---

4 Engels in a letter to Mehring, *ibid.*, p. 476.

5 See E.Kh. Stepanian, *Ob otnositel'noi samostoiatelnosti ideologii* (M., 1961); K. Opałek, *Problemy metodologiczne nauki prawa* (Warsaw, 1962), p. 317ff.; K. Gryzbowski, "Z zagadnien metodologii doktryn politycznych," *Czasopismo prawno-historyczne*, no. 1 (1965).

6 "Although I studied jurisprudence, I pursued it as a subject subordinated to philosophy and history." See note 1 above, p. 424.

this view of Marx were K. Kautsky,[7] W. Sombart,[8] and B. Croce.[9] On the other hand, treating Marxism as a particular secularized eschatology[10] or religious morality[11] or contending that a religion of the people has been substituted for Marxism-Leninism[12] is an outright distortion of Marx's ideas. One can agree with R.C. Tucker that "the Marxian revolutionary idea has a clear moral meaning," but his contention that "there is a close relationship between revolution and religion" and that "Marx may be characterised as a revolutionist of religious formation" and his idea is to be looked upon more as religious than as ethical in nature,[13] is essentially groundless.

It is incontestable that Marx's philosophical anthropology derives from the rationalist traditions of the Enlightenment. His remark that "all of history is nothing but a continual transformation of human nature" brings out an essential element of Marxian axiology.[14] Many reasons concurred to account for the fact that Marxian philosophical

---

7 K. Kautsky, *Ethics and the Materialist Conception of History* (4th ed.; Chicago, 1918), p. 202.

8 W. Sombart, *Braun's Archiv für Soziale Gesetzgebung und Statistik*, V (Tübingen, 1892), p. 489.

9 B. Croce, *Historical Materialism and the Economics of Karl Marx* (London, 1922), pp. 113ff.

10 M. Buber, *Paths in Utopia*, transl. R.F.C. Hall (London, 1949), p. 10.

11 R.C. Tucker, *Philosophy and Myth in Karl Marx* (Cambridge, 1961), pp. 14-21.

12 K. Hulicka and M.J. Hulicka, *Soviet Institutions. The Individual and Society* (Boston, 1967), p. 32.

13 Tucker, *The Marxian Revolutionary Idea* (New York, 1969), p. 32.

14 H.J. Laski, *Karl Marx* (New York, 1933), p. 46; A.D. Lindsay, *Karl Marx's Capital. An Introductory Essay* (London, 1947), p. 114; W. Suchecki, "Równość społeczna jako element demokracji socjalistycznej," *Studia Iuridica*, VII (1979), p. 19.

anthropology, with the evident conclusions to be derived from it concerning, among other things, the importance of studies on man's value system, has not been fully allowed for in Marxist jurisprudence thus far.

The conditions in which the Soviet system of law had been developing were so remote from Marx's predictions about the future revolution that not only general assumptions but certain specific factors had to be considered, such as the actual level of economic and cultural development of Russia at that time, the size of the working class, the state of social consciousness, both of workers and of the internally unhomogeneous peasantry, the weak parliamentary and local government traditions, and also of law-making and administration of justice. Notwithstanding the efforts made to transplant the experiences of the Paris Commune, all attempts to this end ultimately failed, *e.g.*, in the question of absolute renunciation of the principle of separation of powers and even division of duties among the legislature, executive, or judiciary, or in the question of abolition of a regular army and its replacement with a people's army, or lastly in the question of institutional safeguards against estrangement of the officials from the people.

One of the most widely followed orientations in the pre-revolutionary period was legal positivism, primarily in its German variant. The existing system of government favoured this trend in Russia, just as in other countries.[15] Conservative

15 This presumably accounts for the influence that German positivists, specifically P. Laband, exercised on such authors as Yatsuka Hozumi in Japan. See R.H. Minear, "Japanese Tradition and Western Law. Emperor, State, and Law in the Thought of Yatsuka Hozumi," *Law in Japan* (Cambridge, Mass., 1970), p. 210. Naturally, a number of distinct features come into this. One of the characteristics of the Asian tradition was "the merger of politics and ethics," the absence of the concept of law in East Asia, with politics subsumed under ethics in keeping with the political theory of Confucius.

juristic elements in Russia had a decided partiality for the German brand of legal positivism, suitably adjusting it to local conditions. The liberal trend had an ardent advocate in L. Petrazycki, a Polish jurist lecturing in St. Petersburg until 1917. His psychological conception of law inspired many authors both in the Soviet Union and in other East European countries, Poland in particular. The ideas of Léon Duguit also contributed to some extent. On the other hand, a Marxian jurisprudence had really not developed, even outside university centres. Lawyers, theoreticians, and practitioners alike, were rather suspect as to their intentions in the eyes of the working class leaders.

Soviet jurisprudence did not take shape in a void, and in spite of its revolutionary roots it could not entirely escape the existing trends in legal thought. A similar phenomenon is observed in other socialist countries. Thus, criticism of existing legal conceptions occurred simultaneously with attempts to reconcile them with the exigencies of legal theory and practice. Among the prominent authors who contributed to developing a new Soviet jurisprudence were P.I. Stuchka, E.B. Pashukanis, and M.A. Reisner. Stuchka defined law as a system of rules compatible with the interests of the ruling class and suitably protected by its organised forces. In his view, civil law was a reification of the parties to legal actions.[16] Attempts to develop some of his ideas were made later by A.V. Venediktov and S.I. Bratus. Pashukanis, although he criticised Stuchka, did not differ from him so much in his assessment of the role of Soviet administration and law; however, his argument that "all real law is private law" was different. Under the guise of law based on equality are the interests of those who by virtue of ownership of the means of production exercise power over others. In a socialist society, private law relations are superseded by an order serving the community. Everything therefore be-

---

16 P.I. Stuchka, *Izbrannye proizvedeniia po marksistsko-leninskoi teorii prava* (Riga, 1964).

comes administration, but its essence is discretion and utility, not a body of fixed legal rules. In this way, law as understood in Western countries disappears.[17] It should be noted, however, that a certain neglect of form in law-making activity occurred in the early years of Soviet rule. There was no clear-cut division of functions among the agencies issuing legal regulations. Specifically, much fascination with the ideas of the scientific organisation of labour, in the American style in particular, was manifest.[18] An efficient administrative machinery was rated higher than even the best provisions of law. This approach should be viewed, however, in the light of the poor performance of the administration at that time. In 1920, Lenin described the Soviet state as a "worker's state with bureaucratic deformity."[19] He criticised the state apparatus in very strong terms again in 1922.[20]

All that signified eulogy of pragmatism and efficiency, but at the same time the fascination with "the Russian revolutionary sweep" and with the earlier idea of "revolutionary sense of law" was blended with elements of faith in the superordinate values of socialism, such as elimination of all forms of alienation, creation of conditions for man's self-realisation or the idea of social justice and universal brotherhood.

The process in which all existing political structures and the legal order were being demo-

---

17 E.B. Pashukanis, *Law and Marxism: A General Theory* (London, 1978); W. Friedmann, *Legal Theory* (London, 1944), pp. 231-233.

18 American efficiency was held in high esteem. In 1924, Stalin remarked "the combination of the Russian sweep with American efficiency is the essense of Leninism in Party and State work." J. Stalin, *Zagadnienia leninizmu* (Warsaw, 1947), p. 77.

19 V.I. Lenin, *Sochineniia,* XXXII, pp. 7, 214.

20 See Suchecki, "Niektóre zagadnienia ewolucji państwa radzieckiego", *Państwo i prawo,* no. 2 (1962), p. 205.

lished was bound to be accompanied by criticism of the foundations of legal positivism, with an emphasis on the role of the revolutionary consciousness of the masses, on their sense of law, so strongly associated with the aspiration to social justice. M.A. Reisner, one of the representatives of this trend and follower of Petrazycki's psychologism, endeavoured, after the 1917 revolution, to reconcile psychologism and Marxism.[21] The ideas expounded by these authors were strongly criticised in 1938 by A. Vyshinskii.[22] The charge of legal nihilism against them was to serve definite political aims concomitant with the theory and practice of Stalinism. Notwithstanding many misleading arguments, the conception set out by Vyshinskii basically precluded any discussion of the compatibility of law with the new value system taking shape and with objective social requirements. The proposition that jurisprudence should be based not on positive law but on principles of organisation of social relations[23] was not substantiated in empirical investigations nor in theoretically well-founded postulates *de lege ferenda*. The affirmation of macrosociological tenets, the emphasis on the class character of state and law, did not go beyond very general statements. Recognising the need for the study of legal norms (legal dogmatics), Vyshinskii criticised the formal-dogmatic method and urged the use of a method embracing both the substance and form of legal phenomena, a method that would apprehend them in their development, in their real social meaning, and in action, in short, by the method of materialistic dialec-

---

21 See M.A. Reisner, *Teoriia L.I. Petrazhitskogo, marksizm i sotsial'naia ideologiia* (Spb., 1908), for references to the intuitive, neo-naturalistic theory of law.

22 A.Ia. Vyshinskii, *Teoria państwa i prawa* (Warsaw, 1951); *id.*, *The Law of the Soviet State*, transl. H. Babb (New York, 1948).

23 Vyshinskii, *Zagadnienia teorii państwa i prawa* (Warsaw, 1952), p. 102.

tics.[24] In practice, however, he was an advocate of an extreme dogmatic interpretation of law and social phenomena. For example, invoking Lenin's remark that "politics cannot have priority over economics,"[25] he actually had in mind just the opposite, subordinating Lenin's idea to the Stalinist conception of state and law,[26] baffling any possibility for seeking the real determinants of the operation of law. He treated politics as a concentrated expression of economics, being totally oblivious to the fact that what he was actually saying amounted to a subjective, voluntarist articulation of what exists objectively. Consequently, it was a politics which disregarded the realities of social life. When he argued that law is a political tool of the ruling class and that politics is most directly reflected in it,[27] he had in mind nothing but an instrumental treatment of law arising from immediate political considerations. On the question of interaction between law and morality, he considered that morality is not the determinant factor for law, while law is not the determinant factor for morality. But he contended at the same time that the duty to respect Soviet laws is also a moral duty.[28] Consequently, morality is not a valuating criterion of the law in force, whereas that law itself, being a political tool, has become according to Vyshinskii a valuating criterion of morality. It is regrettable that the practical consequences of this reasoning have not been subjected to thorough criticism. It was founded on such fallacious notions as the alleged existence of a complete harmony between particular and general social interests or the concurrence of a moral and law-abiding posture, and so forth.

Until the XX Congress of the Communist Party

---

24 *Ibid.*, p. 66.

25 *Ibid.*, p. 165.

26 *Ibid.*, p. 30.

27 *Ibid.*, p. 165.

28 *Ibid.*, pp. 174, 176.

of the Soviet Union, when Vyshinskii's conceptions were rejected, they did a great deal of harm; they made for stagnation in Marxist jurisprudence in the Soviet Union and in other socialist countries and contributed to flagrant violations of the rule of law. This could not possibly favour an axiological approach to jurisprudence.

The process of forming a new legal order followed a different pattern in other socialist countries than in the USSR, where initially the experiences of the Paris Commune and Marx's tenet concerning the necessity of demolishing the existing state structure served as a model. It was precisely this tenet more than Marx's other references to bourgeois law holding its ground after the revolution that served as an argument for the necessity of abolishing the existing legal system.[29] The violent social conflicts and the sharp struggle for power in Russia favoured the demolishing tradition. Even before the decree on courts was issued in December 1917,[30] which preserved the existing law "insofar as it has not been abrogated by the revolution and does not contradict the revolutionary conscience and the revolutionary sense of law," people's courts had been created to try cases "according to conscience and their own conviction."[31] Reflected therein was an extreme antipositivist standpoint, giving professional and lay judges a freedom of sentencing without precedent in any other revolution.

As for other socialist countries, they endeavoured to maintain a certain continuity in legislation, specifically where institutions firmly set in parliamentary, local government, and civil rights traditions were involved. In Poland, for

---

29 Marx, "Krytyka Programu Gotajskiego," note 2 above, II, pp. 407-408; Suchecki, "Równość społeczna w socjalizmie," *Państwo i prawo*, no. 7 (1979), p. 43.

30 *SU RSFSR* (1917), no. 4. item 50.

31 *Istoriia sovetskogo ugolovnogo prava 1917-1947* (M., 1948), p. 101ff. S. Erlich, *Ustrój zwiazku radzieckiego* (Warsaw, 1954), p. 276.

example, the terms of the 1921 constitution were incorporated in the constitution of 1947, with some amendments made consequent upon a national referendum held in 1946. The 1932 criminal code, supplemented with provisions of the so-called Small Criminal Code, the civil code, and other acts retained their validity. Jurisprudence, just as the practice of administration of justice, recognised the necessity of adopting an interpretation of law that would meet the altered political and socio-economic conditions. Regardless of whether it was called a democratic or socialist interpretation, it was essentially a dynamic interpretation, where the valuation factor played a significant role.

Jurisprudence in Poland before World War II reflected various West European trends, including legal positivism (A. Peretiatkowicz, Longchamps de Berier, Ohanowicz), normativism (W.L. Jaworski, S. Rundstein, W. Sukiennicki), social solidarism (W. Makowski) and psychologism (L. Petrazycki, J. Lande, E. Jarra, H. Pietka); natural law theory had many followers in Catholic circles. There was no clear trend with a Marxist orientation. Under the circumstances, in the early post-war years a decline in the status of jurisprudence which was incapable of following up the changes taking place in the system of government was experienced.

Several orientations in jurisprudence appeared in post-war Poland, which can be classified as follows: (1) attempts to further jurisprudence along old lines (this approach was subjected to strong criticism by the First Congress of Polish Science); (2) attempts to make use of the ideas of the authors named above for the new jurisprudence; (3) acceptance of the tenets of Soviet jurisprudence without going deeper into the substance of Marxian methodology, with all the negative consequences which emanated in Soviet jurisprudence under A. Vyshinskii in 1938; (4) lastly, an orientation which, eschewing what could be called "facade marxism," has endeavoured to develop a methodology enabling an all-round study of law, in the area of normative systems and as social phenomenon, a psychic phenomenon reflecting human motivations, and last but not least an axiological phenomenon allowing existing law to be confronted with the image of value ranking as seen by the society. This last trend as an integral whole meets the authentic requirements of both theory and practice, although some authors concentrating on a selected aspect of legal study may create the impression of following one of the Western trends in jurisprudence.

In the course of debates over many years, the position on so-called legal dogmatics has been laid down in more precise terms. It has been recognised as a necessary instrument, specifically from the point of view of precision of legislation and of interpretation of the provisions of law, as well as prevention of licence which leads to violations of the rule of law, although in some quarters its scholarly character has been questioned.[32]

Repeated attempts have been made to determine the attitude of Marxist theory toward legal positivism and natural law theory. Since many elements need to be considered, I shall confine myself of necessity to major issues of a methodological nature. The basic difficulty lies in a differentiated understanding of trends in the history of legal thought, as also in a different approach to particular theses of either legal positivism or natural law theory.

A common feature of all varieties of legal positivism is the tendency to stability of the legal order, the reliability of a legally established state, hence every valuation, whether it be in historical, political, or axiological categories, a confrontation of the law in force with the idea of law, the ideal model of that law, is regarded as being actually outside the purview of jurisprudence. All considerations on the subject

32 See J. Wróblewski, "Prawo i płaszczyzny jego badania," *Państwo i prawo*, no. 6 (1969); *id.*, "Teoria państwa i prawa. Stan aktualny i problemy rozwoju," *Państwo i prawo*, no. 11 (1972).

of justice or fairness in law, just as any other questions concerning the value system, are of a secondary nature. If, however, the views of the followers of this trend be considered from the point of view of the ontology, epistemology, of axiology of law, or from the point of view of such questions as being and duty, fact and value, politics and law or morality and law, rather significant differences of opinion will come to light. To define the attitude to legal positivism, it would be necessary to refer the problem to four areas of law: namely, law-making; bases of the validity of the law; application of the law; lastly, respect for the law.

Consider some examples of definitions of legal positivism:

(1) a system of views, according to which only rules of positive law made by man are binding; hence, the task of jurisprudence is to describe, not to evaluate or map out, the directions of law-making and law application (outside drawing conclusions derived from positive law);[33]

(2) positivism, also called the "imperative" conception of law, is distinguished by the following features: (a) that of a rule or norm of human conduct; that of political authority; that of political sanctions or enforcement;[34]

(3) law is regarded as a set of norms established in one or other form by a sovereign organisation. One of the fundamental postulates is adequate stability, clearness, completeness, and trustworthiness of law. The problem whether or not the established norms regarded as legal norms correspond to some systems of moral, religious, or customary norms is treated as an incidental or

---

33 K. Opałek and J. Wróblewski, "Aksjologia - dylemat pomiedzy pozytywizem prawniczyn a doktryna prawa natury," *Pańistwo i prawo*, no. 9 (1966), p. 253.

34 E.W. Patterson, *Jurisprudence. Men and Ideas of the Law* (Brooklyn, N.Y., 1953), p. 253.

secondary one;[35]

(4) the separation of jurisprudence from ethics is one of the most important characteristics of analytical positivism.[36]

Some authors use the concept "classical positivism." On closer examination, however, the concept appears to be very conventional. Presumably it covers Austin's analytical positivism and the *Begriffsjurisprudenz* of P. Laband, who was even cautioning against any historical investigations, since in his view they lead straight to politics, but R. Jhering with his *Interessenjurisprudenz* or G. Jellinek, to whom the prerequisite of proper functioning of the law is not only the fact of its being safeguarded by the state with the use of coercive measures (*Verbindlichkeit*), but also the belief of citizens in its validity, approach the sociological or psychological positions.

It seems that the survey of the main tenets of legal positivism made by H.L.A. Hart coincides in principle with what is said on this trend by Marxist jurisprudence. Among these tenets the following should be singled out: (1) laws are commands of human beings (it should be added here that they must take the form of acts of will by state agencies; as for the command concept taken from Austin, it means nothing but the ability to enforce specified behaviour); (2) there is no necessary connection between law and morals or law as it is and ought to be. (One should add that legal positivism avoids comparisons in this area); (3) the analysis of legal concepts is worth pursuing and to be distinguished from historical sociological, and from the criticism or appraisal of law whether in terms of morals, social aims, "functions," or otherwise; (4) a legal system is a closed logical system in which correct legal deci-

35 A. Michalska, "The Positivistic Element in the Marxist Definition of Law and its Evaluation," *Contemporary Conceptions of Law* (Warsaw, 1979), p. 104.

36 E. Bodenheimer, *Jurisprudence. The Philosophy and Method of Law* (Cambridge, Mass., 1962), p. 94.

sions can be deduced by logical means from pre-determined legal rules without reference to social aims, policies, and moral standards; (5) moral judgments cannot be established or defended as statements of fact can, by rational argument, evidence.[37] Marxist jurisprudence devotes, however, more attention to the social and political factors that contributed to the development of legal positivism as a doctrine of the stable bourgeois state of the second half of the nineteenth century, a seemingly apolitical trend but in fact vindicating the existing legal order as requiring no politico-ethical justification.[38]

The analysis of the process of decline of legal positivism in Germany after the First World War, as well as the general criticism of it after the last world war by G. Radbruch and others, corroborates the view that this conception obtains only under conditions of a stable system of government, when the requirement of reliability of a legally established state is in the forefront.

The doctrine of legal positivism is comprised of various elements which, depending on concrete historical conditions, assume greater or lesser importance. The references to legal positivism under the socialist system are linked with emphasis on some of its characteristics. For example, some authors perceive positivist elements in the Marxist definition of law. According to A. Michalska, the definition of law accepted in socialist jurisprudence contains an element which places it in the category of definitions based on positivist concepts, namely that law is established by the state.[39] The idea that only the general norms enacted by the state belong to law is a reference to positivist concepts. However, this is not a

37 H.L.A. Hart, "Positivism and Separation of Law and Morals," in R.M. Dworkin (ed.), *The Philosophy of Law* (Oxford, 1977), p. 18.

38 See Opałek and Wróblewski, "Pozytywizm prawniczy," *Państwo i prawo*, no. 1 (1954), p. 5.

39 Michalska, note 35 above, p. 93.

"classical positivist definition," since, under the Marxist definition, state and law are phenomena closely linked together, by which their class character is brought out.[40] As noted previously, Vyshinskii's conceptions approached in many respects the ideas of legal positivism.[41] The similarity was reflected in a static approach to the system of government and the legal order in an effort to guarantee security and positivity of law. This assumed special significance in the light of the abolition of the division into public and private law and the renunciation of moral criteria in evaluation of law, but at the same time treating a violation of law as an infringement of moral norms. On the other hand, one will find in this conception no trace of the idea of *Rechtsstaat*; of the theory of self-limitation of state or declared apolitical attitude.

In this way, the jurisprudence of that time differed only in appearance from legal positivism, which treated law in abstraction from social reality. Some elements of legal positivism have kept reappearing in many studies, such as the ideology of the binding judicial decision, which was very much like the positivist conception of completeness and consistency of the legal system, though dictated more by distrust in the administration of justice than by the need to guarantee liberty of the individual and the rule of law.

The attitude of Marxist jurisprudence to natural law is more involved. It should be made clear at the outset that concealed under this term are widely divergent trends, both in regard to axiological grounds and to the social and political functions. More than once natural law was a weapon in the struggle for changing the existing legal order, but it also served, especially in its supernatural variety, to legitimate and consolidate

---

40 *Ibid.*, p. 96.

41 See my observations on V.A. Tumanov, *Contemporary Bourgeois Legal Thought* (M., 1974) in *Państwo i prawo*, no. 5 (1975), p. 58.

the existing social and economic order. It was an expression of rationalism, but it was also attacked for being metaphysical. In the most general terms, natural law recognises the existence of rules of conduct independent of positive law or constituting at least its evaluating criterion. Natural law doctrine is a positive law-valuating ideology.[42] Ontologically, natural law does not exist parallel to positive law. It is an ideology which can directly shape, under particular social conditions, the substance of norms, thus becoming the law in force. This is the case both in the process of law-making and its application.[43]

Natural law theory stretches to various trends founded on distinct philosophical assumptions. W. Maihofer distinguishes four types of conceptions of natural law: historical, sociological, concrete, and existentialist.[44] In contemporary natural law, the following trends can be identified: conditioned law of nature (*bedingtes Naturrecht*); variable-substance law of nature (Stammler); historically flexible law of nature (E. Spranger); law of nature in the making (*werdendes Naturrecht*, E. Fechner); concrete law of nature (as opposed to abstract, K. English); historical law of nature (as opposed to ahistorical, A. Kaufmann).[45]

E.W. Patterson differentiated the following concepts of the law of nature: (1) any critical or constructive theory of legal valuation, or of the ideals of law; (2) the use of reason in the making and administration of law; (3) principles of human conduct that are discoverable by "reason" from the basic inclinations of human nature, and that are absolute, immutable, and of universal validity for all times and places; (4) a theory of natural

42 Opałek and Wróblewski, note 33 above, p. 254.

43 V. Peschka, *Grundprobleme der modernen Rechtsphilosophie* (Budapest, 1974), p. 94.

44 W. Maihofer, *Naturrecht als Existenzrecht* (Frankfurt, 1963), p. 20.

45 *Ibid.*, p. 13.

rights based upon a prepolitical society and a supposed social compact in which men conferred limited powers on political government and in so doing reserved natural rights; (5) norms of human conduct discoverable by experience and observation as prevalent and useful among different peoples; (6) the capacity to perceive, or any intuitive perception of "justice" or "equity" in concrete situations.[46]

K. Opałek and J. Wróblewski identified in American jurisprudence the following conceptions, outside supernatural conceptions: (1) the source of rules of the natural law is purposefully the nature of reality and man (the dynamic law of nature theory, J. Wild); (2) the source of natural law norms is the philosophy of nature and human nature (philosophic anthropology of F.S.C. Northrop); (3) the source of the law of nature is elementary structural and functional properties of a good social order, L.L. Fuller's *eunomy*; (4) a sense of injustice constitutes the evaluating basis of the making and application of law (E. Cahn's psychological law of nature theory).[47]

Many followers of natural law theory refer to Neo-kantian philosophy (R. Stammler, G. del Vecchio, G. Radbruch),[48] and to the Neothomistic philo-

---

46 Patterson, note 34 above, pp. 333-334. Also see similar classification attempts by G. Gurvitch, "Natural Law," in *The Encyclopaedia of Social Sciences*; Ch.G. Haines, *The Revival of Natural Law Concepts* (Cambridge, Mass., 1930), pp. 333-338; H. Ryffel, *Rechts- und Staatsphilosophie. Philosophische Anthropologie des Politischen* (Berlin, 1969), pp. 207-209.

47 Opałek and Wróblewski, *Współczesna teoria i socjologia prawa w Stanach Zjednoczonych* (Warsaw, 1963), p. 27.

48 See Bodenheimer, note 36 above, p. 126ff. It should be noted, however, that G. del Vecchio, in views expressed after the last world war, makes clear reference to the Thomistic conception of the law of nature. See G. del Vecchio, "Sul diritto naturale," *Rivista internatzionale di filosofia del diritto*, no. 2 (1967), p. 329.

sophy.[49] J. Finnis contends that the dispute over natural law between liberals and followers of Thomas Aquinas "need no longer be regarded as so polarised."[50] The above remark unquestionably has wider implications. While differences on the question of ontology remain, the importance of value-oriented jurisprudence tends to grow generally.

It follows from this cursory survey of natural law conceptions that it is impossible to give an unequivocal answer as to the attitude of Marxist jurisprudence to natural law theory. Nonetheless, it is a fact that Marxist jurisprudence takes up many problems which are raised by various natural law orientations. The contention of some Western authors that the Marxist conception of law comes under "nihilistic theories" which do not recognise the idea of law as being in the realm of ethical values to which the law should aspire,[51] applies only to the Stalinist period.

The view held by Kelsen, to whom the social and political evaluation of existing law appearing in Marxism "must be seen as a variant of natural law,"[52] also is an oversimplification. In Tumanov's view, the constitutive role of the state in giving expression to the class will in legislation, which in the last analysis is determined by the material conditions of life in the particular society, could be taken "as bearing a resemblance to natural law." In reality, it is not a matter of the "natural" or "law." But Marxism has never regarded all problems posed by natural law as being false; it rejects not

---

49 For natural law conceptions deriving from both Neokantian philosophy and Neothomism, see M. Szyszkowska, *Neokantyzm, filozofia społeczna wraz z teoria prawa natury o zmiennej tresci* (Warsaw, 1970); *id.*, *Dociekania nad prawem natury czyli o potrzebach człowieka* (Warsaw, 1972); *id.*, *U. źródeł współczesnej filozofii prawa i filozofii człowieka* (Warsaw, 1972).

50 J. Finnis, *Natural Law and Natural Rights* (Oxford, 1980), p. vi.

51 H. Coing, *Grundzüge der Rechtsphilosophie* (Berlin, 1950), p. 98.

the value approach as such, but rather the idealist and teleological axiology with its separation of values from the real world.[53] A similar view of the problem is taken by A.N. Naschitz: "a nihilistic attitude to values is alien to the Marxist philosophy of law ... While it must be acknowledged that Marxist theories have given little attention to such axiological questions as the autonomous object of their research, the main issues relating to it were discussed by the general theory of law."[54] Tumanov is quite right in acknowledging that law is an expression of important values in itself and an independent value alongside other values. "Marxism does not reject the idea of the inalienable natural rights of man and citizen, but it would be wrong to regard these rights as being derived from the will of the state, as a reflection of objective right." It associates the rights of man with his social being and "is in close affinity with the revolutionary natural law teaching on the inalienable rights of man."[55] Tumanov concludes that "if natural law is seen as a doctrine of the rights of man and citizen, of ideas, values, and their contribution to the evolution of law, then the Marxist teaching on legal consciousness, legal ideals, and the rights of man, could merit, somewhat tentatively, the title of natural law in its materialist interpretation."[56]

Over the past twenty-five years, Marxist jurisprudence has often given expression to its interest in axiology in the law, in philosophy of law, totally neglected at one time. The dispute over the ontology of the law of nature will pre-

---

52 H. Kelsen, "Justice et droit naturel," *Le droit naturel* (Paris, 1959); Tumanov, note 41 above, pp. 284-285.

53 *Ibid.*, p. 286.

54 A.M. Naschitz, "Wert und Wertungsfragen im Recht," *Revue roumaine des sciences sociales*, no. 1 (1965), p. 2.

55 Tumanov, note 41 above, p. 288.

56 *Ibid.*, p. 286.

sumably never come to an end, but what is more important, it seems, is a dynamic approach to law, a continual critical analysis of it, its constant adjustment to the growing opportunities for man's self-realisation and for perfecting the forms of social life. Value-oriented jurisprudence should inspire the legislator to a higher degree than it did hitherto. The proposed "concept of pluralism of normative systems," one "directed against juridical monism," assumes special importance under the socialist system.[57]

A number of issues concerning the application of law, specifically the existence of general clauses and of concepts containing evaluating elements and embodied in the law in force, the occasional incoherence of the system of law due to inflated law-making activity and the existing gaps in the law, give rise to the demand for a "free judicial decision" ideology, which to some extent likens Marxist jurisprudence to the law of nature conception, though perhaps not to such an extent as, for example, H. Rommen would have it, to whom the creative role of the judge consists of invoking the law of nature and natural justice.[58] In light of the changes taking place in the socialist countries, Poland being an example, one will be justified in concluding that chances for the development of value-oriented jurisprudence and thereby the opportunities for more thorough studies of the problems posed by the natural law doctrine have considerably increased as of late.

---

57 S. Ehrlich, "On Pluralism of Normative Systems," *Contemporary Conceptions of Law* (Warsaw, 1979), p. 7.

58 H. Rommen, *The Natural Law* (St. Louis-London, 1949), p. 260.

POLISH SUPREME COURT DIRECTIVES AS SOURCES OF CRIMINAL LAW

S. Frankowski

Prologue

It has often been claimed that one of the essential differences between the common law and the continental family of legal systems is that, in the former, judicial decisions may, under certain circumstances, be considered as a source of law whereas in the latter the courts may not play any law-making role, their function being strictly limited to the application of legislation.

Historically speaking, Polish law belonged to the continental family, although it now forms part of the socialist family of legal systems.

The present paper undertakes to examine the reasons for the existence of the supreme court directives in Poland, to describe their role in practice, to analyse their legal character, to demonstrate that a clear distinction between the law-making function of the Parliament and the law-applying function of the court, the distinction typical of the continental family, cannot be properly drawn in Poland because of the existence of directives, and to substantiate the claim that directives in the field of criminal law should be abolished in Poland because they are incompatible with the principles of socialist legality (rule of law).

The concept of supreme court directives is known only in the socialist countries, although historically this was not always the case. The directives were first introduced in Soviet Russia in 1922, in a period of acute class and political struggles.[1] The Soviet legal machinery then faced enormous difficulties. The courts, the procuracy,

1 N.D. Durmanov, *Sovetskii ugolovnyi zakon* (M., 1967), p. 292.

and other law-enforcement agencies were very inadequately staffed since the well-trained lawyers of the ancient régime did not want to cooperate with the new government which, incidentally, probably would not have trusted them anyway. The laws were not properly drafted; in most cases they were created in an emergency, on an *ad hoc* basis. The activities of the forces opposing the newly emergent social order took various and changing forms. All this led to the introduction of the so-called Guiding Explanations, which may be considered a prototype of the directives now in existence in Poland and some other socialist countries. The Guiding Explanations issued by the supreme court quickly began to fulfil the role they were supposed to perform: they became the vehicle by which it was possible to manipulate criminal repression by directing it in a desired way and to increase (or to mitigate) its severity depending upon the constantly changing needs and circumstances. Achieving this aim through legislation was too troublesome and probably deemed inexpedient by the Soviet authorities.

In 1949, the directives were introduced into the Polish legal system. The reasons behind this move were, to some extent, similar to those existing in Soviet Russia in the early 1920s.[2] The Polish Penal Code of 1932, although its legislative technique was of a very high quality, was not able to meet the new demands which appeared after the war when radical socio-economic changes occurred in Poland. New social needs could not obviously be envisaged by the pre-war legislators. Those needs included the protection of a socialist system of power and of the social property which became the basis of the new economic system. Such phenomena as alcoholism and road traffic offences acquired new dimensions and, in consequence, much greater importance after the war. At the same time, quite a few Code regulations became doubtful

---

2 S. Rozmaryn, "Wytyczne wymiaru sprawiedliwosci," *Demokratyczny przeglad prawniczy*, no. 6-7 (1949), p. 24.

(*e.g.*, on abortion), some even clearly anachronistic (*e.g.*, on duelling and the protection of creditors). In short, it became obvious that the Code was no longer adequate to the new situation. Several regulations of the Code were repealed and a few penal law statutes passed by the Sejm. Many penal law regulations also were incorporated into numerous statutes dealing primarily with other branches of law (mostly administrative and economic law). As a result, criminal legislation became chaotic. It lacked uniformity, coherence, and harmony. Penal law regulations were to be found in many statutes, passed at various times, based on different ideas and premises. It is interesting to note that the Code itself underwent very few alterations. Instead, it was decided to supplement it by other statutes and to fill its gaps and eliminate its inadequacies and shortcomings by judicial decisions, in particular by the activities of the supreme court. The directives were meant to become the main instrument to this end.

While discussing the reasons why the directives were found useful, we must further note that the judiciary in Poland in the late 1940s and early 1950s was still composed largely of the pre-war judges who received their legal education in another historical period and were well-accustomed to the 1932 Code based on the fundamentally different ideological premises of bourgeois liberalism. A great majority of the pre-war judges decided, after some hesitancy, to remain in office and were allowed to do so. They seemed to support the new socio-economic order and the new political régime. Nevertheless, it was feared by the government that they were naturally inclined to construe and apply the old Code and, more importantly, also the new statutes along traditional lines and in the spirit of the old days. It must also be noted that another large segment of the Polish judiciary consisted of a new breed: devoted Party activists whose legal education, acquired most often at specially created quasi-vocational "law academies", did not meet the normally expected standards (this group was, first of all, meant to exercise political influence on the professionals educated before the war). For this group the directives were designed as a useful instrument to guide their activities in a desired way.

If we take all the factors mentioned into account, it will not come as a surprise that in the first period the directives dealt with those problems which could not be satisfactorily solved on the basis of the old, out-dated criminal law: offences committed in a state of intoxication, economic crimes, recidivism, road traffic offences, and hooliganism. This clearly testifies to the fact that the directives were supposed to become, and in fact did become, a useful tool to adapt the inadequate legislation to the new conditions and to streamline the activities of the courts and other law enforcement agencies which were staffed by people who, for various reasons, could not be fully trusted.

In 1969, a new Criminal Code was adopted by the Sejm and came into force on 1 January 1970. The Code was a result of codifying activities which began in the early 1950s. In this process several drafts were prepared and submitted for public discussion. The last draft, of 1968, was eventually adopted after rigorous analysis and revision by many bodies. It was a comprehensive act, not only consolidating existing criminal legislation, but also introducing many innovative ideas. In this situation the continued existence of the supreme court directives became debatable. It might seem that most of the reasons justifying them under the old legislation disappeared when the 1969 Code entered into force. There is no doubt that the new statute reflected the current views of the legislator and was meant to meet all the current social needs. It may also be noted that with the passage of time the level of professional knowledge and ideological reliability of the Polish judiciary has been considerably increased.

One could, perhaps, advance some other arguments favouring the existence of the directives despite the fact that the new criminal legislation had been adopted. For example: what if the new Code contained such serious gaps or mistakes that no interpretation would be able to overcome them ? This argument does not seem convincing, for if this were truly the case, the only proper way to proceed would be to amend the Code in the Sejm. The supreme court directives are not supposed to rectify the errors of the legislature. Another possible argument in favour of the directives is that the directives are intended to bring some uniformity in judicial decisions, eliminate undue disparities both in the interpretation of statutory clauses and in sentencing. This argument may be countered by the following reasoning: the uniformity of judicial practice may be achieved within our legal system through other means, namely by ordinary supreme court decisions, in particular by the decisions which, although theoretically not binding on lower courts, enjoy in day to day practice a great degree of authority and are almost invariably followed by the judges. Incidentally, the importance of the uniformity of judicial practice should not be over-emphasised. From the point of view of equality under the law it is, of course, of great value, but it must be stressed that if the judicial practice is evidently wrong, the fact that it is uniform does not make it correct.

It must be stressed that the very existence of the directives in our legal system is subject to several serious objections.

First, it may be convincingly demonstrated that in practice the directives *function* on precisely the same footing as statutory law. This means that the promulgation of the directives is in fact a law-creating function.[3]

Moreover, as will be demonstrated, the directives contain many guidelines which do not refer

3 A. Stelmachowski, *Wstep do teorii prawa cywilnego* (Warsaw, 1969), p. 298.

only to the application of the existing law. There can also be found statements of a general nature which are in clear contradiction to existing legal rules, allegedly only construed by the supreme court. It is very symptomatic that in the first directives issued in 1950 the supreme court violated the law then in force.

One might raise an objection here by pointing out that all this shows, at best, only that the directives were not properly used in practice and the violation of the law by the supreme court should not be viewed as an argument against the directives *per se*. This reasoning is not fully convincing. We must bear in mind that the borderline between the application (interpretation) of the law and its creation is very thin. The question is not one of a sharp contrast between uncreative judicial interpretation, on one side, and judicial "law-making" on the other, but "rather one of degree of creativity as well as one of the modes, the limits, and the acceptability of law-making through the courts."[4] There exists always the danger of an interpretation so excessive that the boundaries of law are transgressed. If such an interpretation is absolutely binding, it amounts to the creation of a new legal rule, existing independently from and functioning exactly as a statutory rule.

It is clear that when the directives and the statutory rule are in conflict, the judge will usually not hesitate which to choose. He will almost invariably feel obliged to comply with the directives by considering them an authoritative declaration of the existing law. His task is made easier by the fact that the supreme court would always claim that what it is doing is nothing other than interpreting the existing law. However, from a purely theoretical point of view, a judge should declare his obedience to the statutory rule and not follow the directives. This way of proceeding is very unlikely, mainly because of the

4 M. Cappelletti, *The Judge: Lawmaker or Interpreter* (Sydney, 1980), p. 6 (mimeo.).

fact that the supreme court is the highest court of appeal. It is almost certain that the lower court's decision, if contrary to the directives, would be overruled by an appeals court and, ultimately, by the supreme court. Moreover, disobeying the directives would destroy the purpose of their existence.

We may, therefore, conclude by saying that from a *functional* point of view the directives may be viewed as being on the same footing as the statutory rules. One may object, however, by pointing out that the directives are binding only upon the courts and therefore are not generally binding. Lacking this characteristic, they must not be considered legal rules in the strict sense. This objection may be countered in the following way: since the directives are absolutely binding upon the courts and there are no other state organs having jurisdiction over offenders, it means that in reality the directives are binding on all subjects, including citizens.[5]

Now, let us examine the *normative* character of the directives. My contention is that also from a normative point of view the issuance of the directives by the supreme court is the law-making function. According to Article 28 of the Supreme Court Act, the mere violation of the directives may serve as an independent ground for lodging an appeal. If so, the directives are not meant to be limited only to the clarification of the existing statutory rules, but, for example, may also "create new, more specific rules concretizing the way in which more general, statutory rules should be implemented."[6]

Moreover, one can infer from Article 28 of the Supreme Court Act that the legislator obviously envisaged a situation in which a judicial decision is rendered in violation of the directives, statutory rules being left intact. Otherwise, why

---

5 Durmanov, note 1 above, p. 92.

6 W. Swida, *Prawo karne* (Warsaw, 1971), p. 71

would the legislator have provided for the mere violation of the directives as a separate ground for appeal ? And, if so, how can one claim that the directives are not, from a normative point of view, legal rules ? Further, is it realistic to maintain that the directives must always be viewed in conjunction with the statutory rules on the basis of which they were issued ?

In conclusion, we may say that from a functional as well as from a normative point of view the issuance of the directives by the supreme court is, in this author's opinion, an evident example of law-making activity.

This statement leads us to the following observations.

First, is it desirable that the legal order be changed by supreme court activities ? It is sufficient to point out that in this situation we find a clear deviation from one of the fundamental rules of legality in the field of criminal law, namely, that no law should be applied retroactively. A prohibition of this kind, known to the Polish Criminal Code (Article 1) clearly applies only to statutory rules, not to judicial decisions (including the directives).[7] In fact, the situation under review might be considered also as a deviation from the rule "no crime without law," because the criminality of the act may, in reality, be based on the directives. A citizen, by acquainting himself with statutory law, still can not be certain whether the act he is contemplating is not considered criminal by the directives.[8]

Second, we must bear in mind that there are certain domains of social life which must be regulated only by statutory rules. In particular, according to Polish legal theory, only the statute

---

7 S. Pomorski, "Z problematyki tzw. normotworczej dzialalnosci sadow w prawie karnym," *Panstwo i prawo*, no. 8-9 (1969), p. 373.

8 S. Wlodyka, "Prawotworcza dzialalnosc Sadu Najwyzszego," *Zeszyty Naukowe UJ*, no. 31 (1967), p. 176.

(properly promulgated by the Sejm) may define what forms of human conduct are criminal. The issuance of the directives by the judicial body, although based on the Supreme Court Act, is in my view in clear contradiction with the idea of the division of the spheres of competence among state organs. As such, the very existence of the directives does not promote the rule of law.[9]

Third, it has been pointed out in our legal writings that even apart from the directives, other forms of the supreme court's activities, in particular, the issuance of the decisions, may be viewed as a law-making function. The view has been expressed that this kind of activity should be eliminated or, at least, severely curtailed by the strict adherence of the supreme court to the letter of law.[10] If we agree with this view, we should even more forcefully criticise the existence of the directives because of their absolutely binding character.

Fourth, we may also note that the fact that the supreme court promulgates in reality absolutely binding rules may encourage the judges at large not to pay sufficient and desirable respect to the statutory law. The judges are well aware that some day even an interpretation transgressing the accepted limits may be adopted by the supreme court in the directives and become the only correct one. As a result, the statutory law as such would be less respected by all criminal justice personnel (procurators, policemen, etc.) and by the population at large.

Fifth, according to the Constitution, the judges are independent and subject only to statutory law. Is not their independence violated by the absolutely binding directives ?

---

9 Rozmaryn, *Ustawa w Polskiej Rzeczypospolitej Ludowe* (Warsaw, 1964), pp. 164, 170.

10 L. Lustacz, "O pozakonstytycyjnych formach dzialalnosci prawotworczej," *Panstwo i prawo*, no. 7-8 (1957), p. 9.

All this leads to one final conclusion: the directives in the field of criminal law, having lost their raison d'être and being in clear conflict with the rule of law, s h o u l d b e a b o l i s h e d.

So far what has been said is a summary of my article published exactly ten years ago in *Panstwo i Prawo*, a monthly of the Polish Academy of Sciences.[11] The article was written just when the new Criminal Code was in the first few months of its operation. Therefore, it seemed to me reasonable to express the view that the supreme court should, at least, show more restraint and wait with new directives until enough experience had been accumulated on the basis of the new Code. Alas. As I was completing the final draft of the article, in March 1971 the supreme court issued a directive on the conditional quashing of criminal proceedings, a new penal measure introduced by the Code.[12] In a way, the directives were an easy prey: they had confirmed all my doubts. Therefore, I was fortunate to be able to point out in the last part of my article that:

(a) the 1971 directive restricted the scope of conditional quashing beyond the limits envisaged by the Code by declaring without any reservations that conditional quashing may not take place if the offence is of a hooligan character (although the Code knows of no such restriction);

(b) the court felt competent to address the directive not only to the courts, but to other bodies such as social organisations and even the procuracy, formally independent of the judiciary;

(c) the directive was promulgated only one year after the Code had entered into force. How-

---

11 S. Frankowski, "Wytyczne Sadu Najwyzszego w zakresie prawa karnego materialnego-problem otwarty," *Panstwo i prawo,* no. 10 (1971), pp. 619-628.

12 The Directive on Conditional Quashing of 29 January 1971, VI KZP 26/69, *Orzecznictwo Sadu Najwyzszego,* seria karna, no. 3 (1971). [hereinafter: OSN]

ever it would be totally wrong to assume that by 1970 so many difficulties concerning conditional quashing appeared that the court felt obliged to issue the directive. In fact, the motion of the supreme court chairman to issue the directive was dated 12 December 1969, which meant it had been prepared months before the Code entered into force. In this case the purpose of the directive was not to remove the difficulties encountered in practice by the judges, but to elucidate the new rules adopted by the Code without waiting for the difficulties to emerge.

Present

Returning to the subject in 1981, what has happened in the meantime ? In general, my critical remarks evoked little response in scholarly writings, although the article has been included in a popular reader on criminal law. The only author who dealt with them at length was Professor A. Murzynowski, who in his book advanced the following theses:

(a) in practice, the directives are considered absolutely binding upon the courts and have therefore become an additional source of law. In consequence, the scope of judicial independence has been curtailed in a manner not provided for in the Constitution. Under these circumstances, this author's view that the issuance of the directives in the field of criminal law should be discontinued seems to be to a great extent justified;

(b) it is possible, however, to claim that the directives are not absolutely binding, but that they are presumed to offer the only correct interpretation of law, which means that if the court deems the directives contrary to statutory law, it should disregard them;

(c) a judgment passed in violation of the directives may be appealed. Article 28 of the Supreme Court Act does not state, however, that such a judgment must be overturned. All it says is that one may lodge an appeal because the directives had been violated;

(d) anyway, in the future it is recommended that the supreme court promulgate directives only in exceptional cases when the danger of conflicting interpretations of the law is imminent.[13]

It seems that Professor Murzynowski's original ideas regarding the binding character of the directives have not found any reflection either in legal theory or, especially, in judicial practice. There can be no doubt that the supreme court's directives have to this day been considered absolutely binding by all criminal justice agencies in Poland.

My critical remarks expressed in 1971 in no way influenced the practice of the supreme court. On the contrary, in the period 1970-1981 more directives were issued than in the period 1950-1969. Altogether, on the basis of the new Code fifteen directives plus the so-called Leading Guidelines (to be discussed separately) were issued compared to seven issued before 1970. The number itself is surprising. One might expect that the new legislation is better adapted to contemporary conditions and that the need to employ the judicial machinery to make it work smoothly will arise much less often.

When analysing the directives issued under the 1969 Code one finds, first, that they have gradually changed in format and style. In the very beginning, in the 1950s, the directives were considerably shorter, being confined to one or a few legal problems. In the 1970s, the supreme court's ambitions were much greater: the directives deal no longer with particular legal issues causing problems in judicial practice, but attempt to provide a fairly comprehensive treatment of a given legal institution (*e.g.*, military arrest) or, more often, of a given type of offence (*e.g.*, economic or traffic offences). In short, the supreme

---

13 A. Murzynowski, *Istota i zasady procesu karnego* (Warsaw, 1976), pp. 259-262.

court has undertaken the role of a university professor. The directives now read more like a university textbook. At the same time, the supreme court has not ceased to assume the role of legislator. From this point of view, the directives' structure is very characteristic. In most cases they consist of the following:

(a) an introduction in which we find explained the reasons, purposes and aims of the directives,

(b) a few general rules of primary importance, printed in bold letters, each numbered (with Roman numerals) and called Theses,

(c) each primary rule (the Thesis) is followed by justifying reasons, often phrased like legal rules, each numbered (with Arabic numerals) and named Points.

As a result, one can easily refer to a given Thesis or Point by indicating, *e.g.* Thesis III, Point 5, of the directive X.

Therefore, from a structural point of view the directives resemble to some extent American penal codes annotated (the Theses being the statutory rules, the Points the annotations). It is pertinent to stress, however, that the rules contained in the Points are also binding (whereas the annotations are not).

One can find in the directives of the 1970s, as well as in those of the 1950-60s, examples of rules either changing the existing statutory legal order or filling gaps in legislation.

For example:

(a) in the directive on burglary (1980)[14] there are some novel statements which are contrary to well established scholarly opinions respected in judicial practice. The supreme court claims that "... burglary is predicted neither upon the fact that intent to appropriate the goods origi-

14 The Directive on burglary and audacious theft of 25 June 1980, VII KZP/48/78, *OSN*, no. 8 (1980), item 65.

nated before the act of breaking-in nor upon the fact that breaking-in precedes the appropriation of the goods" (Thesis II, Point 2).

According to this concept, burglary is, therefore, committed in a situation when X breaks into Y's apartment which he mistakes for his own, and then appropriates (takes away) Y's goods found inside; and also in a situation when X consciously allows himself to be locked inside a bank building and then breaks out of the building with the money found unprotected inside the bank. Especially the second example clearly demonstrates that the law of burglary has been considerably widened by the court. No one had ever thought that the breaking-in might also include breaking-out;

(b) the directive on rape (1972)[15] contains the rule that in certain situations a person may be deemed a perpetrator of rape "committed with other persons" (Article 168(2), Criminal Code), if this person "being present at the place of rape shows by his attitude the readiness to take an active part on the side of other perpetrators, creating in this manner the victim's belief that any further resistance is aimless ..." (Thesis III).

This definition clearly transgresses the limits of the concept of a perpetrator as defined by the Code (Article 16). Moreover, at first glance it is very risky to make responsibility for rape, as a perpetrator, dependent upon the mental state of the victim (so if a victim was short-sighted and did not notice X's "attitude," X should not be found guilty, at least not as a perpetrator);

(c) the directive on road traffic offences (1975)[16] contains a statement that the fact that a driver was tired should not, as a rule, be consid-

---

15 The Directive on rape of 21 December 1972, VI KZP 64/72, *OSN*, no. 3 (1973), item 18.

16 The Directive on road traffic offences of 22 February 1975, V KZP 2/74, *OSN*, no. 3-4 (1975), item 33.

ered a mitigating circumstance (Thesis XXXVII). The Code takes no stand on this issue.

Another characteristic feature of the directive promulgated in the 1970s is the emphasis on penal policy, or, to be more specific, on sentencing. Despite the fact that the Code contains several articles laying down sentencing guidelines (Articles 50-52, 54, 57, etc.), the court felt obliged to give much additional advice on how to mete out penalties for particular categories of offences and toward particular categories of offenders. The guidelines recommended by the court are based on a very definite philosophy of punishment. It is obvious to the supreme court that criminal punishment is an effective measure in dealing with offenders. For example, in the directive on rape the court announces that "punishment is one of the important measures in combating criminality". Similar statements may be found in the directive on road traffic offences ("Order and safety on the roads depend to a great extent on the application of appropriate criminal repression" (Thesis XXVIII)) and on recidivism[17] ("Appropriately severe criminal repression ... must constitute one of the vital elements in the prevention and combating of recidivism" (Thesis IX)).

No wonder that pursuant to this very simplistic idea the supreme court encourages the courts, on almost every occasion, to increase the severity of punishment. This is in fact a recurring theme found in nearly all of the directives promulgated under the new Code.

For example:

(a) the directive on rape provides that although the most important sentencing factor is the social danger of the act, the young age of an offender also speaks in favour of several penalties to be applied. The court explains that contrary to a commonly held view, youth must not be considered a mitigating circumstance, since very often a

17 The Directive on recidivism of 22 December 1978, VII KZP 23/77, *OSN*, no. 1-2 (1978).

young offender needs a longer confinement for the sake of treatment (resocialisation) (Thesis III);

(b) in the directive on offences against social property (1975)[18] the supreme court urges one should not forget that the appropriation of social property of considerable value is an extremely grave crime and, as such, requires a severe penalty based on the idea of proportionality and on general prevention considerations. "Every assault on social property violates the rule of just distribution of the national product; therefore, it attacks vital interests of each citizen. Consequently, the criminal law protection of social property is, at the same time, the protection of the human rights of the man who, under socialism, creates new goods through his honest work," adds the court. The supreme court also warns the courts that the penalty imposed may approximate the lowest level of penalty provided by the law under which the offender is sentenced only when there exists a clear predominance of mitigating circumstances (Thesis I). It must be explained that Polish judges always used to impose penalties in the lower range in cases of an average gravity. The implementation of the supreme court's guideline would certainly lead to the application of harsher sentences;

(c) the directive on burglary and particularly audacious theft (1980) deserves a more thorough discussion because it exemplifies in an excellent manner the supreme court's way of thinking about punishment.

When analysing particularly audacious theft the court turns its attention to the fact that the penalties imposed in practice do not differ from those meted out in cases of simple theft. Further, the court looks for the causes of this, in its view, regrettable situation. It finds that such factors as the young age of an offender and the insignificant value of stolen goods are very often

---

18 The Directive on offences against social property of 26 September 1975, VI KZP 14/74, *OSN*, no. 10-11 (1975).

regarded as mitigating circumstances. In the opinion of the supreme court, this practice is in most cases evidently wrong and should be discontinued. If a young offender does not attend any school and does not work, the educational goal of punishment (resocialisation) should be given primary consideration. To achieve this goal "it is often necessary to apply long-time treatment in an institutional setting" (Thesis II, Point 2). As regards the insignificant value of stolen goods, it must be emphasised, claims the court, that this should not be a major sentencing factor. It happens very often in the case of audacious theft that the offender wants to steal as much as possible but takes whatever he finds. Besides, it must be remembered that, apart from the value of goods stolen, the offender usually causes other damage by his actions. For example: the theft from a state-owned shop makes it necessary to close it (or one part of it) to make an inventory. The court points out that factors like these should not be overlooked. Finally, the court gives a long list of aggravating circumstances which are usually unduly disregarded by the courts in the process of sentencing.

There is no need for lengthy comment on the supreme court's attitude toward sentencing. It is obvious that the clearly predominating goal of the directives is to increase the severity of penalties. In every instance the court favours the particular sentencing guideline (proportionality, general deterrence, or reform of the offender) which would enable the courts to impose more severe penalties. It may be said very briefly that what the supreme court has been recommending in recent years is exactly opposite to what we find in any criminal law textbook published in Poland since 1956, namely:

(a) it is wrong to assume that criminal sanctions are effective methods to prevent and combat criminality, especially in such areas as the national economy, traffic, and sexual behaviour;

(b) there is no proof that imprisonment is

more effective than any other way of dealing with offenders (except that it may isolate an offender from society);

(c) imprisonment is particularly unsuitable to reform the offender. It is especially obvious that longer periods of confinement result in moral as well as physical degradation;

(d) imprisonment of young offenders is particularly harmful.

Despite the binding character of the directives, the courts have not been eager to follow them in the field of sentencing. If the directives were given full effect, it would have resulted in a too drastic, in the opinion of the judges, severity of the system.

Therefore, for a long time the courts have been reluctant and have been resisting the pressure to apply more severe measures. Being aware of this mood, the supreme court in October 1979 passed a Resolution [*uchwala*] called a Leading Guideline[19] [*zalencia kierunkowe*] in which it referred to the four recently promulgated directives: on rape (1972), on road traffic offences (1975), on the appropriations of social property of considerable value (1975), and on mismanagement (1976).[20] The court declared the four directives were not properly implemented in practice. The main message of the Leading Guideline is very clear: the lack of the full implementation of the directives "brings harmful results which, to a great extent, make the activities aimed at the restriction and elimination of criminality less effective." The court claims that the criminal repression should be intensified to control criminality. Professor K. Buchala, commenting upon the Leading Guideline, has aptly observed: "it is highly doubtful whether this is exactly the ideology of socialist criminal

19 The Resolution of the Supreme Court of 17 September 1979, VII KZP 32/78, *OSN*, no. 11-12 (1979).

20 The Directive on mismanagement of 27 February 1976, VI KZP 10/75, *OSN*, no. 4-5 (1976).

law over sixty years after the victorious socialist revolution in Russia and the ideology of the 1969 Polish Criminal Code."[21] The same commentator points out that the Leading Guidelines were adopted without any legal basis. The prerogatives of the supreme court are described in the Constitution (Article 61), in the Supreme Court Act (Articles 1, 2, 8, 10, 28), and in the Code of Criminal Procedure. There is not a single clause in which the Leading Guidelines have been mentioned. Professor Buchala concludes by saying that the Leading Guidelines (in fact: the super-directives or the directives above the directives) were adopted in violation of existing law.

We shall not dwell at length on the substance of the Leading Guidelines. It is necessary to stress, however, that on a few occasions they go much further than the directives in emphasising the need for severe penalties, in particular for longer prison sentences. In general, the supreme court seems to stress more strongly than in the past the objective character of criminal responsibility in the domain of sentencing: the greater the harm caused, the more severe the penalty imposed. The idea of individualised punishment, that is the punishment depending primarily upon the personal characteristics of an offender, is not favoured by the supreme court.

One final remark: to dispel any doubts about the legal character of the directives the court stated the following: "The violation of the directives may result in the quashing or in the change of a judgment (Article 28, Supreme Court Act). In consequence, the directives of the supreme court are absolutely binding upon all the courts and, as such, must be implemented in full." The scholarly controversy on this subject has been resolved by the supreme court itself. But what of the venerable Latin maxim that nobody is allowed to be a judge in his own case ?

---

21 K. Buchala, Gloss on the Leading Guidelines, *Panstwo i prawo*, no. 4 (1980), p. 177.

Conclusions

The directives of the supreme court play a vital role in the functioning of the Polish criminal justice system. In practice, they are absolutely binding upon the judiciary and other law enforcement agencies. But they have encountered strong criticism. Some scholars point out that the very existence of the directives in the field of criminal law can not be fully reconciled with the socialist rule of law. In particular, it has been pointed out that the supreme court, by issuing the directives, usurps the law-making role which theoretically belongs only to legislative bodies (the Sejm, with respect to statutes). Further, the directives violate the independence of judges who should be subject only to statutory law. The directives also have been severely criticised for their content: the emphasis on extremely severe penal measures is not viewed by a majority of Polish scholars as a sound penal policy to be followed in a rational society.

It may be expected that in a more favourable political climate the use of the directives will be severely curtailed, and eventually one may even see their complete abolition.

THE ROMANIST TRADITION OF CIVIL LIABILITY IN CONTEMPORARY POLAND

W. Wolodkiewicz

The concept of civil liability does not always have a common meaning in modern legal doctrine. In its broadest sense, liability is necessarily linked with sanction.[1]

The connection of certain legally relevant events with corresponding civil law sanctions is treated in a generalised way by modern law. In the law of obligations, the civil law sanction, which as a rule results when damage is caused, depends on the character of the event which gave rise to the legal obligation. Such factors as the extent of the obligation, the burden of proof, and succession depend on the source of the obligation (contract or tort). Notwithstanding this general approach, there are different rules in various civil law systems. They depend on the socio-economic system of the state, its historical traditions, and many other factors.

Many statutes in modern law, highly abstract in nature, enumerate general categories of legally relevant events on which liability is based. The following are some examples from the Polish Civil Code:

- *Article 415*: "A person who has by his own fault wronged another person shall be obliged to redress the damage;"
- *Article 471*: "A debtor shall be obliged to redress the damage resulting from non-performance of an obligation or improper performance unless the non-performance or improper performance results from circumstances for which the debtor was not responsible;" and

---

1 See A. Stelmachowski, *Wstep do teorii prawa cywilnego* (Warsaw, 1969), pp. 242ff.

- *Article 472*: "Unless specific provisions of the Act provide otherwise, the debtor has the obligation to apply ordinary care."

The first of these rules constitutes the basis for tortious liability, and the other two, for contractual liability. In these rules the obligation of the debtor is linked, in substance, with the fact of having caused damage. The difference between the two systems of liability for damage consists in the fact that the contractual liability system binds the parties under a previously concluded contract. Non-performance of the contractual obligation creates the obligation of redress. In the tortious liability system the duty of redress arises from the fact of having caused the damage when the duty of certain behaviour had not been stated.

In Polish law, the main difference between the so-called system of tortious liability[2] and contractual liability is manifested in the difference in burden of proof: in the event of a tort, the tort-feasor's fault, in principle, must be proved by the plaintiff; in the event of damages resulting from non-performance or improper performance, the defendant (debtor) is obliged to prove the lack of fault.[3]

---

2 Tort [*delictum*] is treated here in its broad sense, *i.e.*, damages resulting from extra-contractual conditions.

3 Polish law knows cases of liability irrespective of fault of the person causing damage; in the field of tortious liability, *e.g.*, liability for *effusum vel deiectum* (Article 433, Polish Civil Code), liability for damages caused by an activity of an enterprise (Article 435, Polish Civil Code), liability for damage caused by motor vehicles (Article 436, Polish Civil Code); in the field of contractual liability, *e.g.*, liability arising from sale warranty (Article 556, Polish Civil Code) and delivery warranty (Articles 609, 612, Polish Civil Code), resulting from renting (Article 664, Polish Civil Code), liability of persons

The principle of fault is a basic prerequisite of responsibility, especially in the nineteenth century civil codes.[4] Exceptions from liability based on fault become more frequent in modern civil law in spite of the sometimes dramatic arguments advanced by proponents of a theory of liability based solely on fault. The concept of fault is itself subject to objectivisation caused by the application of different standards of behaviour which, if not abided by, give rise to the obligation to redress the damage.[5]

The increasing hazards brought about by modern life (connected, for example, with industrial production or the use of motor vehicles) resulted in the introduction of responsibility based on objective prerequisites (sometimes called strict responsibility, or liability based on risk) by legislators, or in judicial decisions, or sometimes suggested by scholarly writings.[6]

---

running hotels for objects brought in (Article 846, §1, Polish Civil Code).

4 W. Warkałło, *Odpowiedzialność odszkodowawcza* (Warsaw, 1972), p. 207; W. Czachórski, *Prawo zobowiazań w zarvsie* (Warsaw, 1968), p. 115. See, for example, Article 1382 of the French Civil Code as far as tortious liability is concerned, and Article 1315; §1295 of the ABGB (without the differentiation of the two systems of liability); §823ff. of the BGB. Similarly, the 1964 RSFSR Civil Code, Articles 222 and 444 (in the latter it is characteristic that the debtor's fault is alleged as a rule).

5 G. Marton, *Les fondements de la résponsabilité civile* (Paris, 1937), pp. 13ff.; G. Viney, *La déclin de la résponsabilité individuelle* (Paris, 1965), pp. 205ff.; Stelmachowski, note 1 above, pp. 252ff.

6 The development of the French approach in the field of liability for *effusum vel deiectum* may serve here as an example. The first redaction of the French Civil Code contained a regulation modelled upon the Roman *actio de effusis vel deiectis*, which in the last version of the Code was deleted. On the basis of the Code Civile, liability for damages caused by throwing

The basic notions and institutions of modern civil law systems were shaped under the influence of, broadly understood, the reception of Roman thought,[7] which had and still has significant meaning for the law of obligations. This is true of both the legal systems of the socialist and the capitalist Continental countries.

In Roman law a general theory of civil liability was never developed. Nevertheless, some basic elements as grounds for liability, elaborated in classical Roman law and then generalised in the law of post-classical period and in the studies of *ius commune*, have influenced the development of the modern civil law.

We have in view here two different grounds for liability, the contractual liability and the tortious liability mentioned by Gaius in his *Institutiones*.[8] They were supplemented by the same author through the so-called *variae causae obligationum*.[9] This last group of events was divided

things or pouring liquids off a building can be claimed under Article 1384. This regulation in its literal wording provided for liability for damages caused by objects over which one has custody. Presumption of fault, which could be removed by proof to the contrary, was the basis for liability. In French scholarly writings, liability independent of any fault is accepted on the basis of Article 1384. See H.L. Mazeau, and A. Tunc, *Traité théorique de la résponsabilité civile* (Paris, 1958), II, pp. 108-109; W. Wołodkiewicz, Gloss to the decision of Polish Supreme Court, *Nowe prawo*, no. 7-8 (1969), p. 1286.

7 J. Bardach, "La réception dans l'histoire de l'état et du droit," *Le droit romain et sa réception en Europe* (Warsaw, 1978), pp. 30ff.

8 Gai. 3.88: *Nunc transeamus ad obligationes. Quarum summa divisio in duas species diducitur: omnis enim obligatio vel ex contractu nascitur vel ex delicto.*

9 D.44.7.1pr.: *Obligationes aut ex contractu nascuntur aut ex maleficio aut proprio quodam iure ex variis causarum figuris.* See Wołodkiewicz, "*Obligationes ex*

in Justinian's law into causes similar to contracts and those similar to delicts,[10] called quasi-contracts and quasi-delicts. These terms have been worked out by the glossators.

An action started with *actio in personam* was the sanction for all these events in the Roman law. The problem of protection of contracts and of the right of persons damaged by delicts is basic in Gaius' discussion about the *actio in personam*. The author, offering a definition of the *actio in personam* (Gai. 4.2), writes: "*In personam actio est, qua agimus ... quotiens litigamus cum aliquo qui nobis vel ex contractu vel ex delicto obligatus est.*"[11]

Initially, the grounds for the protection of different contracts in the Roman law were based on a mode of proceeding at the conclusion of the contract. Acts resulting in contractual liability were divided by Gaius into those committed by *re*, *verbis*, *litteris*, and *consensu*.[12]

---

variis causarum figuris Ricerche sulla classificazione delle fonti delle obbligazioni nel diritto romano classico," *Rivista Italiana per le Scienze Giuridiche,* XIV (1970), pp. 160ff.

10 I.3.13.2: *Sequens divisio in quattuor species diducitur: aut enim ex contractu sunt aut quasi ex contractu aut ex maleficio aut quasi ex maleficio.*

11 I purposely avoid here the controversial matter of whether this sanction was based in classical Roman law on the *ius civile* system only or whether it was based on the *ius honorarium* as well. Personally, I would accept the broad application resulting from the classical law of bringing an *actio in personam* for events whose protection also rests on the *ius honorarium* system.

12 Gai. 3.89: *Harum autem quattuor genera sunt: aut enim re contrahitur obligatio aut verbis aut litteris aut consensu.* It remains an open question to decide whether this classification which was subordinated by Gaius to contracts was not an initial classification of all obligations. See Wołodkiewicz, note 7 above, pp. 135ff.

The absence of a uniform concept of contract in classical Roman law may be attributed to a number of complex reasons. Roman lawyers of the Republican period and of the early Empire were not interested in creating theoretical models of contract. However, in their everyday practice they encountered different legal transactions which resulted in encouraging the praetor to permit certain *actiones* resulting either from the *ius civile* or from protecting a definite factual situation recognised by a praetor by starting *actiones in factum*. Even before the codification of a praetorian edict, the practical difference in a trial between the *actiones in ius* and *in factum* was not, from the structural point of view, very important: the *actio* based either on civil law or on the praetor's *imperium* was started in the *formula* proceedings by the praetor himself. There were no practical needs for creating the category of a contract as a juridical act recognised and protected by civil law. It is generally known that in Roman law the word *obligatio* was a synonym for *actio*. So in practice the classification of *actiones* rather than the divisions and definitions of different events causing the *obligationes* were meaningful. First, the division of the *actiones* into *iudicia stricti iuris* and *iudicia bonae fidei* was significant. This resulted from the system of praetorian edicts. To indicate that practical reasons made it necessary to classify the *actiones* rather than the obligations, one has to take into account that the division of *actiones* into *in rem* and *in personam* was very old.[13]

It is significant that Roman legal theory before Gaius lacked the term *contractus* (*contractus* being a noun) to designate a certain category of legal events.[14] The use of the word *contractus*

13 This division existed in the ancient times of the development of the procedure *per legis actiones*. Cf. Gai. 4.12 and ff.

14 Labeo's (D.50.16.19) and Pedius' (D.2.14.1.3) definitions do not emanate from the noun *contractus*, but they constitute a participial form of the verb *contrahere*.

by Gaius was prompted by an attempt at classification rather than at defining a general category. Through the rhetorical device of definition *per divisionem* used by this author, general categories were significant only as points of reference (*loci*), for further detailed classifications.

Proper consideration of the term *contractus* can be found only in Ulpianus. In his reasoning, agreement of the parties is the basic element of the contract. The agreement itself, to have full legal consequences, *i.e.*, to be enforceable in an action rather than to be the ground for an *exceptio*, had to possess an established *nomen* and be supported by a *causa*.[15]

Gradually, however, along with the process of clarifying the concept of *contractus*, the process of extending the coverage of the term of a contract as an actionable convention became evident. Actionability of those contracts which did not fit into an established category (whose *nomen* was not stated) became possible. One could find this in all sorts of *nova negotia*, whose actionability was based on unclassified conventions for mutual performance, as well as in the development of actionability of different kinds of informal conventions (*pacta*,

---

For jurists the word *contrahere* did not mean a certain group of legal events causing *obligatio*. They used the participial form of the verb *contrahere*, connecting it with the word *obligatio*, wherein an action described by the word *contrahere* (to enter into an engagement, to make something) was carried into effect. For full particulars and further arguments and bibliography, see Wołodkiewicz, "*Contrahere - Contractum - Contractus* dans le droit romain classique," *Le droit romain et sa réception en Europe* (Warsaw, 1978), pp. 298-301.

15 Ulpianus (D.2.14.1.3): *Conventionis nomen generale est ad omnia pertinens, de quibus negotii contrahendi transigendique causa consentium qui inter se agunt ...*; Ulpianus (2.14.1.4): *Sed conventionum pleraeque in aliud nomen transeunt ...*; Ulpianus (D.2.14.7.4): *sed cum nulla subest causa propter conventionum hic constat non posse constitui obligationem ...*

transactiones). The possibility of bringing an action based on the agreements was a step in the direction of departing from the formalism of the old Roman law which regarded only formal acts (in the field of obligations and others) as effective.

One may venture the view that the idea of the principle of freedom of contracts dates back to classical Roman law. The principle "*pacta conventa quae neque dolo malo, neque adversus leges plebis scita senatus consulta decreta edicta principum, neque quo fraus cui eorum fiat, facta erunt, servabo*" (D.2.14.7.7) expressed by the praetor in his edict was initially merely an ideological declaration rather than a legal principle.[16] In fact, however, the idea expressed by the praetor in the edict could be realised in the oldest law by achieving the actionability of different settlements reinforced by performing *sponsio* and its derivative forms. In the classical Roman law there also existed legal measures for the realisation of this principle, *i.e.*, by the possibility of starting an *actio in factum* by the praetor.[17]

The generalisation of the principles of contractual responsibility in Roman law was achieved late in the Justinianic period (after the Justinian codification had been finished), and then in the glossators' writings.

The Greek paraphrase of Justinian's *Institutions* by one of its authors, Theophilus, identifying finally the meaning of *contractus* and *pactum*, provided for the first time a generalised definition of contractual liability. According to Theophilus, "a contract is a convention and consent of two or more persons aiming at constituting an obligation

16 The guiding principle of the edict, as Ulpianus stated it (D.2.14.1pr.), was *aequitas naturalis: Quid enim tam congruum fidei humanae, quam es quae inter eos placuerunt servare ?*

17 See Papinianus (D.19.5.1pr.): *nonnumquam evenit, ut cessantibus iudicis proditis et vulgaribus actionibus, cum proprium nomen invenire non possumus, facile descendemus ad eas, quae in factum appellantur.*

through which one owes something to the other."[18] Theophilus' view constituted a genuine turning point for the further development of the modern term "contract." It also provided a wide range of interpretations. Theophilus coined his concept of the contract by taking the elements both of *pactum* as an informal convention, which was expressed for the first time by Ulpianus,[19] and of identifying the contract with a mutual obligation.[20]

A sixth century gloss from Turin influenced to a certain degree by Theophilus' reasoning did not repeat the view expressed in the paraphrase. In the Turin gloss there are only some elements of the definition of the contract given marginally when defining the category of "quasi-*contractus*." They stress the intention of the person concluding the contract to cause effects in the form of creating an obligation.[21]

---

18 *Theophilus Institutionum graeca paraphrasis,* ed. E.C. Ferrini (Berlin, 1884): συνάλλαγμα δέ ἐστι δύο ἤ καὶ πλειόνων εἰζ τὸ αὐτὸ σύνοδόζ τε καὶ συναίνεσιζ ἐπὶ τὸ συστήσασθαι ἐνοχὴν καὶ τὸν ἕτερον τῷ ἑτέρῳ ποιῆσαι ὑπεύθυνον.

19 D.2.14.1.2: *Pactum autem a pactione dicitur ... et est pactio duorum pluriumve in idem placitum et consensus.*

20 Which could result from the interpretation of Labeo's opinion included in D.50.16.19: *Labeo libro primo praetoris urbani definit, quod quaedam agantur, quaedam gerantur, quaedam contrahantur: et actum quidem generale verbum esse, sive verbis sive re quid agatur, ut in stipulatione vel in numeratione: contractum autem ultro citroque obligationem, quod Graeci* συνάλλαγμα *vocant, veluti emptionem, venditionem, locationem, conductionem, societatem: gestum rem significare sine verbis factam.*

21 See P. Krüger, "Die turiner Institutionenglosse," *Zeitschrift für Rechtsgeschichte,* VII (1868), p. 76; fr. 438 (= ad. I.3.27pr.): *Quasi contractus est quod quidem a contractu separatur nec delicto subiacet, legalem tamen habet confirmationem: hoc autem non est definitio sed subscriptio, eo quod tam ex distractu quam ex constitutione rerum substantiam,* capit. fr.

The influence of Theophilus' paraphrase on the further development of the law in Western Europe is quite possible, although it is not known how it worked.[22] It is attested to by the fact that Theophilus' views are acknowledged in the literature of the glossators, *i.e.*, two centuries before the Greek manuscript was discovered.

In the definitions of contracts from the glossators' era there is only one element of Theophilus' definition present: namely, equalisation with *pactum*. The element of mutuality is missing.

The definition included in the twelfth century epitome *Exactis regibus* which equates *contractus* and *pactum* is characteristic in this respect, too.[23]

---

439 (= I.3.27.1): *Hoc ergo significant, quia in contractibus nullum ignorans obligatur.*

22 The Greek text of Theophilus' paraphrase was discovered in the fifteenth century. Its Greek editions and Latin translations were disseminated in the middle of the sixteenth century. The influence of Theophilus' ideas in the times of the glossators can be explained by the fact that *Institutiones* were the most popular and most widely studied part of Justinian's codification. See M. Conrat (Cohn), *Geschichte der Quellen und Literatur des römische Rechts im früheren Mittelalter* (Leipzig, 1889), p. 333ff.; F. Patetta, *Contributi alla storia del diritto romano nel medio Evo* (1891), p. ii, BIDR, IV, pp. 45ff. (= Studi sulle fonti giuridiche medievali; Turin, 1967, p. 81); F. Calasso, *Medio evo del diritto* (Milan, 1954), I, pp. 285-287; *id.*, *Il negozio giuridico*, 2d ed. (Milan, 1967), p. 173.

23 Conrat, *Die epitome exactis regibus* (Berlin, 1884), p. 97 (VII.1): *Contractus est duorum vel plurium in idem consensus. Et idem est contractus quod pactio, inde dictus quod paciscendo prius diversas in idem contrahimus voluntatem.* Also see p. 124 (IX.18): *Nasci dicuntur ex contractu que nascitur ex pacto, ex quasi contractu que neque ex pacto neque ex maleficio, sed tamen maiorem cum pactis habent affinitatem quam maleficiis.*

The author of *Summa Institutionum* at the turn of the twelfth century ("*Iustiniani est in hoc opere*") identifies *contractus*, *consensus*, *pactum*, and *conventio*. He divided contracts into actionable and inactionable ones.[24]

Identification of *pactum* and *contractus* also occurs in *liber iuris florentinus*[25] at the turn of the twelfth century. There is a similar statement in Accursius' gloss.[26]

In writings of French jurists and humanists of the sixteenth century a distinct differentiation is made between the contract as a source of an obligation and the *pactum* which does not result in legal consequences. Cujacius comes back to the classical concept of a sharp distinction between *contractus* and *pactum*.[27]

---

24 *La Summa Institutionum "Iustiniani est in hoc opere"* (Manuscript Pierpont Morgan 903), ed. by Pierre Legendre, *Ius Commune* (Frankfurt, 1973), II, pp. 90-91: 3, 6, 34-40: *Contractus, consensus, pactum, conventio idem significant. Contractus dictus est quasi simul tractus, idest cum ex diversis motibus duo vel plures ad idem animo obligandi consentiunt, contractum appellari constat. Set quia contractus quidam habent legalem formam, quidam non, hoc modo possumus dividere. Contractus alii obligatorii sunt ex quorum obligatione nascitur accio, alii non.*

25 Conrat, *Das florentiner Rechtsbuch. Ein System römischen Privatrecht aus der Glossatorenzeit* (Berlin, 1882), p. 35 (lib. IV, tit. 1): *Pactum est duorum vel plurium consensus in idem dandum vel faciendum quod alter contrahentium spe vel acceptione admittit.*

26 Accursius' gloss, ad D.44.7.1pr.: *De actionibus quae oriuntur ex pactis in continenti apositis: dicunt quidam quod sunt ex variis causarum figuris: sed potest dici ex contractu, cum sint obligatoria talia pacta vel conventiones. Nam et in ipsum pactum est contractus* (Accurs.).

27 J. Cujacius, *Opera* (Naples, 1772), VIII, p. 318: *Contractus actionem formant, non etiam gignunt novam actionem. Falsum est etiam quod ait: pactum esse con-*

Similar ideas were expressed by Doneau, who though stressing the element of agreement contained both in contract and in *pactum*, says that not every agreement constituted a contract. The purpose of creating an obligation is the basic element of contract, which distinguishes *contractus* from *pactum*.[28]

In the edition of *Corpus Iuris* with a commentary by the humanist Gothofredus, the centre of gravity in the definition of contract moved to the element of mutual (bilateral) obligation, which arises from it. It is interesting that the commentator makes use of the Greek paraphrase of *Institutiones*.[29] Gothofredus considers only an agreement which calls for a mutual obligation to be a proper contract (*contractus proprius*). *Mutuum* or *stipulatio*, which result in a unilateral obligation, are considered to be improper contracts (*contractus improprius*). *Transactio*, *solutio*, and *liberatio* also belong to the group of improper

---

tractum, hoc falso ipso falsius est. Semper accurate pactum et contractum separatur. Contractus enim parit obligationem, pactum non parit obligationem, neque tollit, nisi legitimum sit, id est, nisi ex causis certis et quibusdam legibus exceptis, quibus etiam ex pacto nudo nascitur, vel tollitur obligatio, neque contractus (nisi vis esse ridiculus) voces pacta, nec retro etiam pacta contractus: haec vocabula nunquam permiscentur.

28 H. Donellus, *Commentarius de iure civili* (Frankfurt, 1595), lib. 12, p. 22: *Contractus est duorum vel plurium consensus in hoc ut unus alteri quid det aut faciat, iure ad eam rem et praestationem comprobatus (...). Est enim omnis contractus conventio (...). Conventio autem et pactio idem valent. Est autem pactio duorum pluriumve in idem placitum et consensus (...). Sed non omnis consensus in idem, id est etiam in hoc ut quid fiat, contractus est (...). Contractus autem contrahendae obligationis causa est, unde et nomen (...).*

29 *Corpus Iuris Civilis cum notis Dionysii Gothofredi* (Frankfurt, 1663), Commentary to D.44.7.

contracts.[30]

In another place, the gloss reads as follows: "*contractus proprio est qui utriusque contrahentes obligat. Improprie in quo unus, magis improprie, distractus.*"[31]

The seventeenth and eighteenth century representatives of the natural law school developed consistently the principle that the creation of an obligation constituted a step in the recognition of the autonomy of the parties' intentions. It is expressed by Pufendorf: "*solus consensus obligat.*"[32] The identification of contract with an agreement is clearly seen in Domat's and Pothier's writings.[33]

Classical Roman law also failed to develop a generally accepted notion of a tort (*delictum*). There were various factual situations giving rise to responsibility based on different grounds. Four torts (*delicta*) quoted by Gaius in *Institutiones* (*furtum, rapina, damnum iniuria datum* and *iniuria*) constitute an example of precisely defined blameworthy acts which could be prosecuted by means of private *actiones in personam.*

Besides these "civil law torts" (*delicta*), as they are often called in modern Roman law doctrine, quoting Gaius,[34] there were many *actiones poenales* introduced by *ius civile* and *ius honorarium* and later by the emperor's law. The praetor also extended legal protection through the application of *actiones utiles* whereby he could go beyond the instances of responsibility precisely defined by the *ius civile.*

---

30 C.I.C. edition quoted, gloss to D.50.16.19.

31 C.I.C. edition quoted, gloss to I.3.14 (= 3.13).

32 See Calasso, *Il negozio giuridico*, note 22 above, pp. 338-339.

33 *Ibid.*, p. 340.

34 Which is not accurate because not all of the torts (*delicta*) mentioned by Gaius base their actionability on *ius civile.*

The existence of *dolus* (*furtum*, *rapina*, *iniuria*) or broadly comprehended *culpa* (*damnum iniuria datam* and some "quasi-delicts") could constitute grounds for responsibility in different factual situations. Responsibility could sometimes be independent of the subjective attitude of a responsible person (some quasi-delicts).

In the period of classical Roman law the number of causes which could give rise to private *actio poenalis* increased. Some kinds of torts could be used in a generalised way. The development of the responsibility for damages to property regulated by the *lex Aquilia*, as well as the responsibility for *dolus* provided in praetorian law, are examples.

The *lex Aquilia* in its initial wording regulated well-defined cases of destruction and damage to property committed unlawfully and through a direct act of the perpetrator (*damnum iniuria corpore corpori datum*). Such notions as causality, damage, fault, and the basing of responsibility on any degree of fault (even the slightest) were worked out through an extensive interpretation of the *lex Aquilia*.[35] The *lex Aquilia* contributed to the development and to the generalisation of the grounds for tortious responsibility through the application of *actio utilis*. The term "Aquilian responsibility" is, even now, a synonym of tortious liability (for example, in the French approach).

Responsibility for *damnum iniuria datum* made possible the generalisation of the development of responsibility for *dolus*. At first, *dolus* offered grounds for the application of a proceeding exception (*exceptio doli*). At the end of the Republic, the praetor Aquilius introduced an independent penal action (*actio poenalis*) protecting a person who suffered a loss because of a dishonest act of some other person.[36]

Despite these and other instances of general-

---

35 See D.9.2.

36 See Cicero, *de Officiis*, 3.14.57-60.

ised concepts of specific torts, the term *delictum* was never finally generalised in Roman law.[37]

The texts included in the Justinian codification do not attempt to supply a definition and grounds for tortious responsibility.[38] The first attempt to define a tort is in the Greek paraphrase of *Institutiones* elaborated by Theophilus. The attempt is connected with the distinction between tortious responsibility (*delictum*) and that approximating tortious responsibility (later called quasi-delict). According to Theophilus, tortious responsibility is based on *dolus* in causing the damage, whereas "quasi-*delictum*" is characterised by the existence of mere fault.[39]

This reasoning was continued by the glossators. On the other hand, responsibility based on *dolus* in the case of torts and the responsibility based on *culpa* (*imperitia* also included) constituted a ground for distinguishing between torts and quasi-delicts according to Accursius' gloss.[40]

The fact that in *Summa Azonis* the discussion of all torts occupied a page, whereas "quasi-

---

37 R. Villers, *Rome et le droit privé* (Paris, 1977), p. 418.

38 See I.4.1; D.47.1 - which discuss features of tortious responsibility only; D.47.2ff. - which discusses specific torts (*delicta*).

39 Theophilus, note 18 above, I.4.1 and I.4.5. Comprehensive discussion of quasi-delicts, their grounds and formation would go far beyond the limits of the present paper. See Wołodkiewicz, "Sulla cosidetta responsabilità dei 'quasi delitti' nel diritto romano ed il suo influsso sulla responsabilità civile moderna," *Atti del III Congresso Internazionale della Societa Italiana di Storia del Diritto* (Florence, 1977), III, pp. 1277ff.

40 Accursius, gloss to I.4.5: *Obligatio ex quasi delicto oriri dicitur, quando non ex dolo malo, sed magis imperitia quodam et minus provide delinquitur.* Accursius, gloss to D.44.7.5: "*peccasse*": *alias delinquisse: Vere peccavit quia imperitiae culpae annumeratur.*

delicta" were discussed on two pages offers an interesting illustration of the consequences of the fact that the glossators based responsibility for the latter on *culpa*.[41] Justification for founding responsibility on fault was based on a broad understanding of the concept of "quasi-delicts."

Basing the difference between the *delicta* and "quasi-*delicta*" on the occurrence of a *dolus* or *culpa* as prerequisites of responsibility was elaborated by the post-glossators, then by humanist jurists and by the representatives of the natural law school. Cujacius' discussion of the problem is initially based on the criterion of this distinction, though he sees the inconsistency of basing responsibility on *culpa* or *dolus*; he argues that in the *lex Aquilia* responsibility was based on *culpa*.[42]

A definition submitted by Pothier which influenced the grounds of tortious responsibility in French theory and legislation could be significant: "On appelle délit le fait par lequel une personne par dol ou par malignité cause du dommage on quelque tort à une autre. Le quasi délit est le fait par lequel une personne sans malignité, mais par une imprudence qui n'est pas excusable, cause quelque tort à une autre."[43]

Modern civil codes elaborated in the nineteenth and twentieth centuries had to classify civil responsibility somehow while providing for it. The greatest impact of the Justinian approach in this respect can be observed in the French

---

41 *Summa Azonis*, ad I.4.5 (ed., Basel, 1575), pp. 1083-1087.

42 Cujacius, note 27 above, VIII, p. 331: *Et haec damnorum genera, quae sunt maxima omnium, culpam augent, et convertunt in maleficium: alias vero culpa, quae alio modo laedit alterum non est maleficium, nec vindicatur actione legis Aquiliae, quae est civilis sed actione in factum praetoria.*

43 Pothier, *Traité des obligations*, p. 116.

Civil Code. The Code accepted that quadripartition of sources of civil responsibility (contracts, quasi-contracts, torts, and quasi-delicts) as programmatic, adding an obligation arising *ex lege*.

The usefulness of such classifications was widely discussed.[44] In recent doctrine, contractual obligations are contrasted with obligations resulting from other events which are not contracts. The 1896 German Civil Code and the 1933 Polish Code of Obligations both followed this approach.[45] In the newer Codes there are usually no separate provisions devoted to the classification of sources of obligations.[46]

In legal theory, the systems of responsibility are usually divided into contractual and tortious ones, irrespective of how they are regulated by statutes. This division is very strongly criticised. Some authors assume the decline of civil responsibility in modern law. They also believe that civil responsibility is too simplified. The

44 M. Planiol, "Classification des sources des obligations," *Revue de législation et de jurisprudence*, XXXVII (1904), pp. 224ff.; *id.*, *Traité élementaire de droit civil* (10th ed.; Paris, 1926), II, pp. 268ff.; E. Betti, *Cours de droit civil comparé des obligations* (Milan, 1958), pp. 12ff.; T. Mayer-Maly, *Studien zum Vertrag II*, *Festschrift Wilburg*, *J.W.* (1965), pp. 133ff.; *id.*, *Studien zum Vertrag III*, *RIDA*, XII (1965), pp. 438ff., 450; P. Schlesinger, "Quasi contratto e quasi delitto," *NNDI*, XIV, p. 636.

45 Article 1, Polish Civil Code: Obligations result from a declaration of will and acts and other events which are connected by the act with the existence of an obligation. See R. Longchamps de Berier, *Zobowiazania* (3d ed.; Poznan, 1948), p. 16; W. Czachórski, *Prawo zobowiazań, w zarysie* (Warsaw, 1968), pp. 168ff.

46 See Article 1, 1933 Polish Code of Obligations and Article 353, 1964 Polish Civil Code which lack such classifications *expressis verbis*. Similarly, Article 106 of the 1922 RSFSR Civil Code and Article 158 of the 1964 RSFSR Civil Code; the latter also lacks such systematization.

authors associate these facts with the development of statutory general clauses, as well as with the development of all types of social, commercial, and industrial insurance.[47]

It is suggested the hitherto existing fundamental systems of civil responsibility (contractual and tortious) be replaced by other classifications. There are no reasons for maintaining the distinction between contractual and tortious responsibility in modern law because the obligation of compensation for damages results from the infringement of the right of the other person.[48]

All these objections put forward by modern civil law theory do not entitle us to question the usefulness of the division into two systems of responsibility: one, resulting from the non-performance of a contractual obligation, and the other one based on the commission of damage by a tort. The two systems of responsibility are accepted both in theory and by the majority of civil codes which reflect different kinds of social and economic relationships. Legal differences in regulating these two kinds of responsibility have had great practical significance.

Modern civil law which serves different social and economic relationships introduces new institutions and reshapes the existing ones. But it constantly revolves around the terminology moulded in the Roman law or on the grounds of the Roman law. It manifests perennial values of Roman law which, though established for totally different socio-economic conditions, still serves as a common language for lawyers working in different states and various legal systems.

---

47 See Mazeau and Tunc, *Traité théorique de la responsabilité civile* (Paris, 1965), I, p. 16; Viney, note 5 above, p. 15; Stelmachowski, note 1 above, pp. 265ff.; A. Szpunar in *Studia cywilistyczne* (Cracow, 1970), pp. 30-31.

48 Marton, note 5 above, pp. 251, 254, 400; Warkałło, note 4 above, p. 5.

TRESPASS AND *INIURIA*

A. D. E. Lewis

This paper examines the almost universal assumption of English-speaking Roman lawyers that Roman law in the classical period afforded a remedy *in personam* for the invasion of property rights in land in the form of the *actio iniuriarum*. The modern English common law provides such a remedy in the action of trespass. Trespass lies for any deliberate and direct physical invasion of rights in property, whether the property be land or goods. An action of trespass lies equally if you break down the doors of my house or smash my best china tea-set or even for an attack, an assault, on my person.[1] Despite this wide field of application of the modern action of trespass, the word trespass has acquired a much more limited meaning in ordinary speech. Trespass has come to mean quintessentially trespass to land, and trespassers are those who invade my land. The English equivalent to notices prohibiting entry on to private property - *Défense d'entrer, Eintritt verboten* - is the circumlocution: "Trespassers will be prosecuted;" anyone found trespassing will be proceeded against at law.[2]

---

1 On the general conception of liability in modern trespass, see, for example, P.S. James and D.J. Latham Brown, *General Principles of the Law of Torts* (London, 1978), pp. 119ff.

2 The word prosecute appears in this context as a grave juristic solecism. Prosecute is apt to describe criminal law proceedings but it is no criminal offence in modern law to enter another's land if no damage be done. It is rather a trespass for which a civil suit for damages will lie. Notices announcing that trespassers will be sued might prove less efficacious. Winfield was prompted by this anomaly to dub such notices "wooden lies": *Tort* (8th ed.; London, 1967), p. 323. The reference has been altered by subsequent editors of his work. (I am grateful to Mr. D.E.C.

The English action of trespass is, in Roman law terms, a personal action rather than one which formally protects rights *in rem*. There are in fact no true actions *in rem* in the modern common law, no remedies which are formal equivalents of the *vindicatio*. This is the result of an historical development which is briefly traced below. It is not, of course, the case that such rights are not protected, far from it, but rather that property rights are indirectly protected by actions which are formally *in personam*. Although no contemporary practising lawyer would confuse the two, the action for the protection of title in land and the action to restrain interference with the land are close cousins: they are both actions of trespass. The use of one type of remedy to cover both *in rem* and *in personam* rights has had the result that any entry on to another's property can be the subject of an action of trespass, even if no actual quantifiable harm is caused. In the context of the real right this is understandable, for any interference with my rights as owner threatens my ownership and is properly met with a *vindicatio* to assert my claim. But it is far from clear that any remedy for breach of obligation is required just because someone has entered my land. If such an entrant causes harm, for example, by invading my privacy or damaging my crops, then indeed an action should lie, but for the damage done and not for the mere entry. By its adoption of a single remedy to cover both *in rem* and *in personam* claims the common law has lost sight of this distinction.[3]

Consider the following two passages from a standard students' book, Nicholas' *Introduction to Roman Law*:

> "It was *iniuria*, for example, to prevent another without lawful justification, from moving freely in a public place, or

---

Yale, Christ's College, Cambridge, for information on this point.)

3 B. Nicholas, *Introduction to Roman Law* (Oxford, 1962), p. 216.

> from fishing in the sea or other public water. It was likewise *iniuria* to interfere with his use of his property or to enter unauthorised into his home or on to his land."

> "[If I shoot a patridge on your land] I may have committed the delict of *iniuria* in entering on your land, but this will make no difference to my title to the partridge."[4]

It will be contended that there is no authority in the classical texts for the proposition that it is *iniuria* merely to enter on to another's land. Classical Roman law afforded no remedy, save that of justifiable expulsion by the use of force if necessary, for the situation where someone enters my land without my permission but does no more.[5] For any entry which implied possessory or dominial claims there were, of course, the interdicts and *vindicatio*,[6] but it is absurd to imagine their being used against a mere trespasser who would no longer be on the premises by the time an action could be brought. For any damage, physical or otherwise, which resulted from the entry, on the other hand, there were appropriate *in personam* actions, under the *lex Aquilia* for *damnum iniuria datum* for most physical harms and the *actio iniuriarum* for a large range of activities resulting in harm to the plaintiff's well being. But for any entry on to land to be actionable as an *iniuria* the harm to the plaintiff's well being must be demonstrated; it does not occur immediately on the trespasser's entry.

---

4 *Ibid.*, p. 131. Other writers adopt similar, if more circumspect, positions; for example, J.A.C. Thomas, *Textbook of Roman Law* (Amsterdam, 1976), p. 369.

5 The defence of property might on occasion even justify invading another's property, as in the case where I pull down my neighbour's house as a fire-break: D.9.2.49.1; cf. D.43.24.7.4.

6 See, generally, Thomas, note 4 above, pp. 133ff.

The Classical Texts

There is no systematic treatment of our problem in the classical jurists, and such texts as there are raise the matter tangentially. This suggests a general point in view of the large measure of protection afforded to property rights in Roman law. Reticence to speak generally of one apparent means of protection cannot fail to be significant. If the *actio iniuriarum* were an automatic choice for a landowner or occupier whose property had been invaded, then we would expect to hear more directly about it.

Turning to the examination of the short list of texts which do discuss *iniuria* in the context of the invasion of property rights, some general observations about the scope of the *actio iniuriarum* must be made. For the history of *iniuria* from the Twelve Tables to the classical period, the general argument of Birks[7] is adopted and on that basis the following propositions advanced:

(1) The word *iniuria* in the Twelve Tables is used adverbially to characterise the unlawfulness of damage done. This meaning is incorporated in the text of the *lex Aquilia* in the phrase "*damnum iniuria datum.*" For this reason, if for no other, the word *iniuria* continued to bear the general sense of "wrongful" throughout the classical period, as is evidenced by the explicit statements of the jurists.

(2) Special or substantive *iniuria* was developed within the Praetor's Edict as an extension of the Twelve Tables provisions: the field covered was that of personal injury and insult, the eventual rationale of both being construed as *contumelia*.

(3) Texts which appear to be granting an *actio iniuriarum* for interference with property by entry upon it are in fact giving a remedy for the *contumelia* occasioned by the entry and not for the

7 P.B.H. Birks, "The Early History of *Iniuria*," *Tijdschrift voor Rechtsgeschiednis*, XXXVII (1969), 194.

simple wrongfulness of the entry.

Examining these points in turn:

(1) *That iniuria had a general as well as a special meaning*

Inasmuch as this is evident from the plain words of the texts, this is scarcely worthy of demonstration.

Ulpian 56 *ad edictum* D.47.10.1pr.

Iniuria ... est quod non iure fiat, omne quod non iure fit, iniuria fieri dicitur: hoc generaliter. Specialiter autem iniuria dicitur contumelia.

Paul *lib. sing. iniuriarum* Coll.2.5.1 (= Inst.4.4pr.)

Generaliter dicitur iniuria omne quod non iure fit: specialiter alia est contumelia, ...

The texts are cast in terms of the meanings of the word *iniuria*, general or particular. But the contrast is also between a general and a conceptualised use. *Iniuria generaliter* simply means unlawful and can be appropriated to describe any conduct which should be so stigmatised. But *iniuria specialiter* expresses a substantive legal concept otherwise termed *contumelia*, contumelious conduct, the outlines of which are to be found in the Praetor's *edictum generale*.[8]

(2) *That the central core of substantive iniuria in the classical period was personal injury and insult*

For Labeo, quoted by Ulpian in book 56 *ad edictum*, *iniuria* is committed either by deed or by words:

---

8 Birks, *ibid.*; D.47.10.15.26.

D.47.10.1.1

Iniuriam autem fieri Labeo ait aut re aut verbis: re, quotiens manus inferuntur: verbis autem, quotiens non manus inferuntur, convicium fit.

The distinction *re/verbis* is glossed to mean either by use of one's hands or without the use of hands.[9] This explanation of the distinction is to be taken literally. Some contumelious *iniuriae* are occasioned by the use of physical violence, some are not. The stock *formula* in the Edict dealing with *iniuria* is quoted by Paul in his *liber singularis iniuriarum* (Coll.2.6.4):[10] "*quod Auli Ageri mala pugno percussa est.*" This did not, of course, preclude extension to other types of physical violence "*an fuste an lapide,*" as Paul himself explains, but it strongly suggests that Labeo had such an example in mind.

Ulpian understood the Labeo text in this sense. In the very next sentence from his book 56 he equated "*quotiens manus inferuntur*" with "*in corpus inferri*" because "there is an *iniuria* in respect of the body when someone is beaten."

D.47.10.1.2

Omnemque iniuriam aut in corpus inferri aut ad dignitatem aut ad infamiam perti-

9 The gloss may be by Labeo himself, by Ulpian, or by an intermediate hand. That it was known to Ulpian is shown by an allusion to it in another passage (D.47.10.5pr.). Since Ulpian, however, adopted a different analysis himself (D.47.10.1.2, cited *infra*), it seems better to attribute the gloss to Labeo or an intermediary.

10 The text of Coll.2.6.4 is as follows:

Certum non dicit qui dicit pulsatum se sive verberatum. sed et partem corporis demonstrat et quem in modum, pugno puto an fuste an lapide. sicut formula proposita est: "quod Auli Ageri mala pugno percussa est". illud non cogitur dicere dextra an sinistra, nec qua manu percussa sit.

> *nere: in corpus fit, cum quis pulsatur: ad dignitatem cum comes matrona abducitur: ad infamiam, cum pudicitia adtemptatur.*

Where Labeo had adopted a twofold classification *re/verbis*, Ulpian added a third category. Neither of Ulpian's non-physical examples seems to be a simple illustration of *iniuria verbis*. Whereas Labeo had distinguished with reference to the method used in committing the *iniuria*, Ulpian looked rather to results. Either the body is harmed, or dignity affected, or reputation impugned.[11] Labeo's analysis, though made in relation to the unified substantive *iniuria* of the Praetor's Edict, is still influenced by the origins of *iniuria* in the various decemviral provisions against different kinds of physical violence and verbal assaults. Ulpian's analysis reflects the subtler juristic development of the praetorian *iniuria* which concentrates rather on the resultant harm to the victim. In this analysis, the organising notion of *contumelia* is advanced as an explanation of the general harm caused by the divers injurious acts. But the more sophisticated notion was developed out of the earlier *iniuria* which meant physical violence or insult and it remained linked to it for two reasons. First, the reshaping of the jurists' understanding of *iniuria* was essentially a redefinition of existing *iniuriae* in terms of result: insult occasioned by physical blows, by affront, or by verbal attacks on reputation. Any acts which had the effect of arousing feelings of *contumelia* in the plaintiff were actionable as *iniuriae*, as the heterogeneous

---

11 It is of some interest that the abduction of *comes matronae* is offered as an example of an affront to dignity rather than as a physical assault. In his seventy-seventh book *ad edictum* (On the Edict), Ulpian quotes Labeo to the effect that such abduction can occur not only where force is used but also where a companion is persuaded to abandon her mistress (D.47.10.15.18).

collection of examples in the texts witnesses.[12] Second, and on the other hand, the edict which the jurists were expounding carried as a stock *formula* "*quod Auli Ageri mala pugno percussa est*."[13] In these circumstances, it was not possible to invert the delict completely and redefine it in terms of result. Means were important, for as Paul points out, the claim must be certain and "he does not speak clearly who says that he was beaten or struck."[14]

We find Ulpian quoting Labeo's older analysis side by side with his own, because it was important not to lose touch in the new analysis in terms of result with the means by which the *contumelia* was brought about. It remained true for the classical period that *iniuria* might be occasioned either by physical blows or by insulting conduct. Here another factor entered, one that has a comparative parallel in English law as we shall see. A deliberate physical assault on the person, as contemplated by the Twelve Tables' provisions and the stock *formula* of the Praetor's Edict, gives rise to a remedy for the damage necessarily caused without further reflection.[15] That some physical and compensatable damage occurs as a result of a bodily assault needs no argument. But interference with other interests, for example by insulting conduct, needs some demonstration beyond the mere fact of the insult's being given. It must, for example, be received by the victim and actually perceived by him as contumelious.[16] It would

---

12 Examples are selling a pledge (D.47.10.15.32), calling someone a debtor (h.t.15.33), and calling on a solvent debtor's sureties to pay (h.t.19).

13 Note 10 above.

14 *Ibid*.

15 There might be justifications in terms of the defence of persons or property as in the Twelve Tables' provisions on nocturnal and diurnal thieves (Tab.VIII.12, 13; D.9.2.4.1, 48.8.9, Coll.7.2.1).

16 D.47.10.11.1; Inst.IV.4.12.

be surprising if the mere entry on to another's property could be construed as contumelious conduct without some further characterisation of the act as insulting, and it is my contention that the texts do not require us to draw any other conclusion.

(3) *The texts on entry to land and iniuria*[17]

Paul 4 *ad edictum* D.47.10.23

Qui in domum alienam invito domino introiret, quamvis in ius vocat, actionem iniuriarum in eum competere Ofilius ait.

Whoever enters another's house without the owner's permission, albeit to summon him into court, is according to Ofilius liable to the *actio iniuriarum*. On a first reading, one might take this Paul-Ofilius text to be saying that, although one is allowed to summon another to court in accordance with the rules in the Twelve Tables, using such force on a reluctant defendant as is necessary for example,[18] one is nevertheless not permitted to enter his house for this purpose. Laying hands on someone would in normal circumstances amount to an actionable *iniuria*. The Twelve Tables' provisions relating to defendants who drag their feet give an exception to this general rule. This text, it might be argued, shows that no such exception exists in the case of the *iniuria* of entering another's house *invito domino*. Accordingly, the argument runs, the text demonstrates the existence of a general rule prohibiting such entry on pain

17 Omitted largely for reasons of space is consideration of the *lex Cornelia de iniuriis* (Ulpian, 56 *ad edictum*, D.47.10.5pr., 5). It can be shown that the problems of the *lex* are not germane to the present issue concerning edictal *iniuria* and I hope to provide a demonstration elsewhere.

18 The Twelve Tables provided that if a defendant drags his feet (*pedem struit*) when the plaintiff properly summons him to court (*in ius vocat*), then he could be seized (*manum endo iacito*): Tab.I.1, 2.

of an *actio iniuriarum*.

This interpretation of the text regards the phrase *quamvis in ius vocat* as a mere explanation that there is no exception in such a case from the general rule. If this interpretation reflects even Paul's understanding of the text, then it provides clear justification for the view I am concerned to criticise. But we cannot take such a simple view of the text. In the first place, extracting the broad statement "whoever goes into another's house without the owner's permission commits an *iniuria*" from the text leads to the conclusion that the *actio iniuriarum* is available irrespective of the presence or absence of the owner; it is the mere entry which constitutes the delict. But the words *quamvis in ius vocat* show that for Ofilius the owner is in fact present in the house. The erstwhile plaintiff has entered in order to summons him. So any general principle ascribed to the text must be limited to cases when the owner is present. But there is no way of extracting such a limited general principle from the text whilst at the same time cutting out the reference to summoning. (Of course if there were an established general principle that entry on to another's property was an actionable *iniuria*, then this text would not be incongruent. But no such general principle has been established and this text is no authority for it.)

The second reason for not taking a straightforward view of this text is that it comes from Paul's fourth book *ad edictum*. Paul dealt with the delict of *iniuria* in his fifty-fifth book.[19] His fourth book concerned summoning into court.[20] This strongly suggests that the summoning is in some way integral to the delict in question. For assistance on this point, we can turn to another text of Paul from his first book *ad edictum*:

---

19 O. Lenel, *Palingenesia Iuris Civilis* (Leipzig, 1889), I, col. 1072.

20 *Ibid.*, col. 974.

D.2.4.21

Sed etsi is qui domi est interdum vocari in ius potest, tamen de domo sua nemo extrahi debet.

Although one who is at home can on occasion be summoned to court, yet he ought not to be dragged from his house. The full implications are not immediately clear. Is the summons somehow invalidated if the defendant is dragged reluctantly out ? This seems unlikely. Better is the suggestion that he should not be dragged out because this amounts to an *iniuria*, despite the Twelve Tables rule on those who drag their feet.[21] The exception does not apply in the case where the defendant is taken from his house, presumably because of the implication that the defendant was so afraid to appear in public for fear of being summoned that he has stayed at home.[22] To be dragged from one's home to court implies an unwillingness to appear going beyond the normal reluctance of a defendant to a lawsuit that amounts to a gross insult to character. The same might even be said of an entry to summon someone. D.2.4.21 says that one might on occasion (*interdum*) be summoned at home, our earlier text, D.47.10.23, suggests that the mere fact that one is engaged in such a lawful summons does not exempt one from an *actio iniuriarum* if the summoning be done so as to impugn character. The effect of *quamvis* in this context is to make it clear that, despite the fact that the plaintiff has a liberty to summon the defendant to court within the limits of the Twelve Tables' provisions, nevertheless he may not enter the latter's house in such a way as to suggest that the defendant is unwilling to be summoned lawfully. It is an entry for this purpose which constitutes *iniuria*. A similar interpretation is to be given to the next text, also from Paul.

---

21 Note 18 above.

22 "If Caesar hide himself, shall they not whisper
'Lo, Caesar is afraid' ?"
W. Shakespeare, *Julius Caesar*, II.2.100.

Paul 40 *ad Sabinum* D.47.2.21.7

Qui furti faciendi causa conclave intravit, nondum fur est, quamvis furandi causa intravit. Quid ergo ? qua actione tenebitur ? Utique iniuriarum: aut de vi accusabitur, si per vim introivit.

Paul asks what action is to be available against one who enters in order to steal but who is not yet a thief (presumably because he has not yet contrectated). Obviously, he says, the *actio iniuriarum*. On the traditional view, it is argued that the *actio iniuriarum* "obviously" lies here because any unauthorised entry amounts to edictal *iniuria*. But again we must take the whole situation contemplated by the text into account and not accept the text as authority for a broader proposition than is necessary to explain it. The entry is not just an unauthorised one but one by a thief who contemplates active interference with my property. When one's house is robbed, one suffers two distinct harms, the loss of the goods stolen (for which in Roman law there is available the *actio furti* together with the reipersecutory actions) and a sense of outrage and shock. The latter harm can occur even if no goods are actually stolen. Although the absence of material loss may go some way to assuage one's feelings, the outrage persists. It is this feeling which lies at the heart of the classical jurists' attempt to reshape edictal *iniuria* in terms of result rather than cause: to express the outrage felt when one is physically assaulted (over and above any material damage done for which there might be no remedy in the classical period),[23] or when one is defamed or made vulnerable in one's self-esteem. In all these cases, the *iniuria* seen in terms of result is an implication arising from the actual behaviour of the defendant: an implication that can be

---

23 It is generally held that the classical law offered no remedy, even under the praetorian extensions to the *lex Aquilia*, for corporal damage to a free person. See F.H. Lawson, *Negligence in the Civil Law* (Oxford, 1950), pp. 21-22.

rebutted in certain cases.[24] The *iniuria* does not consist solely in the act itself but also in the reaction of the victim. It is the natural reaction of the attempted robbery victim that makes the entry of the intending thief an actionable *iniuria*.

The third and last text from the classical period underlines the point that it is the implications of what is done rather than what is done that is of significance. It is not strictly a text on physical entry to property but concerns mutual relations between neighbours.[25]

> Iavolenus 9 *ex posterioribus Labeonis* D.47.10.44
>
> *Si inferiorum dominus aedium superioris vicini fumigandi causa fumum faceret, aut si superior vicinus in inferiores aedes quid aut proiecerit aut infuderit, negat Labeo iniuriarum agi posse: quod falsum puto, si tamen iniuriae faciendae causa inmittitur.*

Labeo denied that there was an *actio iniuriarum* where the owner of one flat blew smoke in his premises for fumigation and smoked out his superadjacent neighbour and equally where the one above threw or poured anything down on to the property below. Iavolenus, however, says that the action does lie so long as what is done is done *iniuriae faciendae causa* - with the intention of effecting an *iniuria*. Since this can scarcely mean "with the intention of committing a wrongdoing", it must be taken as a reference to an intention to cause an edictal *iniuria*. Iavolenus thinks it in no way improbable that such things could be done with the intention of embarrassing one's neighbour.

---

24 "*dissimulatione aboletur*" Ulpian 57 *ad edictum* D.47.10.11.1. This is usually held to imply that failure to demonstrate one's sense of outrage immediately and openly leads to loss of the action.

25 Nevertheless, the principles to be applied to invasion of property by an agency seem to apply *a fortiori* to the principal.

Presumably he has in mind the situation which can arise in the case of bad relationships between neighbours in which almost any act can be an occasion for offence. But it is the offence intended and taken to be such which constitutes the actionable *iniuria*.

What then did Labeo mean ? For Labeo, as we have seen, *iniuria* was a matter of causes not of results. The more sophisticated theory which enabled all cases of edictal *iniuria* to be subsumed under one rationale was not available to him. Faced with a problem where something has occurred which merits compensation, Labeo denies that the *actio iniuriarum* can be used as a general remedy for wrongs. Iavolenus may have been genuinely surprised to read what Labeo had written when he came to make an epitome of his posthumous works. For Iavolenus *iniuria* was an established substantive category. How could it possibly have occurred to Labeo that the *actio iniuriarum* was in issue unless there were overriding factors, such as ill-feelings between the parties ? Labeo must have been taken to have denied the *actio iniuriarum* even if there was a contumelious insult and sufficient intention. This is, of course, wrong and Iavolenus reacts with surprising but appropriate force - *quod falsum puto*. If the act were one *iniuriae faciendae causa* then it is actionable. Iavolenus' statement can be generalised to apply to all acts including entries in to property, they can amount to actionable *iniuriae* so long only as they be done *iniuriae faciendae causa*.

One final reflection on the classical law, and this from Ulpian:

> Ulpian 18 *ad edictum* D.9.2.5.1
>
> *Iniuriam autem accipere nos oportet non quemadmodum circa iniuriarum actionem contumeliam quandam, sed quod non iure factum est, hoc est contra ius, id est si culpa quis occiderit: et ideo interdum utraque actio concurrit et legis Aquiliae et iniuriarum, sed duae erunt aestimationes, alia damni, alia contume-*

> *liae. Igitur iniuriarum hic damnum accipiemus culpa datum etiam ab eo, qui nocere noluit.*

Faced with the occurrence of the word *iniuria* in the text of the *lex Aquilia,*[26] with which his eighteenth book was concerned, Ulpian states the standard distinction between *iniuria* meaning *contumelia* and *iniuria* meaning unlawful. Where both actions are available, the *actio iniuriarum* and the *actio* on the *lex Aquilia,* they lie for different types of loss. The latter for *damnum* as defined in the *lex,* the *actio iniuriarum* for the *contumelia. Contumelia,* for Ulpian, is not only the organising rationale for the cases which fall under edictal *iniuria,* but also the standard by which the damages are to be assessed. What then is the actionable damage when someone enters upon my land ? To the extent that there has been *contumelia* as a result of the entry an *actio iniuriarum* will lie.

Actions of Trespass for Invasion of Landed Property Rights in the Common Law

The assumption of English Romanists that the *actio iniuriarum* lies for mere entry on to another's property with nothing more is rather surprising in view of the state of the texts. What then can have prompted it ? I suggest that it is the rather remarkable position of the common law remedy for this situation which has been responsible.

The early history of the action of trespass has been the subject of investigation by English

---

26 The relevant text of the first chapter of the *lex Aquilia* is given by Gaius 7 *ad edictum provinciale,* D.9.2.2pr.: *Lege Aquilia capite primo cavetur ut qui servum servamve alienum alienamve quadrupedemve pecudem iniuria occiderit, quanti id in eo anno plurimi fuit, tantum aes dare domino damnas esto.*

legal historians in recent years.[27] Trespass, Latin *transgressio*, had originally no specialised meaning. Just as *iniuria* in the Twelve Tables, it referred generally to wrongful conduct. An action in trespass was an action for wrongdoing. In fact the early common law as administered in the King's courts did restrict the ambit of trespass claims but for jurisdictional rather than juristic reasons.[28] The common law courts in the twelfth century were not courts of general jurisdiction. Lacking any formal legal restrictions on their competence, they were nevertheless loath to extend their interest beyond that which was broadly of royal or governmental concern. As a result, the earliest types of trespasses (wrongs) to come before the common law courts were allegations of violence occasioning a breach of the King's peace and of corruption and violence by royal officers.[29] Originally, *vi et armis contra pacem Domini regis* was meant literally; wrongs committed in other ways, fraud or insult, for example, were of no concern to the common law administered in the King's courts.[30] Such wrongs were not therefore without remedy, but redress had to be sought from the customary local courts. The trespasses commonly litigated in the King's courts included violent entry on to land, assault and the forcible carrying off of goods.[31] Plaintiffs anxious for various reasons to get other types of case before the more efficient and impartial forum of the

---

27 See, above all, S.F.C. Milsom, *Historical Foundations of the Common Law* (London, 1969), pp. 244ff. and the references cited at p. 410.

28 *Glanvill, Tractatus de legibus ... Anglie*, I, 2; X, 5; XIV, 8 (ed. G.D.G. Hall, London, 1965).

29 Milsom, "Trespass from Henry II to Edward III," *Law Quarterly Review*, LXXIV (1958), pp. 195, 407, 561; A. Harding, "Plaints and Bills," *1972 Legal History Studies*, ed. D. Jenkins (Cardiff, 1975), p. 65.

30 Note 28 above.

31 Cf. J.H. Baker, *An Introduction to English Legal History* (2d ed.; London, 1979), p. 57.

King's court would have to present their complaints as if they concerned violent breach of the King's peace. In a well-known case in 1317 we find an allegation that the defendant, having the plaintiff's wine barrel in his possession, had with force of arms, to wit, bows, arrows, and staves, drawn off a quantity of wine and replaced it with water against the peace of the Lord King.[32]

In the middle of the fourteenth century, for reasons which remain obscure but which are probably connected with the increased business being brought before the King's courts, the courts relaxed their attitude to the types of wrong that could be permitted a hearing.[33] Not only violent wrongs against the peace, but other wrongs could thereafter be legitimately and undisguisedly brought before the King's courts. A wrong committed with force of arms against the peace continued to be litigated as before and came to be labelled an action of trespass. Wrongs occasioned in some other way, early examples are the provision of negligent veterinary or medical treatment where the consent to the treatment barred an allegation that the harm had been done in breach of the peace,[34] were litigated in a form which required the detailed setting out of the facts giving rise to the claim or case. These, then, became known for the sake of distinction as actions of trespass on the case or just case for short. The distinction had some practical purpose. The original trespass claims had covered activities that were,

---

32 *The Case of the Tun of Wine* (1317) Y.B. 10 Edward II (*Selden Society, LIV*), p. 154.

33 The change occurs around the year 1370: Milsom, note 27 above, p. 250, attributes it to a deliberate decision to admit a wider range of cases honestly. The first reported case is *Waldon* v. *Marshal* (1369) Y.B. Mich. 43 Edward III, f. 33, pl. 38.

34 In *Waldon* v. *Marshall, cit.* n. 33, the point was expressly taken by counsel for the defendant who had wrongly supposed that the plaintiff's writ suffered from this inconsistency.

on the face of it, objectionable, inasmuch as they involved the use of force. There was every sense therefore in allowing the plaintiff to state his problem simply, leaving it to the defendant to justify his use of force on the plaintiff or his goods if he could.[35] In the newer types of case, the conduct of the defendant was frequently wrongful only *sub modo* and it was reasonable to expect the plaintiff to set out the circumstances in his claim.[36]

If the mode of pleading had been the only difference between trespass and case, then all would have been well and the history of English law significantly different. But the difference between the old claim of trespass and the new one in case was fixed also in a range of procedural distinctions, not least in the mode of summons appropriate to bring the defendant before the court. Because its ancestry lay in cases brought where the King had a genuine interest in the maintenance of his peace, trespass *vi et armis* commenced with an order for the seizing of the defendant to bring him to court as if the proceeding were, in modern terms, criminal rather than civil in nature. In actions on the case where this dimension was *ex hypothesi* lacking, plaintiffs could only hope for summons of a reluctant defendant by the dilatory procedure of seizure of property, a sanction which might well prove inefficacious.[37] In later times, this distinction came to be an embarrassment, not least because it was impossible to bring both actions simultaneously, although it might very well be unclear to all parties which

---

35 The origin of such complaints was the oral and informal presentation of complaints to the King's justices. See Harding, note 29 above.

36 This was expressed by a judge in an early case saying that the plaintiff had a good claim *en son cas*: (*The Farrier's Case* (1372) Y.B. Trin. 46 Edward III, f. 19, pl. 19).

37 D.W. Sutherland, "Mesne Process in the Early Common Law," *Law Quarterly Review*, LXXXII (1966), p. 482.

remedy was appropriate to the plaintiff's claim. In a case in 1773, *Scott* v. *Shepherd*,[38] the plaintiff was injured by a firework thrown originally by the defendant and passed on by a succession of intermediate parties all anxious to avoid injury to themselves or their goods. What action was appropriate for the plaintiff's claim ? Trespass, on the ground that the harm was a direct result of the defendant's violent act in throwing the firework ? Or case, on the basis that the defendant had indirectly caused the harm that actually occurred, or because he had acted negligently rather than deliberately with regard to the plaintiff ? These difficulties arose because in a rational age it was felt there must be some rational basis for such an apparently fundamental distinction as that between trespass and case. *Scott* v. *Shepherd* settled that if the damage were direct and forcible the proper remedy lay in trespass, whereas if the damage were indirect or consequential the remedy was in case.[39] There remained in all this some sense that the harm remedied in trespass must be obvious and not require special demonstration, either because it happened immediately or because the defendant had intended it.

Forcible trespass to land had been amongst the earliest of wrongs to be remedied in the King's courts. In the beginning the force was very real, for in feudal society land is a source of power as well as wealth. Well into the sixteenth century many local disturbances were occasioned by disputes over property.[40] The common law knew a large

---

38 *Scott* v. *Shepherd* (1773) 2 W. Blackstone 892. For a detailed comment, see M.J. Prichard, "*Scott* v. *Shepherd* (1773) and the Emergence of the Tort of Negligence," *Selden Society Lecture 1973* (London, 1976).

39 On the later developments towards the modern notion of trespass, see Prichard, "Trespass, Case and the Rule in *Williams* v. *Holland*," *Cambridge Law Journal*, XX (1964), p. 234.

40 A parliamentary petition of 1429 speaks of the daily occurrence of acquisition of property by forcible

range of remedies for the protection of landed property rights, both title and possession.[41] The actions appropriate to try title were inherently unwieldy, and it became common for a plaintiff to prefer recovery of possession in a possessory action to the rigours of proof in an action on title. If the plaintiff recovered possession, then his opponent could always have recourse to the action on title if he were prepared to take the burden of proof upon himself. The situation is on all fours with that described by Gaius in his Institutes as between the *vindicatio* and the possessory interdicts.[42] Procedure in the possessory action at common law was similar to that in trespass except for the remedy: the possessory action gave specific recovery of the property, the trespassory action only damages. For a complex series of reasons,

---

entry: *Rotuli Parliamentorum* (Record Commission, 1767-77) iv. 422. The *Paston Letters*, ed. N. Davis (Oxford, 1971-76) offer a wealth of material on the lawlessness of the petty gentry. See especially I, pp. 52, 336, and 398-405. By the sixteenth century, however, the legal records are a poor guide to social reality, owing to the growth of fictitious pleading. This is so even in courts dealing ostensibly with criminal matters: J.A. Guy, *The Cardinal's Court* (Hassocks, 1977), pp. 54ff.

41 The common law real actions, the writs of right, were amongst the earliest remedies to be available in the King's courts. The assize of novel disseisin, the action for recent dispossession, was probably available from 1166. In the thirteenth century the writs of entry extended the possessory remedy to cases of less recent dispossession, limiting the need to bring the writ of right with its attendant difficulties of proof of title. On the complex issues raised by the transformation of feudal land-holding relations into common law remedies for ownership and possession, see Milsom, *The Legal Framework of English Feudalism* (Cambridge, 1976).

42 Gaius, *Institutes*, IV.148.

only recently unravelled,[43] the action of trespass came to supplant the possessory and proprietary actions at common law during the fifteenth century. In 1413 it was still being said that trying title to land in a trespass action was improper, but by the end of the sixteenth century devices had been perfected which enabled the question of title to be settled satisfactorily in an action of trespass.[44] These devices, an endless source of delight to *cognoscenti* and puzzlement to students of a more rational system of law, involved the creation of two wholly fictitious persons and an account of their mutual though imaginery dealings. One who wished to try a title to land whilst himself out of possession would first create an imaginary lease of the land in question to an imaginary lessee, John Doe. The real plaintiff would next call into being an imaginary individual, Richard Roe, who would be supposed to have thrown John Doe out of his imaginary occupation of the land. A letter was then written to the actual occupant of the property as if from the fictitious Roe, setting out these events and informing him that an action was pending by Doe against Roe in which Doe was claiming recovery of the land held under lease from the genuine plaintiff and from which he had been forcibly and wrongfully (as he alleges) ejected by Roe. Roe asks for the genuine defendant's help in defending this action, for, as he points out, recovery of the term of his lease by Doe would put him into occupation of the land even as against the real occupant as well as demonstrating that the genuine lessor of the land to Doe had a right to lease the land and therefore a better right to the title than the actual occupant. If the defendant-occupant does nothing, he will lose the land because Roe will not, for obvious

---

43 Sutherland, *The Assize of Novel Disseisin* (Oxford, 1973).

44 The case in 1413: Y.B. Hil. 14 Henry IV f. 35, pl. 52 cited in Baker, note 31 above, p. 203. The first evidence of the new practice is in *Gerrarde* v. *Worsley* (1580) Dyer 374a.

reasons, defend the action but lose by default. The ousted occupant would then have to commence proceedings himself, bearing the burden of proof, if he wishes to undo the harm these fictitious entitles will have done him. Alternatively and advisedly, he can apply to the court for leave to defend on Roe's behalf the action brought by Doe. But this will only be allowed him if he consents to accept the fictions as true, in other words to have the issue of title tried in an action of trespass.[45]

The existence of these fantastic charades may well have been influential in suggesting to the jurist Bentham, writing at the end of the eighteenth century when they were at their height, that all property rights could be construed as exceptions to the imposition of duties *in personam*.[46] Together with the characteristics of trespass *vi et armis* actions in other contexts, namely, that they are concerned with obvious damage, the effect was to create the notion that in the common law any entry on to land was remediable in trespass because, in the first place, there is no need in such actions to prove damage specially and, in the

---

45 A.W.B. Simpson, *Introduction to the History of the Land Law* (Oxford, 1961), pp. 138-141. The reality of these fictions has left its mark in the form of citation of the cases in which they were used: e.g. *Doe d. Smith* v. *Roe* (1852) 8 Exch. 126 (Doe on the demise or lease of Smith against Roe).

46 J. Bentham, *Of Laws in General* (Collected Edition, ed. H.L.A. Hart; London, 1970), pp. 176ff:

> Now in the list of offences against property the radical one seems to be that which we have styled wrongful occupation of property: it is to that offence that the law, by which the most simple and elementary species of proprietary right is created, corresponds ... Annexing then the expression of will to the act thus expressed, we have the whole substance of the law; which amounts to this "Let no one, Rusticus excepted" (so we will call the proprietor) "and those whom he allows meddle with such or such a field."

second, most trespass to land actions were brought in a context where it was an essential ingredient in the procedure that the formal and fictitional trespass should threaten the actual tenant's property rights. In the result, the common law lost sight of the need to prove damage in order to ground an action for peaceable invasion of land and with it any notion that the remedy in trespass for such conduct occasioning no damage and challenging no property rights is in any way peculiar. English Romanists would appear to have made the mistake of assuming that classical Roman law was equally myopic.

CURRENT DEVELOPMENTS IN POLISH ECONOMIC LAW

J. Okolski

In Poland the system of contracts between state enterprises and other units of the socialised economy is basically governed by the 1964 Civil Code. The duality of civil and commercial law disappeared in Poland after the 1964 codification of civil law. It is, however, worthy of note that certain parts of the Polish pre-war Commercial Code of 1934 have been retained with regard to companies and partnership generally and to foreign trade.

The 1964 Civil Code also regulates traditional civil law relations. It applies in principle to all civil law relationships, including units of socialised economy, traders in domestic and international commerce, and some special relationships. Article 1(1) of the Civil Code provides: "The Code shall regulate civil law relations between units of socialised economy, between individuals, and between units of socialised economy and individuals."

The most extensive exceptions to this provision can be found in the articles applicable to the relationships between units of socialised economy, namely, state enterprises, cooperatives, companies in which the state holds more than 50% of the shares, and other socialist economic organisations. For this area of our economy a new branch of law, called economic law, has been developed, which covers the legal structure of economic organisations and, more specifically, contracts between those organisations called the units of socialised economy.

Nevertheless, it should be emphasised that at the time when the Civil Code was enacted in Poland, the view prevailed that it would be premature, even if theoretically justifiable, to codify economic law separately, and the concept of the unity of civil law has been accepted as a final decision on this issue after discussion of the problem.[1] However, the structure of economic organisations and their contractual relationships are not covered entirely by the Code, which regulates only general principles, and the Code is augmented by many special statutes and provisions.

The legal basis for the creation and operation of state enterprises and associations (which play the most important role among units of socialised economy) is a Law of October 1950, amended in 1958 and 1960.[2] More specific regulations governing important contracts concluded in the socialised sector can be found in the General Conditions of Sale and Delivery 1973[3] and the General Conditions of Building and Construction Works Contracts 1974.[4] These regulations have been enacted on the base of the Civil Code in order to develop and complement the Code rules regarding specific requirements of relationships in the socialist sector of the economy.

The General Conditions of Contracts are of great importance as a source of law in the field of economic relations. It is noteworthy that in some cases these statutes not only complement the Code but also supersede and modify it. According to Article 2 of the Civil Code, in particular situations the Council of Ministers, or other head organs of state administration authorised by it, may provide different rules for relationships between units of socialised economy than those provided for by the Code. This authorisation does not concern the relations between individuals or between individuals and units of socialised economy however much it departs from the above-mentioned

1 See M. Madey and Z. Rybicki, "Legal Aspects of the Reorganisation of Economic Management in Poland," in: *Law and Economic Reform in Socialist Countries* (Budapest, 1971).

2 *DzU* (1960), no. 18, item 111.

3 *Monitor Polski*, no. 36 (1973).

4 *Ibid.*, no. 14 (1974).

concept of unity of civil law. On the other hand, the very existence of such a general exception is an important issue in discussions of the problem of economic law which recently have taken place in Polish legal doctrine.[5]

The current economic reforms under discussion in Poland contemplate decentralisation, giving greater autonomy to state enterprises and enlarging the role of self-government in those enterprises. Obviously, to introduce the reforms into effect it is necessary to make deep and complex changes in the law regulating the Polish economy. There are two crucial issues which are extensively discussed at the present time, and changes are imminent in 1981. Those are: a new legal framework for the operation of state enterprises, and the interplay of the economic plan and contracts between the units of socialised economy.

In Poland, among the various units of socialised economy, state enterprises and their associations play the most important role. The legal form of a state enterprise already existed in Polish law during the inter-war years. However, there is a fundamental difference between the prewar state enterprises in Poland and those of the present time. This difference mainly (although not exclusively) emanates from the type of ownership; the present enterprises act on the base of socialist state property.

According to the principle of the unity of national property, expressed in Article 128 of the Civil Code:

> "Socialist all-national property (state property) shall belong indivisibly to the state.
>
> State legal persons shall, within the scope of their legal capacity in their own name, execute the rights derived

---

5 See Włodyka, *Prawo gospodarcze* (Warsaw, 1981); M. Madey and A. Stelmachowski, *Zarys prawa gospodarczego* (Warsaw, 1980).

from the state ownership of given property components allotted to them."

The unity of state ownership as an economic and constitutional principle is beyond question in our civil law doctrine; however, the issue of the property rights of state juridical persons (including enterprises) in civil law relationships is a matter of controversy.[6] The prevailing opinion is that, regardless of the theoretical controversies concerning the above-mentioned problem, in practice all state enterprises should be considered and treated as owners of products received and the means of production and be fully responsible for their economic activity.

This conclusion can be drawn from a correct interpretation of the appropriate Civil Code provisions, especially Article 33, which establishes the rule that all state enterprises and their associations have legal personality, with all legal consequences, and Article 40, which provides that the state treasury is not liable for debts of state enterprises and their associations, state banks, and other state juridical persons acting on the basis of economic accountability. On the other hand, those units are not liable for debts of the state treasury.

In civil law relations, the most important question is the degree of economic and legal autonomy of enterprises. In other words, to what extent the enterprises can freely make independent economic decisions and shape their rights and duties, and how far they should be bound by the obligatory provisions of normative and administrative acts. The draft law on enterprises should precisely define the scope of interference of supervisory organs of state administration into the domain of enterprise autonomy. The limits of legal autonomy of enterprises should derive only from their legal capacity.

The recent changes in the system of manage-

---

6 See J. Wasilkowski, *Prawo własnosci w PRL* (Warsaw, 1969).

ment of the Polish national economy are intended to provide all state enterprises with necessary operational and legal autonomy. Meaningful progress has been made in that direction. It is noteworthy that foreign trade enterprises and those producing for export or importing goods have the largest degree of independence. The new economic rules being introduced for these enterprises increase the power of their directors to make independent economic decisions in transactions connected with foreign trade.

In recent years, Poland has undertaken to prepare a comprehensive legal framework for foreign investment activities. In 1979, a number of legal acts were passed creating a legal basis for mixed companies established in Poland with the participation of foreign capital.[7] Polish state enterprises and cooperatives may enter into contracts with foreign corporate bodies and individuals in order to establish joint enterprises in the form of a limited liability company in Poland. Prior to concluding the contract, a Polish partner has to obtain a permit issued by the appropriate authorities. Recent Polish legislation on mixed companies is the result of a conscious effort to encourage foreign investment in this country. Experience has shown that Polish and foreign enterprises can cooperate profitably. It is to be hoped that this cooperation will be further stimulated by the new possibilities opened by this legislation.

From the standpoint of the structure of enterprises, there are two kinds: a single-plant, specialised enterprise and a multi-plant, various-branches enterprise.

In Poland, just as in many other countries, the explosive growth of the tendency to concentrate

---

7 For a full account of this legislation, see Z. Burzynski and J. Rajski, "Le régime juridique des investissements étrangère en Pologne," *Droit et pratique du commerce international* [Paris], no. 2 (1980), pp. 171-188.

the production can be observed. This has led to the creation of very large, multi-plant enterprises and associations of enterprises.

An association of enterprises is the basic form for grouping state enterprises. It is an economic organisation performing three functions: first, it is a concentration and grouping by administrative decision of state enterprises; second, it is a superior and supervisory organ of those enterprises; and third, it is an enterprise itself with legal personality.

It follows from the above-mentioned activity of the association that there are two kinds of relationships between state enterprises: vertical and horizontal. Vertically, an enterprise is subordinate to the director of the relevant association; this is a matter of administrative and financial law. However, the vertical relations directly affect the horizontal relationships, which are, by their nature, of a civil law character. From the civil law point of view, it is particularly important that the director of the association, until now, has the right to redistribute within the association the components of state property previously allotted to the grouped enterprises. Moreover, a decision of an association director in the present system can create the so-called "fait du prince" for the grouped enterprises, directly affecting commercial contracts.

In addition to associations of enterprises, there are in Poland other economic organisations called "combines". It is a specific form of multi-plant enterprise created as part of the trend toward concentration of production in order to solve the difficult problem of cooperation between enterprises. A "combine", just as the association, has legal personality; however, what differentiates the combine from the association of enterprises is the fact that the "members" or the parts of the combine (plant establishments) do not constitute legal persons. Although those establishments have certain economic autonomy, they have no legal autonomy; they can act only within the scope of power delegated to them by the director of the combine.

Contracts consequently are concluded in the name of "combine". Nevertheless, this formal standpoint encounters certain difficulties in practice since the components of a "combine" in many cases have enough economic power to encourage them to act as an independent entity, so they draw up contracts by themselves and assume obligations. Despite the lack of legal personality, they in fact have legal capacity.

This situation requires a new approach to the traditional civil law instruments available in our legal system. The existence and development of new economic structures, and the creation of new large and powerful economic organisations consisting of units having a significant degree of economic independence, raises special legal problems. Some question the traditional legal institution of legal personality, which does not seem to be useful in certain cases. Undoubtedly, there is an urgent necessity to find new legal forms allowing those entities comprising a part of large economic organisations to act autonomously and to participate in trade operations. At the moment, they undertake independent economic activity, although formally deprived of legal capacity by present legislation.

As already noted, the reorganisation and proper regulation of state enterprises is under discussion in Poland. Various suggestions are being considered for changes in the structure of our economy. There is no doubt that the former centralised structure proved to be inefficient. Among various proposals, one enjoys substantial support among Polish economists and lawyers. This approach would enlarge the autonomy and independence of enterprises by liquidating the supervisory organs of enterprises, such as the associations of enterprises and the "combines". Under this proposal, the present associations of enterprises endowed with administrative power should be replaced by associations of enterprises created not by administrative decision as was done until now, but by the agreements and contracts between those enterprises economically interested in the creation of such associations. Those agreements would differ from traditional commercial contracts, having mixed elements of administrative and civil law relations and being within the domain of economic law. Obviously, such changes would not be possible without profound alterations in the methods of managing the national economy.

Another aspect of economic reform being discussed is the interplay of the economic plan and contract. Contrary to the free market economy concept, the socialist economy is of planned character. Not only is all production and distribution of raw materials according to the economic plan, but the exchange of goods between units of the socialised economy is subordinate to the plan. State-owned industry is directly influenced by the planning system, and in the so-called private sector the indirect results of central planning are present.

Specific commands of the national economic plan and subplans impose certain duties on the relevant branches of the economy. They are addressed to all units of the socialised economy, such as state enterprises, their associations, cooperatives, and corporations in which the state is shareholder of at least 50% of the shares. These planned tasks are first elaborated in enterprises on the basis of their economic production capacities, in accordance with their needs and market demand, and then submitted as drafts to the planning organs through all levels of the economic administrative structure. The central organ of economic planning, after considering those proposals submitted by associations of enterprises and taking into consideration the benefit of the state, determines the obligations, which are then transmitted back through administrative decisions to particular enterprises. This method of planning combines central planning with enterprise initiative.

Recent changes in the economic system make

planning more flexible. The number of so-called directive targets has been greatly reduced. The planned tasks are generally defined by the plan through the system of indicators which allow an enterprise to make its own decision within the limits thereof. Nevertheless, the planning system clearly influences contracts concluded between units of the socialised economy, and hence they are partly pre-determined by the plan. On the other hand, the draft plan has to be anticipated very often by previously concluded contracts, *i.e.*, long-term cooperation contracts, construction contracts, and so forth.

Contracts between units of the socialised economy can be classified according to the way they are concluded as compulsory or planned contracts and as free contracts in the traditional sense. In the first category, enterprises or other units of the socialised economy are obliged to enter into contractual relationships. The duty of drawing up a contract between state enterprises results most frequently from administrative decisions or can be imposed by law. The obligation to conclude a contract applies primarily to all producers or sole disposers in certain branches or to those who perform building and construction work. The associations of enterprises or other supervisory units conclude so-called agreements for coordination of deliveries or establish a distribution list for goods which are in short supply. A distribution list is mainly a result of rationing raw materials; it may, however, apply also to other goods which are not generally available on the market. A similar situation exists in the field of building and construction. There is an investment and building plan which imposes the obligation to make a relevant contract. The contracts are merely instruments of executing those plans.

Special provisions of the Civil Code (Articles 397-404) establish general rules regulating the said obligation. Accordingly, when on the basis of these provisions a given enterprise has the obligation to conclude a contract with another enterprise, the object of which and the time of conclusion having been specified, the other party may demand to have this contract concluded. If an offer is communicated to the party under obligation, a failure to answer by the offeree is considered to be an acceptance of the offer (Article 400). This is an exception to the general rule that the offeree is under no duty to answer and his mere silence by no means indicates assent. If an offer is rejected, the offeror may sue the enterprise under obligation in a so-called "precontractual dispute", and the precontractual adjudication proceedings may lead to the formation of a definite contract. Another exception from general Code rules is that any attempt by the offeree to change the terms of the offer does not amount to a rejection of the offer. An offeror can submit a statement of divergencies and again, in the event of disagreement, a relevant arbitrazh commission may lead to precontractual adjudication proceedings to an agreement unless it is considered that the contract had been concluded on terms derived from the statement of divergencies.

A change in the economic plan may directly influence the contract. The aforementioned rules are respectively applicable if an enterprise is obliged to change or to rescind a contract. Decisions of supervisory organs following changes in the economic plan may cause performance of the contract to be impossible or impracticable. In the event of such an unforeseen order, a debtor is excused from performance under defined conditions. It should be pointed out that in such cases it is possible to make liable for damages the superior organ which issued the administrative decision influencing the performance of the contract.

These brief remarks allow us to conclude that the degree of contractual freedom in the socialist economy in Poland is strongly limited. Our doctrine attempts to justify this by the view that Polish civil law takes into consideration not only conflicting interests of immediate contracting parties, but, by limiting bargaining power, discovers and elevates the common social interest to the most favourable level. Also, there is a particular need for protection of consumer interests and those of smaller enterprises that justifies to a certain extent the intervention of legislation into various economic relationships, including many types of contracts.

In recent discussions on the economic reform, it became rapidly obvious that the category of so-called planned or compulsory contracts can not be maintained to such an extent. It is possible that the economic reform will introduce a radical change in the planning system which could lead to their abolition or at least to the significant diminution of their role.

The economic reform in Poland currently discussed contemplates a new system of planning. The enterprises would draw up their plans independently. Only a few tasks should be imposed by the national economic plan on enterprises. In this process the regulatory system and the market will orient the enterprises with respect to the central objectives of the national plan. The enterprises should then conclude contracts according to certain plan indicators and adapt their own plan to the contents of those contracts. In this way we should achieve the reversed relationship between the plan of the enterprises and the contracts. The content of a contract should be decisive for the plan of the enterprise.[8]

The introduction of a new economic and planning system requires changes in our civil law, particularly the provisions concerning the duty of concluding contracts between units of the socialised economy. We hope that under the new system contracts between those units will be a much more practical and active instrument of the planned economy and also will contribute to the enrichment of the contractual system through the introduction of new contracts and by enlarging the freedom of contract.

---

8 See L. Vékás, "Economic Management and the Law of Contracts," *Acta Juridica Scientiarum Hungaricae*, no. 15 (1973), pp. 417-437.

THE CHANGING CONSTITUTION IN BRITAIN

D. Oliver

Walter Bagehot made his name as the man who perceived and wrote so elegantly and wittily about the contrast between the dignified and efficient constitutions.[1] Since Bagehot wrote *The English Constitution* in 1867, both the dignified and the efficient constitutions have changed, and the contrast between the two has become yet more striking. Lawyers now at least recognise that the monarch has an almost exclusively formal and symbolic role, and accept that legislative supremacy and the control of government lie with Parliament, while the policy-making function belongs to the government. Political scientists, however, have a quite different perception of the system, or at least of the "efficient" system. The perceptions of students of politics tend to vary according to their political standpoints, but there is broad agreement among them that all too often actual political power does not lie in Parliament or with the Cabinet; that Parliament does not control the government; that real power often rests with organisations that do not form part of our formal constitution at all: pressure groups, the extra-parliamentary political parties, and international organisations; and that consequently our theoretical "checks and balances" are misdirected. It is this contrast between constitutional theory and political reality that forms the subject-matter of this study.

Experience in recent years, and since 1974 in particular, has directed public attention to the importance of pressure groups and political parties in our system of government. The general election of March 1974 was fought, in part at least, on the issues "Who governs Britain - the government or the unions ?" and "Who can best

---

1 W. Bagehot, *The English Constitution* (London, 1963), pp. 61-65.

handle the unions ?". My speculation would be that the next general election will have as a major issue the question "Who governs in the event of a Labour majority in Parliament - the government or the extra-Parliamentary Party's National Executive Committee ?". It was this issue that gave rise to the split in the Labour party after the special conference in January 1981.

There is considerable current controversy about the relationships between political parties and governments, and between pressure groups - particularly trade unions - and governments, and between political parties and pressure groups. The influence of pressure groups, in particular, has increased as a reaction to the extension of the arm of the state since the Second World War into areas of what were previously predominantly private activities. The government's economic power has accordingly increased enormously: this vast economic power has enabled governments to influence the behaviour of private individuals and organisations in almost any area in which they might wish to become involved, often without being subject to any effective parliamentary control. And with the growing realisation, both in and out of Parliament, of the government's ability to avoid control have come a growth in the activities of pressure groups; moves in the Labour party to substitute party control of government; and pressure in Parliament to assert more effective democratic control. We are living through a period of struggle for control of government. And constitutional theorists and politicians are waking up to the dangers inherent in the divergence between the dignified and efficient constitutions. Constitutional lawyers, and others, are having to face up to the fact that their traditional theory may not be appropriate to deal with political realities in the 1980s and seek a new theoretical framework that will provide an adequate system of checks and balances.

According to conventional theory, the executive has the policy-making function and should be concerned to govern in the public interest and with the consent of the electorate at large. Events since 1974 have demonstrated that in many circumstances policy decisions are not freely made by governments but may be thrust upon them or made for them by other organisations: trade unions and civil servants, for example. According to our traditional constitutional theory, Parliament should be and is in a position to check and supervise and control the executive effectively. Yet in the period 1974 to 1979 this assumption was shown not to be well founded in two respects: the government, by use of the whip system, Prime Ministerial patronage, and the Prime Minister's right to seek a dissolution at the moment of his choice, found ways of controlling Parliament rather than the other way round; and on a number of occasions the government by-passed Parliament altogether and, either unilaterally or in collaboration with extra-Parliamentary organisations, developed and implemented policies which did not require, and could not in fact have commanded, the consent of Parliament. The Social Contract of 1974-1977 and the anti-inflation policy 1977-1979 illustrate the point.

Although the principal subjects of this paper are political parties and pressure groups, it is not perhaps necessary to produce precise definitions of "political party" and "pressure group." Richardson and Jordan argue that:

> "A common distinction between a political party and a pressure group is that a political party is interested in assuming governmental responsibilities over a wide range of issues whereas a pressure group seeks to further a far narrower range of issues and does not wish to become the government ... We would argue that parties themselves are a forum for group struggles and no profound satisfactory distinction can be made between the party and group."[2]

---

2 J.J. Richardson and A.G. Jordan, *Governing Under Pressure* (London, 1979), p. 17.

This view seems to me to be convincing. But whether or not one agrees that there is no real distinction between political parties and pressure groups, it has not generally been true of the members of *national*, as opposed to *Parliamentary*, political parties in Great Britain that they have been interested in assuming governmental responsibilities. Indeed, any claim by extra-Parliamentary members of a political party to assume governmental responsibilities or dictate to government would be entirely inconsistent with our traditional constitutional theory. Under our present system, members of the government are required to make their own judgments on political questions and to accept responsibility for them. Governmental responsibilities are assumed by the person who can command a majority in the House of Commons, and by the team appointed by him or her: all members of the government must take a seat in one or other House of Parliament. But there is no constitutional requirement that Members of Parliament must belong to a political party. While it is true that for decades now Parliament has divided fairly strictly along party lines, it is not true that the members of the Parliamentary parties are in any way mandated by the national political parties: indeed, such mandating would be inconsistent with our theoretical constitutional system, which requires that Members of Parliament should be representatives of all their constituents and not delegates of any sectional interest.[3] This is the philosophy of Edmund Burke, and it is fundamental to legal constitutional theory.

This important constitutional principle is

---

3 See, for example, *Report of the Committee of Privileges*, H.C. 118 of 1946-7; 440 H.C. Deb., 5S c. 284ff. [The Case of W.J. Brown]; Lord Hailsham of St. Marylebone, *The Dilemma of Democracy* (London, 1978), chapter viii; B. Smith, *Policy Making in British Government* (London, 1976), p. 181: "Only parties ... can define the public interest and represent the national constituency."

currently under attack and may well change:[4] but hitherto the Parliamentary parties, that is, Members of Parliament, and their leadership, have been broadly independent both of their mass membership and of the extra-Parliamentary party organisations. Smith accounts for this characteristic of the system by asserting that:

> "In neither party can the Parliamentary leadership afford to appear dominated by party members if they are to convince the electorate that they can form a government responsive to national needs and interests regardless of party. The very nature of Parliamentary democracy, in which two teams of political leaders compete for office in a continuous election campaign, means that the party rank and file mainly exist to support and serve, but not dominate, their leaders."[5]

Pressure group activity is clearly a permanent feature of the political scenery. In modern industrial democratic societies, individuals have little chance of influencing the decisions and actions of government, or indeed of any powerful organisation, unless they work through an interest or pressure group. Hence it is clearly desirable for the individual that pressure groups should flourish. But there are problems inherent in the activities of such groups. Their activities could undermine or challenge the effectiveness of a country's formal legal constitution. Richardson and Jordan argue that because of the power of groups "increasingly Western governments are finding difficulties in the application of policies or decisions arrived at in a perfectly constitutional manner."[6] The tension arises because pressure groups do not readily fit into a system where

---

4 See the publications of the Rank and File Mobilising Committee for Labour Democracy, especially *Mobilise for Labour Democracy* (London, 1980).

5 Smith, note 3 above, p. 78.

6 Richardson and Jordan, note 2 above, p. 4.

legislative power rests with representatives of geographical areas rather than of interest groups and should not favour sectional interests at the expense of the general good. If real power rests with pressure groups rather than with the electors in geographical areas, the principal political control of our system - the requirement for regular elections - is misdirected, for pressure groups do not depend for their power or their legitimacy upon those elections.

The argument that pressure groups can frustrate the formal organs of a constitution illustrates the obvious truth that formal constitutions may with the passage of time and changes in society cease to mirror or control the *actual* distribution of power in society. This process is bound to lead in due course to adjustments either of the actual or of the formal distribution of power if there is not to be continuing tension between legal and political theory, and political reality. But a major difficulty in making formal adjustments to the system is that perceptions of how the system actually works differ widely according to the political or social standpoint of the observer.

Recent History: 1974-1979

In the general election of March 1974 no party obtained a clear majority in the House of Commons. In October 1974 a second election was held; this time Labour had a majority of three in the House of Commons. This majority was lost by March 1976 as a result of defeats in bye elections and the disappearance of John Stonehouse, a Labour Member of Parliament. In 1977 a pact was made with the Liberal party in Parliament, and the government continued in office, despite its insecure position, until defeated in the general election of May 1979.

Throughout that period the effects of the lack of a real majority and the intractable problems of the economy combined, led the government to resort to unpopular and controversial techniques in order to implement their policies. First, they relied on strong party discipline in order to get their measures through Parliament; second, they found ways of by-passing Parliament if Parliament's consent to their policies was not forthcoming; and third, they moderated some of their party's most radical manifesto policies in order to secure the co-operation of groups on whom they were dependent, notably the trade unions and the International Monetary Fund, and to secure the support in Parliament of the Liberals and other minority parties.

"Elective Dictatorship"

In order to implement its policies by legislation, the government had to rely strongly on party discipline in the Parliamentary Labour party. The techniques resorted to were well established: the whip system; Prime Ministerial patronage which placed in the Prime Minister's gift over a hundred appointments amongst members of the House of Commons who took the Labour Whip; and on the doctrine of collective responsibility, which requires all members of the government to support the government in Parliament. A Prime Minister has the right to ask for a dissolution at any time; this constitutional right can be used by a Prime Minister as a threat to bring wayward back benchers to heel, since Labour, throughout much of this period, could expect to lose in a general election. All of these techniques have been well-known and much used weapons in the armoury of government for many years, but taken with the fact that the government had won only 39.2% of the vote and had no real majority, the tactics came to be resented in many quarters as oppressive and undemocratic. Lord Hailsham in his Dimbleby Lecture in November 1976,[7] in typically robust and colourful language, coined the phrase "elective dictatorship" to describe the system. But it was not only in right wing circles that the government's tactics were resented. Similar sentiments underlie the campaign currently

7 Hailsham, *Elective Dictatorship* (London, 1976).

being conducted by the radical, or so-called left, wing of the Labour party for reform of the constitution of the Labour party in order to ensure that a future Labour government will be accountable to Parliament, and not in control of it. And the House of Commons has reacted by setting up a new Select Committee System aimed at controlling government effectively.

The By-passing of Parliament

The principle of government by consent is at the heart of any democratic system. Consent is given normally in the form of legislation and supply. However, since the Second World War, with the extension of the arm of the state into innumerable areas of what were once purely private activities, it has become increasingly apparent in a number of important areas that governments do not need the consent of Parliament in the form of legislation as a necessary precondition for implementation of their policies. This development flows from aspects of government power which increase in importance with the extension of socialism, in the sense of bringing into public ownership property formerly in private hands.

Governments (and other public bodies) can implement new policies without direct recourse to Parliament in a number of ways. First, by invoking the wide discretionary and rule-making powers that they possess under existing legislation which over the years has entrusted governments with ever-increasing powers of this kind. The phenomenon is well documented elsewhere. These powers can be, and have been, resorted to in order to implement policies not themselves directly sanctioned by Parliament. They give enormous potential for arbitrary policy-making and policy implementation.

The second aspect of government power which enables the executive to by-pass Parliament derives from the public ownership of enormous quantities of land and other resources: public housing, schools, nationalised industries, coal, oil, and minerals, and so forth; and from the government's receipt of vast sums in revenue. In making use of their property holdings, over which they have broadly the same rights as private owners, and in spending revenues (for example, on capital projects, on procurement, on grants, subsidies, and on the wages and salaries of public employees, on benefits and allowances to the poor, the old, the sick, the disabled, and the unemployed) governments are clearly in a strong position to bargain and to influence the behaviour of the population or of particular organisations, individuals, or groups that are dependent upon them; and by this manipulation to implement policy decisions, often without Parliament's approval, let alone its express legislative authority. In using this type of power to influence behaviour, governments are not using the traditional tool of the governor - the rule-making power - but rather the power of ownership. A serious defect in our constitutional system, in my view, is the absence or inadequacy of political or legal checks on the exercise by governments, or others, of this power of ownership.

The anti-inflation policy of 1974-1979 is a particularly compelling illustration of the use of economic and bargaining power without Parliament's consent. The government decided that a necessary ingredient in a counter-inflation policy must be wage restraint of some kind. Such a policy was clearly likely to be unpalatable to the population generally and particularly to trade unionists. Acute difficulties flowed from the fact that the trade unions have traditionally been strong supporters of the Labour party both politically and financially. A wage policy is therefore necessarily difficult, if not impossible, to enforce without the co-operation of the trade unions and their members. Such a policy may also be electorally disastrous for the Labour party.

In May 1975, when the government was keen to contain inflation, Jack Jones of the powerful Transport and General Workers Union proposed to the government that the unions would comply with and supervise a voluntary wage restraint policy in exchange for government assistance on various matters including unemployment and some price control. The union side of the bargain was that wage claims would be limited to an agreed level. The government agreed. This "social contract" operated relatively well for a year and was renewed in the Summer of 1976. This time the Trade Union Congress agreed to hold wage claims down to an agreed norm, and the *quid pro quo* from the government was an increase in personal tax allowances. This agreement held for a year, but by the Summer of 1977 it was clear that, for various reasons, the trade unions were not in a position to renew the social contract, and an "orderly return to free collective bargaining" was agreed.

From a constitutional point of view, the significance of the social contract from 1975 to 1977 was enormous. No legislation was required in order to implement the major conditions of the contract; the policy was formulated by agreement between the government and a powerful pressure group, and the group itself implemented and policed the policy. Parliament was by-passed in the processes both of formulating and of implementing the policy. Some legislation was required to deal with price controls and measures to deal with unemployment and to fix the personal tax allowance increases promised by the Chancellor of the Exchequer in return for the second year of restraint; but Members of Parliament of all parties protested that Parliament was being used as a rubber stamp for policies agreed outside any of the conventional constitutional institutions and consequently free from our so-called system of checks and balances. The government, by resort to its control over Parliament through the whip system and Prime Ministerial patronage, was able to bargain with the legislative and executive power which should rightfully be the provinces of Parliament, and the Parliamentary executive respectively.

The "social contract" caused the government to be accused of acting unconstitutionally. To express the conventional constitutional view one could not possibly better the words used by Lord

Hailsham in voicing the reaction of some to this period:

> "... what (a policy of wage restraint) certainly is not is a bargaining counter to be traded for slabs of public policy between the TUC and the government. Either the public policy traded away is in the public interest, or it is contrary to the public interest. If it is not in the public interest it should not be pursued even if nothing is offered in return. If it is in the public interest it should be pursued even if something very attractive is offered for giving it away. The government has no mandate to trade away public interests as part of a bargain with sectional interests and it may be added that sectional interests can have no mandate from their members to trade away their legitimate interests in return for slabs of public policy. A contract in this sense is a double abomination. It sacrifices the interest of the public to a section of the public, and it involves both an assumption of power by the leaders of that section which is not warranted by any democratic principle, and a disregard by both sides of those whose interests are not represented."[8]

It may be that in this passage Lord Hailsham is under-estimating the necessity that a government may face of bargaining in order to secure co-operation, in other words, in order to govern by consent. Politics is, after all, the art of the possible. On the other hand, Hailsham is expressing neatly the conventional constitutional theory upon which much of our constitutional law is based. He gives precedence to the public interest over sectional interests; and he makes a plea for the interests of those who are excluded from participation in the policy making process by the govern-

---

8 Hailsham, note 3 above, pp. 62-63.

ment's by-passing of Parliament.

From 1977 the government was no longer able to count on the unions for co-operation in the policy of wage restraint. So it devised a "counter-inflation policy" which relied for its efficiency on the government's power as owner of resources, rather than its rule-making power, which requires Parliamentary consent.

The government decided to use its contracting and statutory powers, which had nothing to do with pay or prices policy, in order to enforce the policy both on the private and the public sector. It required government contractors to sign pledges to abide by this and all future pay policies and refused to contract with those who would not give this pledge. The government refused Export Credit Guarantees to firms that had broken the pay "norm". It drew up "black-lists" of firms who had broken the pay norm and who would therefore be refused future government contracts or other assistance.

Parliament was not in a position to prevent the government from pursuing this most unpopular and arbitrary policy. The policy was never tested in the courts, but in some respects at least it may have been quite lawful.[9] Yet certain powerful organisations were able to break it. Ford threatened to abandon their plans to build a factory in an area of high unemployment in Wales unless released from the pay norm; the government released them. Mackies in Belfast were permitted to break the guidelines for political reasons. The Winter of 1978-79 was a winter of discontent as public sector workers revolted against the limit on their wage rises, while private sector workers were able to bargain freely and collectively. In the end the policy had to be abandoned, after an adverse vote in the House of Commons on 14 December 1978. But the experience of this period with the counter-

---

9 H.W.R. Wade, *Constitutional Fundamentals* (London, 1980), pp. 55-57; T.C. Daintith, "Regulation by Contract: The New Prerogative," *Current Legal Problems*, XXXIV (1979), pp. 41-64.

inflation policy focused attention on the fact that governments may be more susceptible to control by powerful groups and organisations than by Parliament.

The period 1974-1977 also highlighted another problem, as far as pressure groups were concerned. The leaders of the trade unions, who had agreed to the social contract, put the private interest, as they saw it, before the short-term interest of their members.[10] This experience has been a timely reminder to the trade unions and to other pressure groups of the potential for conflict between their activities as private organisations and their ties with political parties or with governments. There is always a danger from the point of view of the grass roots members of pressure groups that their leaders will join the establishment and neglect the interests of their own members. In the case of the trade unions, from 1975 onwards their alliance with the government resulted in the widespread disaffection of some union members, disaffection both from their unions and from the Labour party.

The tension between the Labour party and trade unions has called in question the relationship between the two. The Labour party is dependent financially on the trade unions. The trade unions have considerable influence on both the policy and the choice of leader of any future Labour government. And yet the aims of the two organisations cannot always coincide; the responsibilities of trade unions are not those of governments. Not all trade union members are Labour supporters, and not all Labour supporters are trade union members. Yet neither side can afford to break the marriage between them. Some take the view that the link should be broken, that it is undemocratic for a political party to be tied so

---

10 Hailsham, note 3 above, p. 63; T. Benn, *Arguments for Socialism* (London, 1980), p. 174.

strongly to a particular interest group.[11] Others pretend that the bond is strong and indissoluble and good for both sides. My own view is that severe conflict is inherent in the relationship between a political party and any trade union movement that is genuinely concerned with its members' interests, and that each should be free to pursue its own ends separately.

The Moderation of Radical Policies

In its election manifestos of March 1974 and October 1974 the Labour party was pledged to a number of radical policies. It promised, amongst other things, a "fundamental and irreversible shift in the balance of power and wealth in favour of working people and their families." A number of promises were not kept. And the shift in the balance of power and wealth in favour of working people had not taken place. The poor were poorer and the rich were richer.[12]

The Labour government would argue in its defence that external circumstances made it impossible for them to implement all the manifesto policies: the lack of a real majority in Parliament, the government's need for aid from the International Monetary Fund and so forth: all pushed the government into modifying its policies; the point would also probably be made that a Labour government with moderate policies commands more support amongst the electorate than a party with radical policies.[13]

The left wing of the Labour party reject such arguments. They argue that many of the pressures on governments to moderate their policies are inherent in the constitutional system and that the

---

11 N. Johnson, *In Search of the Constitution* (London, 1977), p. 166; Hailsham, note 3 above, p. 49.

12 F. Field, "How the Poor Fared," *What Went Wrong?* (London, 1979), pp. 124-136.

13 K. Coates, *What Went Wrong?* (London, 1979), pp. 7-33.

system itself ought to be changed so that these pressures can be counteracted.[14] In particular, they maintain that the extra-Parliamentary Labour party ought to be in a position to draft the manifesto and hold a Labour government to it. In other words, they want to see the system of policy-making and government - the constitution - changed so that socialist policies can be achieved. They feel that socialism cannot be accomplished within the present constitutional framework.[15] They want the system changed in order to attain socialist policies.

The pressures on a government to moderate radical policies are numerous. It is not in my view necessarily an anti-left wing pressure. The critics of the last government identify in particular the civil service, the International Monetary Fund, and capitalist organisations as bringing pressure to bear on the last government to moderate the radical policies on which, allegedly, it was elected.

First, the civil service, whose members are alleged to have an inherent pro-establishment, conservative bias which impels them to pressurise any government to moderate radical policies.[16] It is not possible to gauge what foundation there is for this view of the civil service. But if it should take hold it would have profound implications for constitutional theory, since the remedy offered by the left wing is to substitute party control of government for what they see as civil service control (and other external controls).

The second influence operating on the government of 1974-79 that is blamed for the government's

---

14 M. Meacher, "Whitehall's Short Way With Democracy," *What Went Wrong?* (London, 1979), pp. 170-186.

15 E.g., R. Milliband, *Parliamentary Socialism* (London, 1979).

16 Meacher, note 14 above; cf. Smith, note 3 above, pp. 100-109; F. Rose, *The Problem of Party Government* (London, 1976), pp. 371-372, 417-422.

moderating of its radical policies is the International Monetary Fund. In early Autumn 1976, there was a drop in the value of sterling, coupled with an adverse balance of payments. The government sought a loan from the International Monetary Fund; the Fund imposed strict conditions for the limitation of public spending and restriction of the Public Sector Borrowing Requirement. As a result, the Chancellor of the Exchequer, Dennis Healy, announced a round of public spending cuts, in addition to those that had already been imposed in February and July 1976.

It was partly as a result of these cuts that the government failed to implement its manifesto pledge to effect the "fundamental and irreversible shift in the balance of power and wealth in favour of working people and their families." The loss of working class electoral support for Labour in the 1979 election was put down in no small measure to this series of cuts; hence, the resolve in the left wing to make such measures impossible in the future.

The government's deal with the International Monetary Fund had other repercussions for the system. As with the social contract, the government had agreed a set of unpopular policies that did not require Parliament's consent, without even consulting Parliament, or its own back benchers, on the matter. Back benchers on both sides of the House felt increasing resentment at the government's disregard of their views when at the same time the government was so obviously open to influence from other quarters.

Second, the left wing became profoundly suspicious of the International Monetary Fund (as, indeed, they are of the E.E.C. and other external organisations) and came to regard them as, in effect, agents of capitalism, and therefore necessarily hostile to a Labour government. The view was held in some circles that the I.M.F. was the vehicle by which groups in the City of London, civil servants in the Treasury, and officials of the Bank of England could exert pressure on a

Labour government to adopt policies favourable to capitalism.[17]

Implications of Recent History for Constitutional Theory

In the election of May 1979 the Labour government was roundly defeated. A Conservative government with radical policies and a safe majority was returned. Mrs. Thatcher's government has had little to do with the trade unions and until February 1981 there was little talk in the Press of "deals" between government and pressure groups. In that month the government gave in to the miners over the closure of collieries, and consequently came under pressure from other unions (the waterworkers and civil servants) to modify their policy of reducing public expenditure.

The extra-Parliamentary Conservative party traditionally exerts little pressure on a Conservative government. As Smith puts it:

> "Tory principles of leadership actually endorse the right of the Parliamentary group to be free from non-Parliamentary control (although not influence)."[18]

But this is not to say that all is now quiet on the constitutional front.

Pressure Groups

Pressure groups continue to be important influences on government policy, although the signs are that this present government is less open to pressure from extra-Parliamentary groups than were its predecessors. Whether as a result of this government's attitude to pressure groups

---

17 Meacher, note 14 above, pp. 181-182.

18 Smith, note 3 above, p. 76. And see S.E. Finer, *The Changing British Party System 1945-1979* (Washington D.C., 1980), chapter 3.

is unclear, but some pressure groups are now concentrating their attention on Members of Parliament. It was recently reported that there are ninety-one all-party groups of Members of Parliament that are in receipt of funds from pressure groups.[19] This burgeoning of relationships between back bench Members of Parliament and pressure groups suggests a breaking down of the party system. It also clearly raises questions of Parliamentary privilege.

It seems to be well-established in a number of reports of the Committee of Privileges of the House of Commons over the years, and a number of findings of the Speaker, that a Member of Parliament's duty is to his constituents and to the country as a whole, rather than to any particular section thereof. Hence, it would be wrong in principle for Members of Parliament to allow themselves to be "bought" by sectional groups. The arrangements that Members of Parliament come to with sponsoring organisations are generally required to state specifically that a Member of Parliament's independence is not fettered by the arrangement.[20]

But of course it is difficult to ascertain how independent a Member of Parliament can really be when he is receiving favours from any organisation. Also it would clearly be undesirable if Members of Parliament, and governments, were completely immune from legitimate pressure from the electorate, whether organised into groups or otherwise. A major constitutional problem is how to find a balance between the legitimate and illegitimate influences of organised groups on Members

---

19 *The Times*, 24 December 1980, p. 2.

20 H.C. 118 (1946-47) [The Case of W.J. Brown], cf. Walkland (ed.), *The House of Commons in the Twentieth Century* (Oxford, 1979), chapter iv. H.C. 34 (1967-68) Appendix V. Memorandum by the Study of Parliament Group to the Select Committee on Parliamentary Privilege. And see S.A. de Smith, *Constitutional and Administrative Law* (London, 1977), pp. 308-309.

of Parliament and on governments.

Some of those who object to pressure groups increasing their influence on Parliament and government press at the same time for increased party control of government. This raises the problem alluded to earlier, namely that it is not possible, in Britain at any rate, to draw any meaningful distinction of principle between pressure groups on the one hand and political parties on the other. Some groups of Members of Parliament, especially nationalist groups, could be pressure groups and parties. Some regard the Labour party as the political wing of the trade union movement. Some political parties contain or are made up of groups that could be regarded as parties and as pressure groups: the Tribune group, the Solidarity group, the 1922 Committee, and so forth. If there is no real distinction between pressure groups and political parties, a desire to reduce the influence of pressure groups is not logically consistent with the campaign to increase the influence of political parties on governments.

Select Committees

The new system of select committees has been referred to earlier in this paper. These committees were set up shortly after the 1979 election and were intended to be more effective than the previous select committees in examining, criticising, and controlling the executive. The select committees are particularly important in that they are not governed by party whips and have not divided along party lines in the same way that the House of Commons tends to divide on the floor of the House. They can be seen as an attempt by Parliament to re-assert control over the executive and locate the political struggle in Parliament where the traditional system of checks and balances ought to ensure that the government is genuinely concerned with the public interest and with obtaining the consent of the representatives of the electorate to government policy. In a recent report on the first year of these committees Davies concludes that "we are witnessing improvements to the three major functions of Parliament. The scrutinising of the executives, the passing of legislation and the voting of supply."[21] This last clearly indicates awareness of the need for supervision of the economic power of governments.

The attempt to re-assert Parliamentary control of the executive can in my view succeed only if certain conditions are satisfied. First, Members of Parliament must be genuinely determined to control the executive; they can only succeed if the Parliamentary party system - the whip system and the other methods of party control - is relaxed. This is anathema to the left wing of the Labour party, which requires stronger, not weaker, party control of government. Second, the executive must be prepared to submit to Parliamentary control. Ultimately this means that it must genuinely accept the principle of Parliamentary democracy. Third, extra-Parliamentary groups, on whose co-operation the executive and Parliament are obviously in large measure dependent, must be prepared to accept the will of Parliament and of a responsible executive even if their own interests are to some extent damaged thereby. Again, this is ultimately a question of the acceptance of Parliamentary democracy. Unless the theory of the present system is accepted, the new select committee system is bound to fail. Britain will then move into a new phase of constitutional development, toward either corporatism or government by the extra-Parliamentary political parties, either of which would involve an abandonment of the spirit of present system of Parliamentary executives and ministerial responsibility. Both these options would seem to be undesirable and undemocratic, particularly in a multi-party state.

---

21 A. Davies, *Reformed Select Committees: The First Year* (London, 1980), p. 65. And see First Special Report of the Committee of Public Accounts, vol. 1 (1981).

Reforms of the Constitution of the Labour Party

The traditional Westminster system of democracy is greatly influenced by Burke's theory about the proper function of Parliament and of Members of Parliament. Amongst the left wing of the Labour party this theory is being challenged.

One result of party disillusionment with the last Labour government's performance was the formation of the Campaign for Labour Party Democracy, which seeks to substitute for the Burkean view of Parliament, sectional party control of a future Labour government. To this end the campaigners proposed three reforms of the constitution of the Labour party. First, they desired every Labour candidate to be re-selected between general elections. This has been accepted. The purpose of this is to enable the local constituency parties to monitor the performance of a Member of Parliament, and thus put pressure on him to ensure implementation of Labour party policies by a future Labour government. Clearly, he will be a delegate of his party, not a representative of his constituency. Second, the campaigners proposed that the leader of the Labour party should be chosen by an electoral college consisting of Members of Parliament, constituency parties, and trade unions. This also has been accepted. The importance of this change is that the leader of the Labour party would in all probability be the Prime Minister in the event of a Labour majority in Parliament, and consequently a Labour Prime Minister would be under strong moral and political pressure from the extra-Parliamentary elements in the party to implement party manifestos. It was this change that provoked the setting up of the Council for Social Democracy in January 1981. Third, the campaigners propose that the Labour party manifesto should be drawn up by the National Executive Committee of the party, which should be bound by Conference decisions. At present the manifesto is drawn up jointly by the N.E.C. and the Parliamentary party, and it is said that in effect the Parliamentary party leader has a veto on the policies to be included in the manifesto. It is to overcome this, and to ensure that the National Party can dictate policy, that this third reform is proposed. In addition, the campaigners propose that:

> Prospective Parliamentary candidates should sign an undertaking as a condition of nomination to abide by and seek to implement in the House of Commons the policies of the Party.

It is also now suggested that the Cabinet should be elected by the national party and that the manifesto should be annually renewable. As has been stated before, these reforms have fundamental implications for constitutional theory. First, they clearly represent a rejection of the spirit of Parliamentary privilege and Article 9 of the Bill of Rights and the Burkean philosophy, which require that Members of Parliament should represent all the electorate and should be independent from external sectional pressures. Second, since a Labour government would be bound by the policies in its manifesto, the executive policy-making function of state would have passed from the executive, which is theoretically responsible to Parliament and through Parliament to the electorate, to an extra-Parliamentary political party, which is not accountable in this way to the public. The changes also suggest that it is proper to carry out a manifesto because the electorate will have voted for the manifesto. This seems a highly specious argument. Indeed, Crossman[22] and Finer[23] have both convincingly refuted the idea that manifestos were designed to secure the consent of the electors. Crossman saw them instead as a method by which a government can reinforce itself against civil service pressure to abandon party policies.

Another issue raised by the constitutional reforms of the Labour party is that they appear to deny the present *legal* theory popular with judges

---

22 R.H.S. Crossman, *The Politics of Pensions* (Liverpool, 1972), p. 24.

23 Finer, note 18 above, pp. 125-127.

and academics that the purpose of government is to serve the public interest. Given that the identification of the public interest is not a justiciable issue, since matters of judgment and prediction are involved, the judges are prepared to leave identification to the public interest to the government. But if the judges felt that the government was not accountable to Parliament, they might be readier to enter the field of public policy in order to protect the public from an unaccountable executive. So legal theory is important in relation to the judicial role.

In some quarters, particularly in the Labour party, the very principle that the function of governments is to promote the public interest is rejected. A leading left wing Member of Parliament was reported recently as saying:

> "We want these people (Members of Parliament) to represent their class interests and not this bogus national interest that we hear so much about. I want people in Parliament who are dedicated to carrying out that class interest."

This is consistent with the Marxist view that conflict between the classes is inevitable and that there can be no homogeneity of interest in a class-ridden society. Not everyone has this perception of society, and traditional constitutional theory certainly does not.

An obvious implication of changing the function of government from promotion of the public interest to promotion of sectional interests would be that the consent of the electorate would not be readily given to sectional interest policies. If the electorate believes that the government is concerned with the interests of all, then it will acquiesce in government policy. If it does not believe that to be the purpose of government, then clearly objections will be taken to the promoting of particular sectional interests at the expense of others.

Conclusions

It is not easy to draw any particular conclusions from the foregoing analysis of the relationship between traditional legal constitutional theory and the actual operation of the system of government in Britain. However, it is submitted that recent history indicates that in a number of ways our formal system is not adapted to deal with controlling the actual use and abuse of political power. The reality of the distribution of power does not coincide with constitutional theory which supposes power to rest primarily with the executive and the legislature.

The emergence of the power associated with ownership of property and with spending power highlights the inadequacy of our present constitutional institutions in dealing with possible abuse of this enormous power: at present, this is an area in which pressure groups are better able to control the government than is Parliament. As socialism expands in Great Britain, the problems of control of power will become more acute, and new institutions are bound to come into existence to deal with those problems.

The move among the left wing of the Labour party toward party control of government stems from disillusionment with the traditional constitutional controls of the executive. But the solution offered by these campaigners for reform represents in effect a rejection of the traditional notions of the public interest and government by consent as being the principal aims of government. In their place it substitutes the promotion of sectional interests as the principal aim of government. This alternative is unattractive; but it must be admitted that the difference of opinion between those who are in favour of party control and those who oppose it rests largely on differences in the perception of political reality. It may be that the lawyer's notion of the public interests is unrealistic; and that it is equally unrealistic to expect Members of Parliament to represent all their constituents and not simply their supporters and that the system should be based on a recognition of conflict between classes and interest groups. But if all the proposed changes in the Labour party constitution were to come into effect, a number of important constitutional changes would in due course have to be made. At present, political parties hardly exist in constitutional law, and consequently there are no institutionalised checks on the conduct of political parties. Should there be any such institutionalised controls ? In my own view, obviously there should. If a Member of Parliament professes to be under a duty to represent those who support him only, then there are bound to be calls for the other voters in a constituency to have a representative or protector of some kind. This would in due course strengthen the calls for proportional representation or for multi-member Parliamentary constituencies, so that the minority might have some nominal champion in Parliament.

Finally, it is obvious that there is widespread discontent across the political spectrum with the working of our present system, and a desire for reform. The setting up of the Social Democratic Party since 25 January 1981 was a direct result of alarm at the move in the Labour party towards party control of government, and discontent with the two party system. The Party appear to have substantial electoral support. There have been calls for constitutional reforms of varying kinds from influential and respected public figures and groups over the last seven years.[24] The proper response to this discontent in a democratic society would be an open-minded and critical appraisal by a Royal Commission of the existing system, of its ability to cater for the needs and desires of the people, of the

---

24 See, for example, Sir L. Scarman, in *English Law - The New Dimension* (London, 1974); Hailsham, note 7 above, *id.*, note 3 above; Finer, note 18 above, chapter 6, Postscript; Johnson, note 11 above; Wade, note 9 above; Benn, note 10 above; and Rose, note 16 above, chapter 16.

options for reform, and of the attitudes of the electorate both to the present system and to the options.

POLISH CONSTITUTIONAL DEVELOPMENT IN 1980

L. Garlicki

The year 1980 saw important changes in the Polish political and constitutional system as stabilised during the past decade.[1] The summer crisis led to the conclusion of numerous "agreements" between the Cabinet's representatives and workers' groups. Far-reaching changes occurred in both the communist party and the state leadership, and consequently an extraordinary Ninth Party Congress was held in July 1981. A vast programme of reforms has been adopted. New developments have been particularly visible in the trade union movement, which is actually organised on a pluralistic pattern.

It is obvious that such substantial political changes have been accompanied by many new legal developments. The reforms are still far from being completed, and the new legal regulations are but a beginning; nevertheless, some new acts already have been adopted. As far as constitutional problems[2] are concerned, a reform of the parliamentary procedure has been enacted. Also the above-mentioned "agreements" seem to merit attention. Finally, since this review covers the whole of 1980, the reform of administrative procedure (which preceded the summer events) must be discussed.

---

1 See L. Garlicki, "Polish Constitutional Development in the 1970s," *Comparative Law Yearbook,* III (1980), 247-265.

2 That is, all legal developments which either bring direct changes (amendments) to the Polish Constitution of 1952 (*DzU* (1976), no. 7, item 36) or deal with the structure and powers of the constitutionally established agencies and organs, or with fundamental rights and liberties of citizens.

Judicial Review of Administrative Decisions

Until 1980, the judicial review of administrative decisions did not exist in Poland, save certain categories of cases.[3] The Supreme Administrative Tribunal which existed before the Second World War was not reintroduced by post-war legislation. Consequently, very few administrative decisions were subjected to judicial review, the majority of them being taken exclusively within the administrative branch. The 1960 Code of Administrative Procedure (CAP) introduced some due process guarantees in this field; nevertheless, the only permissible review of administrative decisions was a review by the superior administrative agency.[4]

This situation has been criticised by Polish scholars for many years. The desirability of introducing broader judicial control of administrative decisions was noted by some scholars as early as the mid-fifties; in the last decade, legal doctrine has been virtually unanimous on the point. Many authors have emphasised the importance of judicial review for socialist legality, claiming that the lack of this review deprives an individual of the right of access to the courts. An oft-quoted example during those discussions was that of other East European countries, where substantial changes in the administrative procedure were implemented from the late 1950s. In effect, the judicial review of administrative decisions was established in Hungary, Yugoslavia, Rumania, and Bulgaria,[5] and some changes in this field were also proclaimed

---

3 It did exist in social insurance matters, as well as in a delictual or tort action against the government, if the omission or malfeasance was done by illegal administrative decisions. See M. Wierzbowski, "Administrative Procedure in Eastern Europe," *Comparative Law Yearbook*, I (1977), 228.

4 J. Letowski, "Protection of Civil Rights in Polish Administrative Proceedings," in W. Sokolewicz (ed.), *The Law in Poland* (Warsaw, 1978), pp. 311-338.

5 Wierzbowski, note 3 above, p. 227.

by the 1977 USSR Constitution.[6]

All the foregoing developments have influenced the decision-making process in Poland. Far-reaching proposals to amend the 1960 CAP were submitted in the early seventies, and in 1977 two parliamentary committees began work on a report on the present state of Polish administrative procedure. In autumn 1979 these two committees jointly introduced a bill amending the Code of Administrative Procedure, and finally on 31 January 1980 the CAP-Amendment was adopted by the Sejm.[7] Consequently, one can say that the CAP-Amendment was created by the Sejm itself, which is rather atypical since most of the bills are prepared within the administrative branch and introduced in the Sejm by the Cabinet (the Council of Ministers).

The 1980 amendment vested the judicial branch with the power to review the legality of administrative decisions. The amendment provides for twenty categories of matters in which the judicial review of administrative decisions exists. In other matters administrative decisions are not subjected to judicial review, unless such review is established by special legislation (*e.g.*, social security). The CAP-Amendment remains silent on the general rule that all final administrative decisions may be appealed to the court, as is provided, for example, by the comparable Bulgarian and Rumanian legislation.[8] That position in our regulations is due to the specific political situation that existed in the late seventies in Poland. Since some conservative and bureaucratic circles saw any judicial review as entirely

---

6 Especially in Article 58(2).

7 *DzU* (1980), no. 4, item 8 (see also *DzU* (1980), no. 9, item 26).

8 In all socialist countries some kinds of decisions are, however, excluded from judicial review (for example, decisions relating to the defence and security of the state, to maintaining public order, some tax decisions, and some decisions on foreign relations and contracts).

unacceptable, the 1980 Act had to adopt some compromise solutions. Nevertheless, the present scope of judicial review in Poland may be described as broad, since nearly all important decisions (and over 90% of the total number of decisions issued) are subject thereto. It seems, however, possible to endorse the further development of judicial review of administrative decisions due to the political changes which have taken place in Poland since January 1980.[9]

Exclusive jurisdiction in administrative cases is possessed by the High Administrative Court, which has been established by the CAP-Amendment as one of the so-called special courts. It means that the High Administrative Court acts independently of the existing system of ordinary courts, and, according to Article 61(1) of the 1952 Constitution,[10] its activities may be supervised only by the Supreme Court.

The High Administrative Court sits in Warsaw; the Ministry of Justice also may establish local divisions of this Court in other cities. The Court is composed of its President (Chief Judge) and judges; the number of judges (presently eleven) is determined by the Council of State.[11] All judges are appointed for life by the Council of State upon motions presented by the Ministry of Justice. All Polish citizens who possess regular judicial qualifications,[12] providing they are at least 35

---

9 See L. Garlicki and M. Rybicki, "Nad problematyka wymiaru sprawiedliwości w pánstwach wsółczesnych," *Państwo i prawo*, no. 2 (1981).

10 "The Supreme Court shall be the highest judicial organ and shall supervise the work of all other courts with respect to the pronouncement of judgments."

11 The Council of State is a supreme presidial body elected by the Sejm from among its members. Among its numerous powers, the Council of State appoints judges and surveys activities of all courts in Poland.

12 That is, (1) to guarantee that he will properly exercise the duties of a judge in Poland; (2) to enjoy

years old, are highly qualified in administrative law, have worked no less than ten years as a judge, procurator, advocate, member of the State Arbitrazh,[13] notary, or qualified legal counsel, or as a senior officer in the state administration (in this last instance, however, his previous duties had to embrace legal practice) are eligible. Also eligible are all senior members (professors and docents) of law faculties and other similar institutions.

Once a year the President of the Court is bound to convene a plenary session of all judges of the High Administrative Court (individual cases are decided by three-judge panels and must not be heard by the plenary session). At this session, discussion of current problems in the Court's activities and decision-making should take place. The First President of the Supreme Court, the Minister of Justice, the Minister of Administration, and the Procurator General may take part in the session. The President of the Court has to regularly inform the Council of State about the activities of the Court;[14] he also informs the Prime Minister and the Minister of Justice about important issues of the Court's jurisdiction.

A right to seek judicial review is vested in

---

fully public rights; (3) to be of unimpeachable character; (4) to have completed a university legal education, postgraduate court training, and to pass the appropriate state examination.

13 State Arbitrazh is a specialised agency which hears cases between state enterprises and other economic organisations. See V. Knapp, "State Arbitration in Socialist Countries," *International Encyclopaedia of Comparative Law,* XVI, ch. 13.

14 Neither the content of such information nor the way in which the Council of State discusses them may affect the principle of the independence of judges. See Garlicki, "Die verfassungsrechtliche Stellung des polnischen Obersten Gerichts," in T. Berberich, W. Höll, and K.J. Maass (ed.), *Neue Entwicklungen im öffentlichen Recht* (Stuttgart-Berlin-Köln-Mainz, 1979), p. 200.

the party whose legal situation was affected by an administrative decision. Also the procurator may seek such review. A party may seek judicial review only after exhausting all the ordinary legal remedies available (*i.e.*, after appealing the decision to a superior administrative agency, whenever possible). It is also possible to seek court action in a case of non-feasance by an administrative agency which has failed in its duty to decide the case within a proper time. The Court may then issue an order to the administrative agency to decide the case.

The case is first presented to that administrative agency which has issued the final decision. It is the agency's duty to transfer the case to the High Administrative Court within thirty days, unless it changes the decision by itself. As in all other socialist countries, the powers of the Polish Court are limited to issues of law, and only compliance or non-compliance with the law (substantial as well as procedural) may be examined by the judiciary. The Court hears the case in open session, and each party may be represented by a lawyer (advocate). The Court may set aside the decision if it finds it illegal (contrary to law), but it cannot decide the case on the merits. The case has to be decided *de novo* by the proper administrative agency, which is bound by an interpretation of the law as given by the Court.

All decisions of the High Administrative Court are final; however, some instruments of special review are given to the Supreme Court, where the former Civil Chamber has been reshaped into a Civil and Administrative Chamber.[15] The First President of the Supreme Court, the Procurator General, and the Minister of Justice may lodge with the Supreme Court a motion for a so-called extraordinary review of any judgment of the High Administrative Court. A panel of three Supreme

---

15 The Supreme Court consists of four chambers (Criminal, Civil and Administrative, Labour and Social Insurance, Military), each supervising appropriate decisions of lower courts.

Court judges decides the case *de novo* in such a situation. The Supreme Court may also issue a general (abstract) interpretation of laws which is binding upon all courts, the High Administrative Court included.

The establishment of the High Administrative Court as a special court having exclusive jurisdiction over administrative cases is by no means typical of East European legal systems. In all other socialist countries (except some Yugoslav member republics) the power to review administrative decisions is vested in the ordinary courts. It is pointed out that this approach is based on the quest for the unity of the administration of justice and court organisation.[16] In Poland, however, the prevailing view has been that separate administrative jurisdiction would be more appropriate to the specific character of administrative cases. Since the High Administrative Court is staffed by judges with considerable experience in administrative law, it is believed that it would be easier for them to adjust to their new duties.[17] It seems also that the present Court may be more independent and eager to check any illegal administrative action than the ordinary courts. In other words, one of the reasons for the separation of administrative jurisdiction may be linked to the present structure of the ordinary courts. Finally, the idea of a separate administrative court is firmly rooted in the Polish tradition.

The Summer Agreements

The three agreements signed between 30 August and 3 September 1980 by the Cabinet's representatives and workers' organisations were of crucial importance for the further development of the

---

16 A. Rácz, *Courts and Tribunals. A Comparative Study* (Budapest, 1980), p. 87.

17 See S. Zawadzki, "Teoretyczne i legislacyjne aspekty projektu nowelizacji kodeksu postepowania administracyjnego," *Państwo i prawo*, no. 2 (1980), p. 26.

political situation in Poland. They were followed by numerous other agreements concluded for different branches of industry, enterprises, or even single factories. In very broad terms, it seems possible to say that those latter agreements are similar to "collective bargaining agreements" known to labour law, since they deal mainly with such problems as conditions of work, wage regulations, and so forth. The first three agreements, however, dealt with more general matters of a political (and hence, constitutional) character.

The agreements have recognised the workers' right to establish new trade unions as an "authentic representation of the working class". The new trade unions have to base their activities on the principles of the 1952 Constitution. In particular, they accept the leading role of the Polish United Workers Party in the state system, the existing network of international alliances, as well as the socialist structure of ownership relations in Poland. The new unions must not act as political parties: their activities have to be oriented toward a representation of social and financial rights of the workers. The agreements have further stipulated important changes in state policy concerning freedom of speech and the press, particularly for a relaxation of censorship. Also the unions' right to strike has been acknowledged. Finally, most points of the agreements have dealt with social and economic questions, providing for many specific social benefits and pay rises, as well as some general changes in state policy on these matters. The need for economic reform, prepared and carried out by the government with the unions' participation, also has been recognised. The Cabinet assumed an obligation to initiate legislation necessary to implement all agreed ventures. As far as constitutional law is concerned, two important bills are to be prepared. A new trade union law[18] shall guarantee a pluralist structure

18 On 8 October 1980, the Sejm partially amended the 1949 Trade Unions Act (*DzU* (1980), no. 22, item 83), thus validating the Council of State resolution issued on

of the union movement. In particular, it shall grant to unions a right to strike, determining - among other things - a procedure for pre-strike negotiations and defining conditions under which a strike may be proclaimed. A new act on state control over the press and other publications (censorship law) should, among other things, define the powers of censorship more precisely and establish judicial review over decisions on this matter.[19]

All the above-mentioned regulations, when passed, will introduce considerable changes into Polish constitutional law. Many other parts of the agreements have been or will be transformed into legal regulations concerning labour law, social welfare law, administrative law, and so forth. Thus, the agreements exert a far-reaching impact on the entire legal system. This impact, however, is not direct, since positive decisions of the legislative branch are necessary to implement the new laws.

Can the agreements be regarded as a direct source of law ? In my opinion, the agreements should be considered in both their political and legal dimensions. As far as the former is concerned, the agreements are often described as a *contrat social*, that is, as a political document formulating a basic programme of socio-political reforms in Poland. Since they are mutually accepted by the government (by its political as well as the executive branches) and by workers' organisations, the agreements are binding on them and,

---

13 September 1980 (*Monitor Polski*, no. 22, item 104). The resolution provided a new registration procedure for trade unions. New unions may apply for registration to the Warsaw district court, and appellate jurisdiction has been vested in the Supreme Court. Over fifty unions were registered by the Warsaw court between September and December 1980.

19 The agreement concluded in Gdańsk provided for jurisdiction of the High Administrative Court here. Many take the view that ordinary courts (their civil divisions) are better prepared to decide censorship cases.

according to existing guidelines of political morality, it is their political duty to observe and to enforce the agreements. The bilateral character of these agreements means also that their stipulations must not be changed without the consent of both signatories. Proper enforcement of the agreements is guaranteed by political sanctions, as appropriate, for state agencies and party organisations on one side and for trade unions on the other side. Non-compliance with the agreements may also bring some legal consequences, for example, the parliamentary dismissal of a Cabinet member or dissolution of a union by the court.

The political dimension of the agreements suggests many similarities with a civil law contract. The notion of a "political contract" seems to be warranted. Again it must be stressed that our analyses are on the political dimension. As is recognised by legal doctrine, a modern society contains not one, but many, normative systems.[20] One of them is a system of legal norms, being parallel to other systems, in particular to the system of political norms. The latter norms are mainly established by political and social organisations. To a considerable extent, they exist independently of legal regulations; quite often, however, they deal with the functioning of state agencies, especially Parliament and the Cabinet. Moreover, there is no clear-cut distinction between political norms, constitutional conventions, and legal norms in constitutional law. The agreements as "political contracts" belong to the system of political norms, and they are a new type of such norms, unknown in Poland before the summer of 1980.[21]

The political dimension of the agreements as "political contracts" (*i.e.*, a mutually binding programme for further development) does not explain, however, their legal nature. The very idea of such

---

20 See S. Ehrlich, *Wstep do nauki o państwie i prawie* (3d ed.; Warsaw, 1979), pp. 182-184.

21 Garlicki, "Refleksje nad characterem Porozumienia Gdańskiego," *Państwo i prawo*, no. 1 (1981), pp. 3-13.

agreements has been completely foreign to socialist constitutional law thus far, and no reference to any existing legal concept seems possible on this matter. In my opinion, the agreements cannot be defined either as a civil law contract or as a "collective bargaining agreement" as known in labour law. The former belongs to the realm of private law, whereas the legal nature of their signatories is completely different and appertains rather to public law. The latter have to deal exclusively with problems of labour law (or social policy at most), whereas the agreements also stipulate essential political (constitutional) changes.

Finally, the agreements cannot be considered as normative (legal) acts, that is, as direct sources of law. The power to establish normative (legal) acts is limited to the agencies enumerated in the 1952 Constitution, and an appropriate procedure has to be observed.[22] Even assuming the agreements are the Cabinet's acts, the normative-act theory can not be accepted, since the Cabinet now has power to regulate this subject-matter. Also, the language of the agreements does not indicate any intention to transform them into normative (legal) acts. All three agreements have been written as political documents, and there is no need to squeeze them into legal categories.

The view that the agreements are mainly political norms must not be understood as an attempt to diminish their importance. As has been pointed out, political norms play a very important role in any modern society, sometimes being even more effective than legal ones.[23] As one of many possible examples, the so-called "general principles" of law can be given.

One of the important features of Polish law

---

22 See R. Orzechowski, "The System and Mode of Creating Law in the Polish People's Republic," in *The Law in Poland,* pp. 7-37.

23 See examples given by Ehrlich, "O wielości systemów normatywnych," *Państwo i prawo,* no. 5 (1979), pp. 30-33.

(as well as the laws of other continental countries) is the existence of certain "general principles" (*Generalklauseln, principes généraux*), which permit a judge to refer to usage or to equity, and permit the correction of statutory provisions in the interests of public order or good morals.[24] The task of such "principles" is to introduce some moral, political, or customary norms into the positive law. In this way, the political norms contained in the agreements may be applied by the courts to interpret or even modify legal regulations.

Parliamentary Organisation and Procedure

It seems significant that the summer's political developments have exerted an immediate impact on parliamentary law. The same phenomenon occurred in 1956 and in 1971: political programmes of democratic reforms have resulted in an activisation of the Sejm and have led to essential changes in parliamentary organisation and procedure. Equally distinct has been the opposite trend: any restrictions against an existing level of democratic freedoms has had an immediate effect in a decline of parliamentary activities. In 1980, however, parliamentary reaction has been particularly swift; within three months of the autumn session two important reforms have been completed. The new act on the Supreme Chamber of Control[25] has restored parliamentary supremacy over the Chamber; amendments to the parliamentary rules of procedure[26] have extended the controlling powers of the Sejm.

---

24 See D. Lasok (ed.), *Polish Civil Law* (Leyden, 1977), I, pp. 25ff. Also generally R. David and J. Brierley, *Major Legal Systems in the World Today* (London, 1968), p. 115.

25 *DzU* (1980), no. 22, items 81 and 82.

26 *Monitor Polski* (1980), no. 24, item 109; no. 27, item 145; see the new full text of the rules in *Monitor Polski* (1980), no. 29, item 164.

The Supreme Chamber of Control has been traditionally subject only to the Sejm and the Council of State. The mission of the Chamber has been to supervise the work of the state administration (including the Cabinet and all its members) and to report its findings to Parliament. That system was abandoned in 1976, when the Chamber was linked to the state administration and subordinated to the Prime Minister. The powers of the Chamber were drastically curtailed; it lost the right to scrutinise activities of the Cabinet and the Prime Minister, and its rights vis-à-vis other members of the Cabinet were limited.

The 1976 reform was heavily criticised, and the main task of the 1980 Act has been to revive the Chamber as a subsidiary body of the Sejm. At the same time, some new elements concerning both the powers and structure of the Chamber have been added to the statute. According to the amended Article 34 of the 1952 Constitution, the Chamber is empowered to supervise the financial, economic, and administrative work of all organs of state administration together with the services, institutions, enterprises, and other undertakings for which the state administration is responsible. The legality, efficiency, and expediency of the work is supervised. The Chamber has a right to supervise the activities of cooperatives, social organisations, and units of the non-socialised economy regarding their financial and other duties toward the state. The Chamber can not interfere with the activities of representative bodies, courts, and procuracy agencies. It acts on its own initiative, or on the command of the Sejm and the Council of State, or on request of the Prime Minister. In particular, it is a duty of the Chamber to report annually to the Sejm on how the Budget and the National Economic Plan have been implemented by the Cabinet. The Chamber's report serves as a basis for parliamentary approval of the Cabinet's actions on this matter. In addition to that general duty, the Chamber shall supply parliamentary committees with all relevant information on the work of any minister, institution, or establishment, either on request or on its own initiative.

The above-mentioned powers of the Chamber are similar to those existing before 1976. In addition, the 1980 legislation has provided for some measures which link the supervisory activities of the Chamber with the parliamentary accountability of the Cabinet's members. It is a new prerogative of the Chamber to report to the Sejm charges against any person of high-ranking position in the state administration. The procedure for parliamentary approval of the Cabinet's report on the implementation of the Budget and National Economic Plan also has been modified. The Sejm may grant general approval to the Cabinet, but at the same time it may exclude a member of the Cabinet from such approval.[27]

The Chamber's structure has been entirely reformed. An institution of so-called Presidium (Collegium) of the Chamber, abolished in 1976, was restored. The Presidium is composed of the President of the Chamber (appointed by the Sejm) and members (appointed by the Council of State upon a motion of the Chamber's President). The Presidium is the directing authority in the Chamber; it organises the work of professional staff and other employees of the Chamber, and it takes all important decisions and reports. The Presidium is responsible, through its President, solely to the Sejm. The 1980 Act has introduced two important changes regarding the pre-1976 structure of the Chamber: (1) it is now possible to appoint as a member of the Presidium a person who does not belong to the permanent staff of the Chamber (the Presidium before 1976 had been composed solely of the Chamber's officials). It is believed that, although concrete supervisory activity could be carried out by civil servants permanently attached to the Chamber, a general evaluation and conclusion regarding the Cabinet's work should be done by politicians. Thus the present Presidium of the

---

27 Prior to the 1980 Act, approval could be granted (or refused) only to the Cabinet as a whole and not to particular ministers.

Chamber is composed mainly of members of political parties and social organisations (deputies, university professors, trade union activists), usually with a long experience in political life; (2) the new Act has strengthened the position of the Presidium's members. In particular, the privilege of a quasi-judicial independence has been granted to them.

On 8 October and 21 November 1980 two series of amendments to the parliamentary rules of procedure were adopted by the Sejm. The former dealt with the Supreme Chamber of Control Act and provided for detailed forms of cooperation between the Chamber and the Sejm. The latter is of a more complex character, introducing new solutions to nearly all problems of parliamentary organisation and procedure. The November amendment has been devoted above all to strengthening parliamentary control over the Cabinet as well as over the whole system of state administration. Some important provisions also concern legislative procedure.

As far as parliamentary control is concerned, the most important change has been, of course, the reform of the Supreme Chamber of Control (see above). As noted before, one innovation was an orientation of Chamber activities toward supervision over the Cabinet. Many new provisions of the rules of procedure have the same aim. Assuming that the real power of Parliament is determined by the powers of its committees, the amendments have enlarged them. First, the standing committees[28] received new prerogatives vis-à-vis members of the Cabinet. Any committee may introduce a motion to the Budget and Planning Committee proposing that

---

28 There are twenty-three standing committee in the Polish Sejm. Twenty of them are organised upon a pattern of departmental specialisation: their scope of mandate corresponds to the responsibility of various ministerial departments. The remaining three are: Committee on Legislation, Committee on Mandates and Rules, and the newly established (see below) Committee on Petitions; see A. Burda, *Parliament of the Polish People's Republic* (Wrocław, 1978), p. 103.

the House exclude a particular member of the Cabinet from the annual approval concerning the implementation of the Budget and the National Economic Plan. A Prime Minister's motion to appoint a new member of the Cabinet may be referred to an appropriate committee for an opinion, which should be presented to the House before a final decision.[29] All committees have been vested with a right to summon to their meetings any member of the Cabinet or any other administrative official, providing their activities are related to the scope of a committee's mandate. A new standing committee, the Committee on Petitions, has been established. Its function is to examine voters' petitions (complaints or proposals - over 4000 each year) addressed to Parliament (each deputy is obliged to examine all petitions addressed individually to him) and to submit to Parliament (or other standing committees) conclusions concerning the work of the state administration as a whole or any particular agency. The Committee may direct any petition to an appropriate administrative agency and survey how it is resolved there.

The control powers of the House have been enlarged. The November amendment has expressly provided for - hitherto unknown in parliamentary practice - debates in the House on periodic reports of the Council of State concerning its activities. Since similar reports of the Cabinet have taken place for many years, there has been no need to change earlier rules on that matter. However, the President of the Sejm (Marszałek Sejmu) has been vested with a new right: during a parliamentary debate he may request the Prime Minister to present his position on a given matter.

Three important changes have been introduced

---

29 In Poland the Cabinet's members are appointed by the Sejm (or, exceptionally, by the Council of State with subsequent parliamentary approval) on the recommendation of the Prime Minister. See Burda, *ibid.*, pp. 168-170.

into legislative procedure:[30] (1) the amendments have not provided for an obligatory first reading in the House; the Presidium of the Sejm may refer a bill either to the House or directly to the appropriate committees, where a first reading takes place. The Presidium's discretion has, however, been limited since the new rules of procedure provide that for consideration of constitutional amendments, annual budgets, national economic plans, codes (codifications), and other important bills the first reading should be in the House. If the first reading is held at a committee meeting, all deputies have to be informed. Each deputy has a right to take part in this meeting and/or to submit amendments to the bill, which have to be examined by the committee;[31] (2) the position of the Committee on Legislation has been strengthened. Whereas earlier provisions had stipulated that a final report on a bill should be presented by the committee appropriate for the subject-matter of the bill, upon an opinion presented by a Committee on Legislation, the November amendment provided for a joint report by both committees acting as equal partners. This was merely a codification of the real position of the Committee on Legislation, which is, in practice, one of the two most powerful committees in the Sejm; (3) new rules have provided for committee examination of draft bills. Opinions and recommendations of

---

30 Poland has a procedure of two readings. The first reading consists of a debate on the general principles of a bill and may take place either in the House or at a joint sitting of the Committee on Legislation and the committee appropriate for the subject-matter of the bill. Then the bill is examined by the committees, and finally the second reading is conducted in the House. The second reading is based on committee reports, which are examined before a final vote is taken. See Burda, *ibid.*, pp. 146-152.

31 Each deputy also has a right to submit amendments during the second reading. In the parliamentary practice, however, such amendments were rare because of political limits.

committees are submitted to the Cabinet as a basis for a definite redaction of a bill.

There is no need to specify all changes in parliamentary organisation and procedure. The examples given indicate that a strengthening of the Sejm's position in the governmental process should follow from these changes. Nonetheless, the problem of further reforms exists, as both political documents and legal writing emphasise.

THE JUDICIAL ROLE IN THE REVIEW OF POLICY DECISIONS

R. C. Austin

Introduction

The objects of this paper are threefold: *first*, to examine the exercise of the supervisory review powers of the superior courts in the United Kingdom over the policy decisions of public authorities, including ministers and departments of the central government, local authorities, and other statutory bodies; *second*, to determine whether such examination reveals the existence of certain political or constitutional assumptions underlying those decisions of the superior courts, and *third*, to determine whether such assumptions, if any are revealed, have undergone substantial modification, or even reversal, as a consequence or reflection of, or in response to, the dramatic changes in the nature and functions of government institutions during the past 35 years.

At the outset, however, it is essential to describe what is meant by "policy decisions." The term "describe" rather than "define" is used advisedly, because a clear and comprehensive definition of "policy," if not impossible, has certainly eluded even the highest of our superior courts, the House of Lords, a point amply demonstrated by their Lordships' decisions in *Anns* v. *London Borough of Merton*[1] and *Bushell* v. *Secretary of State for the Environment*.[2] Whilst some similarity may be identified in the use by their Lordships of such contrasting terms as "discretionary"[3] and

---

1 [1978] A.C. 728, [1977] 2 All E.R. 492.

2 [1980] 2 All E.R. 608.

3 [1977] 2 All E.R. 492, 500, *per* Lord Wilberforce.

"operational,"[4] on the one hand, and "national"[5] and "local"[6] on the other, it is clear that the concepts embodied by these terms are not synonymous. The terms are used in an incomplete, descriptive manner rather than as definitions.

Nor is it possible to claim that policy decisions are invariably general and legislative in character, for decisions taken on specific disputes of mixed judicial and administrative character may involve the formulation of new, or the variation of existing, policies. For example, the decision of the Secretary of State on the called-in application for planning permission to construct a fast breeder nuclear reactor and nuclear waste re-processing plant at Windscale in Cumbria, clearly involved the formulation of policies concerning nuclear electricity generation.[7] Issues such as costs, environmental damage, long-term waste disposal, security from theft and/or sabotage, public health risks, and long-term energy needs all combined to make that single decision on a specific case a crucial question of general policy at both local and national level, thus graphically illustrating the near-impossibility of achieving a satisfactory universal definition of "policy decisions."

Nor is it possible to argue that policy decisions involve the formulation of principles, standards, or guides for the future rather than their application in the present, because the essence of policy is its flexibility. Thus, an authority charged with the application of policy in a particular case before it, will frequently be required to modify, adapt, or even abandon a policy when confronted with a situation not foreseen by the original policy-maker. The application of the

---

4 *Ibid.*

5 [1980] 2 All E.R. 608, 614-615, *per* Lord Diplock.

6 *Ibid.*

7 "The Windscale Inquiry." Report by the Hon. Mr. Justice Parker (London, 1978).

policy to a present case may thereby involve its re-formulation.

Despite these reservations, however, it is submitted that *some* general characteristics of policy decisions can be identified.

First, policy decisions necessarily involve the making of choices between various possible options open to the decision-maker. Usually, those choices are not dictated by pre-determined, limited criteria; indeed, the policy decision-maker is frequently free to select his own criteria at the time of making his decision, and to determine what relative importance he attaches to particular criteria. The criteria he considers may involve a wide range of social, economic, environmental, political, or other factors. Policy decisions thus involve the exercise of subjective discretion, with few limits placed on the exercise thereof.

Second, policy decisions are usually directed to the future rather than to the past. They are in most cases predictive of future events, and they determine the future reaction of public authorities to such events.

Third, policy decisions are usually general rather than specific. They are directed to categories, groups, or classes of persons and events rather than to specific individual persons and events. It is possibly *this* aspect of policy decisions which Lord Diplock was really attempting to describe by his use of the terms "local" and "national" in the *Bushell* case.[8]

Fourth, because policy decisions involve the making of choices determined by a wide range of criteria, usually of social, economic, environmental, political, or other character, the policy decision-maker must usually have at his disposal substantial research facilities and expertise, to assist in the compilation and assessment of the wide-ranging information, frequently of a highly

---

8 [1980] 2 All E.R. 608.

complex and technical nature, upon which his decision will be based. This characteristic is in my view one of the crucial determinants of judicial response to policy decisions, and I shall return to this point later.

Fifth, and possibly because of the characteristics already noted, policy decisions are frequently the subject of fierce political controversy, often on ideologically partisan battle lines. The wide range of subjective choices open to the decision-maker, the freedom to select his own criteria, the large numbers of persons and wide range of interests likely to be affected by his decisions, the impact of his decisions upon future events, and the differences of opinion between experts as to the conclusions which should or could legitimately be drawn from the enormous volume of information available or produced by research, often cause policy decisions to become the subject of ideological disputes between the two major political parties, or even within those parties. This last characteristic has been, in this writer's view, another major cause of judicial inhibition in the review of policy decisions, for reasons which will be considered below, connected with constitutional assumptions about the independence and political impartiality of the judiciary.

Another expression requiring some explanation is the phrase "political or constitutional assumptions." The exercise of governmental power in the United Kingdom is not exclusively regulated by written instruments imposing legal restraints on those upon whom such power is conferred. Wide areas of the British Constitution are uncharted by legislation or judicial precedent, the principal sources of law. Instead, those areas are mapped out by numerous common understandings as to the scope of powers and the manner of their exercise. Some of these have become so widely accepted and so uniformly applied that they are known as constitutional conventions,[9] *e.g.*, that the monarch

---

9 For fuller discussion of the nature and content of conventions, see S.A. de Smith, *Constitutional and*

shall not assent to a bill passed by Parliament or that ministers are responsible to Parliament. Numerous other examples of conventions can be given.

In addition to conventions, however, there are certain widely held views of a politically normative character; *e.g.*, that a government, once elected and appointed to office, ought to govern in the interest of the nation at large and not direct its efforts exclusively to the sectional benefit of its supporters. These political norms, though not elevated to the status of constitutional conventions, nonetheless wield considerable influence on the conduct of those in power. Further, the sanctions for breach of both conventions and political norms are generally political rather than legal, although breach of convention may in certain cases lead to legal consequences.[10]

Having attempted to clarify some of the terms, it is now appropriate to return to the three declared objects of this paper.

Judicial Decisions in the Review of Policy

Judicial review of the administrative acts and decisions of public authorities in the United Kingdom has traditionally been subject to curial inhibition when the action or decision which is the subject of review was taken in the exercise of a discretionary power. That inhibition has frequently been transformed into judicial abdication

---

Administrative Law (3d ed.; London, 1977), pp. 44-63.

10 For example, in 1909 the refusal of the House of Lords, in breach of convention, to pass the Liberal Government's Budget led to the passing of the Parliament Act 1911. Further, and more directly, breach of the convention requiring Parliament to be summoned each year would lead to illegal government expenditure and taxation and a breach of the prohibition, contained in the Bill of Rights 1688, against maintaining a standing army in peacetime without Parliamentary sanction.

where the discretion has been characterised by the courts as involving considerations of policy. The view taken in such cases by successive generations of judges was that provided the public authority did not stray beyond the outer boundaries of its often widely defined powers - such boundaries being referred to variously as the "four corners,"[11] the "ambit,"[12] the "proper scope"[13] - and acted in good faith (a largely meaningless limitation),[14] it was free to act as it chose within the confines of those legal boundaries. It was the courts' role to define those boundaries by reference to and interpretation of the empowering statute or instrument, but not to trespass upon the authority's activities within those boundaries. The test was essentially the very broad one of general legality, within which the administrative body had considerable freedom of action.

Thus, for example, in *Westminster Corptn.* v. *London and North Western Rlwy. Co.*,[15] the House of Lords held that the courts could not interfere in the exercise of a discretionary power by a local authority which adopted the policy of constructing public conveniences under the street, thus incidentally and in addition to its power to construct the conveniences, constructing a subway under the street for the purpose of access to those conveniences. Provided the authority was exercising its power to construct conveniences, the court could not interfere with the manner of implementation of

---

11 *Carltona* v. *Commrs. of Works* [1943] 2 All E.R. 560, 564, *per* Lord Greene M.R.

12 *White and Collins* v. *Minister of Health* [1939] 3 All E.R. 548.

13 *Associated Provincial Picture Houses* v. *Wednesbury Corporation* [1948] 1 K.B. 223.

14 de Smith, *Judicial Review of Administrative Action* (4th ed.; London, 1980), p. 290, n. 72. de Smith refers to the courts' "perfunctory dicta about the need ... to act in good faith."

15 [1905] A.C. 426.

that power adopted by the authority.[16] Similarly, in *Associated Provincial Picture Houses* v. *Wednesbury Corporation*[17] where a local authority imposed a condition upon the grant of a Sunday licence, forbidding the admission of children, the court would not intervene unless the authority's decision was so absurd that no reasonable authority could come to such a decision.

Again, in *Carltona* v. *Commrs. of Works*,[18] a wartime case involving the requisitioning of factories under emergency regulations, the court explicitly adopted the "four corners"[19] test and declined to question the content of the decision once it was established that the government authority was acting within the very general legal or statutory limits of its power. It is also possible to identify specific areas of policy decision-making where the subject-matter of the cases has been explicitly characterised as immune from review by the courts, probably on the basis of the highly "executive" and politically sensitive nature of such matters, *e.g.*, immigration and deportation (*Soblen*,[20] *Schmidt*,[21] *Van Duyn*,[22] *Hosenball*[23]) and prerogative powers (or their statutory replacements) in areas such as security, intelligence, foreign relations, defence, states

---

16 *Ibid.* at p. 427, *per* Lord Halsbury: "... it is beyond the power of any court to contest that discretion."

17 [1948] 1 K.B. 223.

18 [1943] 2 All E.R. 560.

19 *Ibid.* at p. 564, *per* Lord Greene M.R.

20 *R.* v. *Brixton Prison Governor, Ex parte Soblen* [1963] 2 Q.B. 243.

21 *Schmidt* v. *Home Secretary* [1969] 2 Ch. 149.

22 *Van Duyn* v. *Home Office* [1975] Ch. 358.

23 *R.* v. *Home Secretary, Ex parte Hosenball* [1977] 1 W.L.R. 766.

of emergency and passports,[24] (*D.P.P.* v. *Chandler*,[25] *Liversidge* v. *Anderson*,[26] *McEldowney* v. *Ford*[27]).

Not all the earlier cases reflect such a consistent judicial approach however, but the exceptions are notable precisely because they highlighted the controversial nature of an activist or interventionist judicial role in the review of policy cases, *e.g.*, *Roberts* v. *Hopwood*.[28]

In that case, where a Labour-controlled local authority, which was empowered to pay such wages as it thought fit, had decided to pay a fair and reasonable minimum living wage in excess of the then "market rates" and had also decided to pay women the same wages as men for the same work, the House of Lords upheld a surcharge upon the councillors by the District Auditor. Lord Atkinson specifically denied the council the right to "be guided ... by some eccentric principles of socialistic philanthropy, or by a feminist ambition to secure the equality of the sexes in the matter of wages in the world of labour."[29] Their Lordships held that in so doing, the councillors had acted unreasonably and thus unlawfully, thereby justifying the District Auditor's surcharge upon the individual councillors. *Roberts* v. *Hopwood* is therefore a clear example of overtly political judicial intervention in a policy decision taken by an elected public authority. But it has been much criticised on both legal and constitutional grounds and

---

24 For further examples, see de Smith, note 14 above, pp. 286-298. See especially p. 297 where de Smith notes that, in such cases, "... the policy content of the power is large and its exercise affects large numbers of people."

25 [1964] A.C. 763.

26 [1942] A.C. 206.

27 [1971] A.C. 632.

28 [1925] A.C. 578.

29 *Ibid.*, p. 594.

is of dubious authority today.[30] Although there are other early examples of judicial intervention in policy decisions, they are few and none is as blatantly political.[31]

Apart from those exceptions, it is possible in my submission to discern a clear and generally consistent pattern of judicial restraint from intervention in policy decisions until the mid-1960s.

Change, when it came, was not borne by the abrupt gust of legal revolution noted by de Smith, who describes the *Padfield*[32] case in 1968 as marking "the emergence of the interventionist judicial attitude that has characterised many recent judgments."[33] A number of earlier decisions had created expanded judicial concepts of jurisdictional restraint on discretion. Taking into account irrelevant or unrelated considerations;[34] acting for improper purposes or motives;[35] fettering or failing to exercise a discretionary power by

---

30 See, for example, R.C. Austin, "Judicial Review of Subjective Discretion - at the Rubicon; Whither Now ?," *Current Legal Problems*, XXVIII (1975), p. 150.

31 For example, *Re Decision of Walker* [1944] K.B. 644, *Prescott* v. *Birmingham Corporation* [1955] Ch. 210 and *Taylor* v. *Munrow* [1960] 1 W.L.R. 151.

32 *Padfield* v. *Minister of Agriculture* [1968] A.C. 997.

33 de Smith, note 14 above, p. 287, n. 47.

34 *Hall* v. *Shoreham UDC* [1964] 1 W.L.R. 240.

35 *Webb* v. *Minister of Housing and Local Government* [1964] 1 W.L.R. 1295.

reason of policy,[36] agreement,[37] or delegation;[38] acting on the basis of no evidence[39] - all these concepts had by 1968 become potent weapons in the arsenal of judicial review. In the areas of town and country planning, housing, and land acquisition for public works, the courts had energetically utilised these concepts to restrain public bodies in the exercise of statutory discretionary powers often couched in subjective terms, and often containing considerable policy elements.

Although a trend towards judicial activism can thus be discerned prior to 1968, the decision in *Padfield*[40] did expand the scope for review by establishing hitherto unexplored grounds for intervention. In that case, the Minister of Agriculture had not clearly acted in a way which gave rise to any of the existing grounds for review. Although his stated reasons were ambiguous and unclear, the House of Lords did not feel able to hold that he had overtly acted for an improper motive or on the basis of irrelevant considerations. Nonetheless, since the Minister's decision appeared to frustrate or defeat one of the purposes of the statute, *viz*., to provide a channel for redress of grievances

---

36 *R.* v. *P.L.A., Ex p. Kynoch* [1919] 1 K.B. 176, followed in *Kilmarnock Magistrates* v. *Secretary of State for Scotland* 1961 S.C. 350 and later followed in *British Oxygen* v. *Board of Trade* [1971] A.C. 610. See also *Sagnata Investments* v. *Norwich Corporation* [1971] 2 Q.B. 614.

37 *Stringer* v. *Minister of Housing and Local Government* [1970] 1 W.L.R. 1282, following numerous earlier authorities.

38 *Lavender* v. *Minister of Housing and Local Government* [1970] 1 W.L.R. 1231, similarly based on numerous earlier authorities.

39 *Webb* v. *Minister of Housing and Local Government* [1964] 1 W.L.R. 1295, followed in *Coleen Properties* v. *Minister of Housing and Local Government* [1971] 1 W.L.R. 433.

40 Note 32 above.

independent of the self-governing statutory body, the Milk Marketing Board, their Lordships held that in the absence of good reasons for so frustrating the object of the statute, the Minister's decision was an invalid exercise of his discretionary power. The reasoning in their Lordships' judgments can be criticised,[41] but their decision clearly established a new ground for review, namely acting without good reasons so as to frustrate or defeat the objects and purposes of the empowering statute. This "purposive" approach to the interpretation, construction, and review of statutory discretionary powers clearly marked a significant step in the expansion of judicial intervention in discretionary policy decisions. An additional consequence of the *Padfield* decision was that it effectively required all administrative decision-makers to provide reasons (indeed, good reasons) for their decisions since the courts could now assume that there were no good reasons (a ground for review) if the decision-maker failed to provide any. Alternatively, if the effect of his decision was to frustrate the objects of the empowering statute, the absence of reasons did not preclude the court from reviewing on that ground, as distinct from the "no good reasons" ground.[42]

The mood of overt judicial activism which was marked by *Padfield* continued in a series of decisions through the 1970s. The *Tameside*,[43] *Eckersley*,[44] *Congreve*,[45] *McWhirter*,[46] *St.*

---

41 See Austin, note 30 above, pp. 168-172.

42 Note 32 above, pp. 1033, 1049, 1053-1054, 1061-1062.

43 *Secretary of State for Education* v. *Tameside M.B.C.* [1976] 3 All E.R. 665.

44 *Eckersley* v. *Secretary of State for the Environment and London Borough of Southwark* (1977) 121 Sol.J. 593; [1977] J.P.L. 580.

45 *Congreve* v. *Home Office* [1976] Q.B. 629.

46 *Attorney-General, ex rel. McWhirter* v. *I.B.A.* [1973] 1 Q.B. 692.

Germain,[47] and *Laker*[48] cases all demonstrated a liberal interventionist approach. Standing to sue was expanded in *McWhirter* and other cases,[49] whilst the "no evidence" rule was enlarged in *Tameside* and *Eckersley* to a "sufficient evidence" rule. The *St. Germain* case extended the review jurisdiction of the courts to prison disciplinary decisions taken by prison governors and boards of visitors, whose decisions had hitherto been unreviewable. *Laker* and *Congreve* illustrated the determination of the courts to restrict wide statutory powers within the limits defined by reference to general principles to which lip-service had always been paid, but to which the courts now attached great significance.

Thus it is possible to discern a substantial reversal of previous attitudes of judicial caution over the past fifteen years. That is not to deny that there are exceptions to this trend. Cases such as *Hosenball*,[50] *Gouriet*,[51] and, more recently, *Bushell*[52] illustrate only too well the continued reluctance of some members of the judiciary to become too closely involved in the examination of either the substance or the methodology of ministerial decision-making at the highest levels of executive policy. Issues such as deportation for national security purposes, the decision whether or not to restrain, by legal process, criminal

---

47 *R.* v. *Board of Visitors of Hull Prison, Ex parte St. Germain* [1979] Q.B. 425.

48 *Laker Airways Ltd.* v. *Department of Trade* [1977] Q.B. 643.

49 See, e.g., *R.* v. *G.L.C., Ex parte Blackburn* [1976] 1 W.L.R. 550; *R.* v. *Metropolitan Police Commr., Ex parte Blackburn (No. 3)* [1973] Q.B. 241; *Arsenal Football Club* v. *Ende* [1979] A.C. 1.

50 Note 23 above.

51 *Gouriet* v. *Union of Post Office Workers* [1978] A.C. 435.

52 *Bushell* v. *Secretary of State for the Environment* [1980] 2 All E.R. 608.

acts proposed by a trade union (namely, the complete blocking of all postal and telephone communications with South Africa), and the assessment of traffic need justifying further extensions to the national motorway network, were seen in those cases as matters of national policy or the public interest upon which ministers of the executive government, and not the courts, were best fitted to make the appropriate decisions. Thus, judicial review was limited to a minimal role; the courts could only ensure that the decision-maker was acting in good faith, within the general scope of his jurisdiction, and in accordance with minimum requirements of procedural fairness. Beyond those limits the courts should not, in such cases, exercise their powers of supervisory review. In each of those cases, explicit reference was made to the policy content of the issues, which therefore required determination by the minister concerned. Policy was variously described as involving considerations of the public interest, of the national interest, of general benefit rather than individual rights. Ministers were accountable to the national forum, Parliament, where such decisions could be reviewed, criticised and (presumably) overturned or altered by dint of the pressure of Parliamentary and public opinion.

The above examination of the case law on judicial review has demonstrated, it is submitted, that after a substantial period of extreme judicial caution, the courts have in the past fifteen years substantially reversed their previous approach to the review of policy decisions. The scope and penetration of, and the grounds for, judicial examination of such decisions has been dramatically expanded in that period. But there remain some areas of policy decision-making which are regarded by some members of the judiciary as prohibited territory, reserved exclusively for the executive government, and subject only to the control of the representative legislature.

Underlying Constitutional/Political Assumptions

It is the contention of this author that the judicial inhibition exhibited prior to the mid-1960s was the product of certain constitutional and political assumptions concerning the appropriate allocation and exercise of power within the framework of British government; further, that the dramatic legal revolution in judicial review which has taken place in the past fifteen years is the consequence of the partial, though not complete, erosion of those assumptions; and that that erosion is the consequence of the political revolution in the role of government since 1945.

What, then, are the constitutional and political assumptions referred to above which underlie the judicial attitude that the courts should not intervene, by supervisory review, in the exercise of policy decision-making powers ? The first is that since by constitutional convention ministers are responsible to Parliament for their acts and decisions and for those of their departments and other subordinate administrative bodies, the courts should leave to the minister or body concerned and to Parliament the making, review, and control of those decisions which the minister or body and Parliament, rather than the courts, are both better-equipped and more appropriate to exercise, review, and control. Policy decisions, as previously noted, are legislative and general in character, apply to large numbers of people rather than individuals, and look to future rather than past events. They set out social, economic, and political goals or objectives and the proposed means of achieving them. These functions are, it was assumed, most appropriately exercised and controlled by those who have the necessary resources of knowledge, research, and expertise, and who are responsible to the public at large, *i.e.*, ministers and Parliament. Judges have neither the information and expertise[53] nor the public account-

---

53 Since the rules of admissibility preclude the submission in U.K. courts of "Brandeis briefs," common in

ability which would justify their intervention in the exercise of policy decision-making powers. Ministers, on the other hand, have the vast resources of information and research facilities and the expertise of civil servants in their departments and other subordinate bodies. They consult widely with outside bodies to obtain information and advice. They have non-civil servant specialist advisers and the Central Policy Research Unit at their disposal in order to ensure a source of information and advice independent of their departments. They can appoint departmental committees, Royal Commissions, public inquiries (either statutory or *ad hoc*), and tribunals of inquiry to investigate particular issues of public concern. Such bodies are not limited by strict rules of evidence, so the range and type of information available to them is not restricted. The members of such bodies are usually selected for their knowledge and experience of and expertise in the subject-matter of the investigation. Ministers are thus better informed and more expertly advised than the courts are or could be, and ministers, via Parliament and the ballot box, are more responsible to the public than the courts are or should be.

This last point leads us to the second major assumption underlying judicial caution, namely that the existence of an independent judiciary, both actually, and publicly seen to be, untainted by political bias or influence, is one of the fundamental pillars of the British Constitution, and is the cornerstone for the protection of individual rights and freedoms. The risk that judicial intervention in policy decisions (which, as previously noted, are frequently the subject of partisan political controversy) will undermine public

---

United States litigation, and since the U.K. judiciary is drawn from a highly specialist practising Bar, most of whom increasingly have no formal education outside the law, it is unlikely that U.K. judges could develop the expertise or acquire the information necessary for the resolution of complex policy questions.

confidence in the independence and impartiality of the judiciary and hence reduce the effectiveness of the judiciary in protecting individual rights and freedoms, is a theme often to be found in judicial utterances, both in and out of court.[54] That perceived risk is a major ground of objection to the enactment of an entrenched Bill of Rights in the United Kingdom.[55] (So, too, is the assumption that politicians, not judges, should exercise and control policy decision-making powers.)[56]

These assumptions, about information and expertise, public accountability, and political independence and impartiality, reflect closely many of the attributes ascribed to policy decisions earlier in this paper. Policy decisions affect large numbers of the public, are future-looking or legislative in character, involve complex multifaceted issues, require extensive resources of information, research, and expertise and are frequently the subject of partisan political controversy. In accordance with the aforementioned assumptions, such decisions therefore should be, and are, taken and controlled by ministers and Parliament rather than by the courts.

But since the courts do now actively intervene in both the procedural and substantive aspects of policy decisions, the questions must be asked, "Do judges still accept those assumptions

54 E.g., *Duport Steels* v. *Sirs* [1980] 1 All E.R. 529, 542c *per* Lord Diplock, 551 and 554a-d *per* Lord Scarman. See also Lord Devlin, *The Times*, 9 December 1975, commenting on the *Congreve* case (*supra*); and Lord Parker C.J., *The Times*, 8 April 1971.

55 See P. Wallington and J. McBride, *Civil Liberties and a Bill of Rights* (London, 1976), pp. 16-17, 35-38, for discussion of this issue.

56 See, e.g., Lord Lloyd, "Do We Need a Bill of Rights ?," *Modern Law Review*, XXXIX (1976), 121-129; G.A.G. Griffith, "The Political Constitution," *Modern Law Review*, XLII (1979), 1-21; Lloyd, "The Controversy Regarding a Bill of Rights," *Israel Yearbook on Human Rights*, X (1980), 347-364.

today ? If not, why not ?". The answers to those questions are not as simple as the questions themselves. Some judges certainly appear to be very sceptical about the effectiveness of ministerial responsibility to Parliament as a control over policy decision-making.[57] Others appear to believe that the recently expanded scope and extent of, and the new grounds for, judicial intervention do not involve any judicial arrogation or substitution of ministerial power, but simply require the minister to act within more explicit and detailed legal boundaries.[58] Both groups appear to believe that judicial independence and impartiality is not threatened by such active judicial intervention.[59]

Why have judicial attitudes altered in this way ? It is submitted that the answer lies in the post-1945 expansion of the role of government. Government ceased to be merely the defender of the realm, the guardian of public order, the custodian of justice, and the keeper of the public purse. The active role of post-war governments embraced health care, public investment in and ownership of industrial concerns, social welfare, housing, agriculture, mineral extraction, public utility services, transport, national road systems,

---

57 E.g., Lord Denning M.R. and Lawton L.J. during argument on the *Gouriet* case, *The Times* (Law Report), 20, 27 January 1977:

"Was he [the A.-G.] then to be answerable to Parliament alone, where he would, perchance, be supported by his own political party ?" (Lord Denning M.R.)

"All Parliament will do is to move to reduce his [the A.-G.] salary by £10 a year." (Lawton L.J.).

58 See the explicit attempts by all of their Lordships in the *Tameside* case to eschew the political aspects of the controversy out of which the case arose.

59 In *Duport Steels* v. *Sirs*, the Court of Appeal asserted that it was merely asserting the will of Parliament, as did the House of Lords, though by a different approach to statutory construction.

employment, and a wide range of regulatory functions. Government became more complex, less centralised, and both created and depended on an immense increase in information and expertise. Ministers no longer know (nor can they, nor could they be expected to) what occurs in their departments except at the most general levels. Most decisions are taken by civil servants acting in the minister's name. The "permanent executive" has thus become extremely powerful, at the expense of Parliament, which has neither the expertise nor the information to act as an effective check on the executive. Nor has it the political will or independence to do so, since it is dominated by the executive's majority within the House. The two-party system has created a rigorously disciplined legislature which is unable to act independently so as to control the excesses of the executive. Collective responsibility has ensured ministerial immunity from censure in the House.

The courts have thus stepped into the breach to a limited extent in order to plug the gap left by the inadequacy of Parliament. A new balance is being sought between legal and political controls. This point of equilibrium between the two may continually shift. For example, as the new select committee system flexes its muscles,[60] the balance may move back towards Parliament. What is certain, however, is that we are unlikely to see again the judicial abdication which characterised the case law on judicial review of policy decisions for the half-century prior to the resurgence of judicial activism in the past decade and a half. Old constitutional and political assumptions as to the nature and respective roles of the executive, legislative, and judicial branches of government have undergone substantial modification so as to reflect the changed character of government in twentieth century Britain.

---

60 See Anne Davies, *Reformed Select Committees: The First Year* (London, 1980).

TRADE UNION FREEDOM IN BRITAIN

R. W. Rideout

British trade unions operate in two main areas on different levels. Most negotiation on terms and conditions of employment takes place locally. It may be conducted by a full time district official but very often it will be conducted by the works representatives (shop stewards) without any intervention from the union as such. Except in the public sector, central negotiation tends only to set minimum and largely inoperative wage rates and to deal with some fringe matters such as overtime rates and holiday entitlement. This is generally acknowledged to have been the main factor contributing to the undoubted fact that the British trade union movement is relatively very strong at workshop level and surprisingly weak at national level. No official steps have ever been taken to correct this imbalance and, indeed, the Royal Commission that reported in 1968 concluded that plant bargaining was the most sensible system because it was nearer to the source of dispute. There is considerable feeling in the United Kingdom now that this judgment was wrong. Some attempts are underway to make the National Engineering Agreement a realistic, and thus effective, instrument to establish actual basic rates of pay. This effort is, however, exceptional and, in any event, limited. The most that is likely to occur in the foreseeable future is a move from plant bargaining to company bargaining (as in British Leyland), so that with the exception of the public sector and of certain "ancillary" terms and conditions local bargaining will continue to set the standard. It is appropriate, therefore, to consider how free British unions are to exercise this power effectively. Since there is no restriction on the freedom to bargain (and almost no legal assistance for it either) this paper will primarily concern the freedom of the unions to back their bargaining power with the sanction of industrial action.

The political influence of the unions, on the other hand, is almost exclusively exercised at national level and, indeed, is usually channelled through the Trade Union Council. Individual unions, however, affiliate to the Labour Party and, if large enough, may influence the adoption of policy at the annual conference. This, incidentally, tends to enhance the insularity of the shop steward's approach, since he has little opportunity to develop a view of wider issues than those directly concerning his company.

The political influence of British trade unions on government is widely regarded as considerable.[1] It began to be noticeable in the sense of direct contact with government, rather than as a result of the exercise of external pressure, at the beginning of this century. Both the Conservative and Liberal parties saw that their future stability depended on appearing to acknowledge the interests of the worker, but the Liberals were initially more successful in developing contact with the unions partly because, at the turn of the century, almost all union leaders were, by conviction and not merely by name, old style Liberals. The record of the Liberal government in 1906 in consulting with union leaders and particularly with what was called "The Joint Board" was impressive by the standards of that time. There is no evidence that this was a facade of interest. Both Asquith and Lloyd George seem to have genuinely believed in the necessity for such contact. Subsequent history reveals that (rather as England's predicament is Ireland's opportunity) the trade unions have achieved most when government has had no option but to seek their support. They may represent eleven million voters, but the polarisation of the political parties has meant that the Labour Party has not since 1918 had to court this support and the Conservative Party has seen no real advantage in trying to do so.

So it was that consultation with trade unions

---

1 See R.M. Martin, *TUC: The Growth of a Pressure Group 1868-1976* (Oxford, 1980).

only reached its presently accepted status during the Second World War. There were even a few isolated occasions on which the unions were consulted on military policy. Conversely, there were many occasions when they were not consulted on matters of direct relevance to them, and a number of these omissions can be attributed to the most famous of all union leaders - Ernest Bevin - when in government.

It has since been accepted, until the past two years, that because people cannot be compelled to work, and British unions in extremity have been known to act together, government can in the end be compelled to listen to them and might as well do so before this extreme is reached. Recently doubt has been cast on this, and such a proposition has come to be regarded as part of a double bluff.

Though it is clear that British trade unions are prepared to take industrial action in support of political objectives, the present government of the United Kingdom is operating on the assumption that they can, in a confrontation with government, only hope to attain their objectives if two preconditions are satisfied:

(i) their members must feel sufficiently sure that their jobs are secure to be prepared to support industrial action. Conversely, it will help the union if the employers wish to make the most of a favourable economic situation by avoiding industrial disruption;

(ii) the public as a whole (including members of trade unions) must be sufficiently impressed by the union's arguments not to oppose such action. In the United Kingdom history suggests that however economically powerful the union may be, it will refrain from industrial action if public opinion is opposed.

Neither of these preconditions pertains in the United Kingdom at present. Consultation (let alone influence) has been deliberately reduced to its lowest ebb since before the war by a government which gives every sign of being unimpressed by union power. The adverse effect this would normally have on the already uneven balance between local and central union power is, however, offset by the fact that the power of the shop steward to deliver beneficial settlements is reduced by at least an equivalent amount.

The law does not greatly impinge specifically upon political action by trade unions. As we shall see, legislative protection from civil liability is granted to action in "contemplation or furtherance of a trade dispute." At first sight this might seem not to extend to industrial action in furtherance of a dispute about government policy, and there was, indeed, considerable academic argument as to whether the General Strike of 1926 was legal. The issue was raised again in a series of cases between 1977 and 1980. The Court of Appeal attempted considerably to reduce the scope of the protection, but the House of Lords overruled those decisions in three significant cases, pointing out that the definition of a trade dispute is very wide and establishing that the test of furtherance is subjective.[2] Most significantly these decisions stated that so long as the action had some connection with a trade dispute the protection would not be lost even though that connection was purely incidental to the primary political object.

As we shall see, special provisions now apply to secondary action, but it can safely be said that no difficulty should be encountered by a union wishing to bring primary political action

---

2 See a neat summary of the Court of Appeal conclusions in *United Biscuits (UK) Ltd.* v. *Fall* [1979] I.R.L.R. 10, overruled in *Express Newspapers Ltd.* v. *McShane* [1980] I.C.R. 42; *NWL Ltd.* v. *Nelson* [1979] I.R.L.R. 478; *Duport Steels Ltd.* v. *Sirs* [1980] I.R.L.R. 116.

within the legislative protection.[3]

Returning to the central theme of this paper - the power of unions to negotiate - it is the view of the present writer that, in or around 1965, British trade unions made a catastrophic error of policy in their approach to the legislature. For a hundred years until that time it had been a keystone of their policy that they had created themselves without legislative assistance and that it was dangerous to accept such assistance in the conduct of their essential activities. It is submitted that the justification for this approach is apparent if we compare the situation in the United Kingdom with that of countries such as the United States, Australia, New Zealand and, probably, the Federal Republic of Germany, where the union movement owes either its establishment or its survival to legislative assistance.

In the United Kingdom, legislation before 1965 might acknowledge the existence of trade unions and occasionally smooth out an obstruction to their operation (as in the case of the effect of delictual liability or problems of amalgamation). Until 1965, it had not granted to them a right within the traditional areas of their collective bargaining activities. In 1965, however, British unions found themselves faced with a problem that they had not foreseen and with which they thought they could not cope. The problem was that of mass dismissal by reason of redundancy. At that time there was no legislation providing for compensation, the common law afforded virtually no job security, and there were surprisingly few collectively agreed schemes of compensation for redundancy. In fact the growth of such collective agreements once legislation had established the basic principle of compensation suggests that the unions could have solved the problem for themselves within two or three years. Whatever the truth may be, the principle of legislative assist-

3 See the remarks of Lord Diplock in *NWL* v. *Nelson* on how this could have been achieved in *Hearn* v. *BBC* [1977] I.C.R. 685.

ance for trade union purposes displaced that of non-intervention in the Redundancy Payments Act 1965. Subsequently, it has received startling confirmation in the Employment Protection Act 1975, where a number of conditions of employment which normally would have been reserved for voluntary negotiation were, at a minimum level, made available to all employees by legislation. Much of the impetus for both these pieces of legislation derived from the potential or actual membership of the EEC by the United Kingdom, but such pressure was either not detected or not resisted by the unions.

The United States affords a glimpse of what happens if non-intervention is replaced by assistance. In Western democracies at least, government policies are not consistent and certainly are not consistently in favour of trade unions. Non-intervention as an accepted policy may leave the unions to fight their own battles, but it also protects them from legislative attack. Such attack, it is submitted, is an almost inevitable outcome of growing strength. If legislation grants rights, in the end it will be concluded that too many have been granted. The tendency is not to withdraw some of these rights, but to attack on another front or grant the other side countervailing rights. History, in my view, will confirm that in the United Kingdom the Industrial Relations Act 1971 was the direct product of the realisation that unions and their traditional pastures were not, by convention, immune from legislative intervention. It failed, and the policy of legislative assistance was resumed, to be replaced again in 1980 by legislative attack which shows every sign of increasing in intensity.

The nature of this attack will be examined in relation to three main indicators of trade union negotiating power in the United Kingdom, two of which apparently have no parallel in Europe. They are the closed shop; the picket; and the immunity of those organising industrial action from civil liability.

It is, and has been for almost a hundred years, perfectly legal in the United Kingdom for a trade union to seek to insist that an employer should engage only its members and the employer to enforce that agreement by dismissal of non-members. The device, as is well known, confers on the unions enormous disciplinary power enabling them to call on the support of an entire workforce. For reasons already discussed, that workforce may not respond, but the risk of loss of jobs if the union call is disobeyed is a great inducement to do so. Until 1971, the freedom arose simply because the employer was more or less free to dismiss when he chose for no reason, provided he gave the employee a short period of notice or wages in lieu. The employer lost that freedom in 1971, when a right to complain of unfair dismissal was granted to virtually every employee. At the same time, freedom to operate the closed shop was notionally curtailed, although the curtailment had no practical effect. In 1974 complete freedom to operate the closed shop was restored save for religious objectors. The closed shop is, however, once again, and this time effectively, assailed by the Employment Act 1980:

(i) exclusion from its operation is granted not only to the religious or conscientious objector, but to anyone who can establish a "deeply held personal conviction" against membership of any trade union or even of a particular trade union. So the closed shop cannot be imposed on him by the threat of dismissal, and this really means that the agreement is unenforceable in such a case;

(ii) new closed shops (and this may well mean also re-negotiated closed shops) can only be enforced by dismissal of those who do not comply if the introduction of the closed shop is supported by a ballot vote of 80% of those *entitled* to vote;

(iii) when a new closed shop agreement is introduced existing employees who are not members of the union in question are protected from dismissal by reason of a refusal to join the union. Unions are not likely to find this limitation intolerable since frequently they voluntarily concede such a provision in negotiations;

(iv) unions operating closed shops may not arbitrarily or unreasonably expel or exclude members or applicants for membership affected by the closed shop.

These statements do little to reveal what is likely to happen because they adopt a practice common in recent labour legislation of establishing "reasonableness" as the standard of behaviour. There is developing in the United Kingdom, however, a hitherto unknown semi-legislative device which we call a "Code of Practice" by which the legislature, possibly through the intermediate stage of an independent agency, seeks to guide the courts as to what is acceptable practice. Such a code has been issued for closed shop agreements. This Code is likely to have a startling effect on the imposition of restrictions on the closed shop. Paragraph 24 provides:

> The employer should have special regard to the interests of particular groups of staff who as members of professional associations are subject to their own code of ethics or conduct. Because the obligations imposed by such a code may be incompatible with the full range of union activities including, for example, participation in industrial action endangering health or safety, the employees concerned *might well reasonably object to joining a union whose rules do not respect such obligations.*

Paragraph 37 says:

> Closed shop agreements should be applied flexibly and tolerantly and with due regard to the interests of the individuals as well as unions and employers.

Paragraphs 48 and 54 virtually invite the courts to hold unreasonable any exclusion or expulsion from the union unless the procedure satisfies certain standards and the reason is not proscribed. They read:

> *Union rules and procedures*
>
> In handling admissions to membership, unions should adopt and apply clear and fair rules covering:
>
> * who is qualified for membership;
> * who has power to consider and decide upon applications;
> * what reasons will justify rejecting an application;
> * the appeals procedure open to a rejected applicant;
> * the power to admit applicants where an appeal is upheld.
>
> *Industrial action*
>
> Disciplinary action should not be taken or threatened by a union against a member on the grounds of refusal to take part in industrial action called for by the union -
>
> (a) or because industrial action would involve a breach of a statutory duty or the criminal law, would contravene the member's professional or other code of ethics, would constitute a serious risk to public safety, health or property;
>
> (b) or because the action was in breach of a procedure agreement;

(c) because the action had not been affirmed in a secret ballot.

If to these restrictions is added, in due course, condemnation of the closed shop by the European Court of Human Rights, the British government will almost certainly increase the level of protection afforded to employees who do not comply with its terms. It may then be possible for British trade unions to answer a question long asked by continental Europeans. Is the closed shop really necessary for the proper exercise of union power or does it, rather, diminish that power ?

Not only the power of unions to regulate and discipline their members is being attacked. Their hitherto largely unhindered power to take industrial action has also recently been subjected to restriction.

British unions, unlike those in any other European country, lay great stress on the persuasive power of the picket line to ensure the effectiveness of industrial action. There has never been any doubt about the right of the police to control misconduct on the picket line. Criminal sanctions are more than adequate, although the physical power of the police to control mass picketing is sometimes in doubt. These sanctions, however, are, in practice, usually only applied to control and not to terminate the picket (though in some circumstances the latter effect could be achieved by them). Short of attempting to instruct the police upon the use of their powers, it is widely felt that to confer upon management a legal right to secure an injunction to prohibit the picketing would be a more effective curtailment. It is worth noting, however, that in its Code of Practice on picketing, the British government has somewhat arbitrarily suggested that normally six pickets should be regarded as the maximum necessary for peaceful persuasion. The inference must be that more may be considered to threaten a breach of the peace.

English law possesses a principle of delictual

liability which offers to the employer a means of preventing picketing. It recognises liability for intentional interference with the contractual rights of another. A picket will almost inevitably interfere with both contracts of employment and commercial contracts, for example, to supply goods or services. Because this liability would effectively be imposed on all picketing so that management could prevent it by developing the "Labour Injunction" so well known in America before the Second World War, there has existed in the United Kingdom since 1906 a statutory immunity from action in contemplation or furtherance of a trade dispute. In 1980 all those picketing otherwise than at their place of work (save for trade union officials who actually represent those employed at the place picketed and who are accompanying such employees on the picket line) were deprived of this immunity. This is designed to allow the civil prohibition to be applied to secondary pickets and, particularly, to a relatively new phenomenon in the United Kingdom: the flying picket. This piece of legislation is fraught with detailed uncertainty,[4] but, more significantly, it is not clear whether the theoretical legal liability can be effectively imposed largely because, in the United Kingdom, mandatory injunctions can, with one exception, only be obtained against named (and, therefore, identified) individuals who may, of course, be replaced the next day by fresh individuals not named in the first injunction.

Against this, however, must be set the fact of central importance to the efficacy of all labour injunctions, that it is possible to obtain an interim injunction if, *inter alia*, it is shown that the activity is likely, when examined at a full hearing, to be found to be unlawful. It is, however, perfectly clear to British trade unions that if this legislation is shown to be ineffective to prevent secondary picketing, the present

---

4 See B. Bercusson, "Picketing, Secondary Picketing and Secondary Action," *Industrial Law Journal*, IX (1980), pp. 220-232.

British government will pass more restrictive legislation. That government has, indeed, already issued a discussion paper on the possibilities of further reduction of immunities.[5] The British trade union movement is obviously very unsure of the amount of support it would receive if it mounted any major challenge to such threats partly, at least, for the reasons already suggested in this paper.

There is, however, a very large body of opinion, even within the present government, in support of the proposition that restriction of union power by these means should not go too far. This is revealed by the handling of the related question of immunity for secondary industrial action. Without statutory immunity this would be subject to exactly the same delictual liability as the consequences of picketing. The same immunity was conferred in 1906 and survived, subject to some judicial attack, until 1980. As we have seen, the House of Lords confirmed the full scope of the immunity after a series of Court of Appeal decisions had sought to restrict it by a narrow interpretation of the qualifying clause "in contemplation or furtherance of a trade dispute".

In 1980, however, the Employment Act apparently removed the immunity from "Interference with the employment contracts of employers not party to the dispute which in turn interferes with commercial contracts".[6] The Act goes on, however, to impose certain conditions upon this removal of immunity which effectively mean that the immunity continues to extend to ordinary secondary action (except, as we have seen, secondary picketing) and is only applicable to what I call "tertiary" action. We may summarise the position thus:

---

5 *Trade Union Immunities*, Cmnd. 8128. January 1981 (HMSO).

6 Bercusson, note 4 above, p. 215.

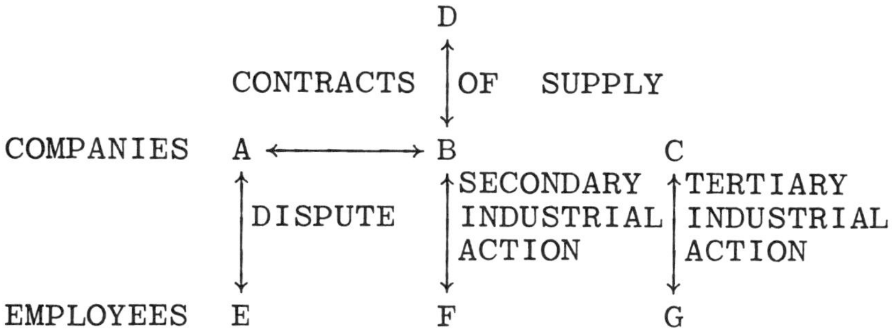

We may examine this diagrammatic situation by the steps imposed by the Act. For the removal of immunity:

(i) the contract interfered with (that between A and B) must be a contract other than a contract of employment. In our diagram and in normal practice it is;

(ii) the action must be "secondary" according to the definition introduced for this purpose. That is:

(a) it must take the form of interference with a contract of employment. The action by F against their employer B like virtually all industrial action affects the contract of employment so those leading it will be interfering with such a contract;

(b) the employer against whom the action is taken must be one not a party to the dispute (B is not a party).

If the legislation stopped there, it would have described and eliminated immunity for the typical secondary action situation.

Even if these conditions are satisfied, however, immunity is not removed if the secondary action is *directly* to prevent or disrupt the supply of goods or services during the dispute between a party to the dispute and the employer subject to the action and *was likely to achieve that purpose.*

So in our typical example the industrial action against B, though secondary, will not necessarily, or perhaps usually, be outside the scope of immunity from action. That will only occur if B has no such connection with A (in which case secondary action would seem rather unlikely), or if the action is not aimed directly at the contracts of supply, or is not reasonably likely to interfere with them. So the only action clearly caught by the removal of immunity would be "tertiary" action against employer C, whom we may imagine to have stepped in to replace the loss of B's goods or services. Even this is still protected if C is an associated employer of the party to the dispute (A), and the goods or services supplied are in replacement of others which would have been supplied by or to A, and the pressure on C is likely to achieve the effect of interfering with this supply.

It should be pointed out that the references to the need for the action to be direct and likely to be effective if immunity is to remain arise from suggestions in the Court of Appeal that, following the House of Lords' interpretation of the test, it was easy to claim immunity for non-industrial purposes by alleging that there was a subsidiary purpose not very likely to be achieved.

This apparent narrowness of the removal of immunity is surprising. It is worth pointing out that liability may arise even in the case envisaged in our diagram:

(i) if the *principal* purpose is not to disrupt contracts of supply or service;

(ii) if the pressure on B *indirectly* disrupts the contracts of another employer D. D may be able to sue;

(iii) any spill-over so that there is a disruption of the supply of goods to or from those not involved in the dispute will not attract immunity. On the other hand, such spill-over will probably not attract liability in the first place since this head of delict requires intention rather than reasonable foresight;

(iv) if there is no contract in existence to supply goods because goods are only supplied as required and employer B, when pressurised, declines to enter into a contract with A. This interference with a future contract is actionable.[7]

The contract could also be terminated subject to re-negotiation, thus making continuation of the pressure actionable;

(v) if the action is considered not likely to achieve its purpose of interference. It is not clear whether the test for this is: giving practical rather than moral support (Lord Denning MR: *McShane* [1979] I.R.L.R. 79 at 82) or: reasonably capable of achieving its purpose (Lord Wilberforce: *McShane* [1980] I.R.L.R. 35 at 38 where he came to a different conclusion than those who had applied this same test in the Court of Appeal);

(vi) if no employer is party to the dispute; that is, the dispute is between an employers' association and the union of which association the employer affected is not a party.

---

7 See [1969] 2 Ch. 106 at 140; [1965] A.C. 269 at 339; [1972] Ch. 630 at 644.

On the other hand, unions could try to avoid liability altogether by ensuring that the employer pressurised was a party to a dispute (for example, as to whether the employees should be required to handle the blacked goods), or by inserting in contracts of employment a provision that the employee be not required to handle blacked goods (in which case there would be no interference with a contract of employment), or by securing that employer B gave no orders to handle the goods, thus depriving A of a remedy (*Thompson* v. *Deakin* [1952] Ch. 646).

Trade unions in the United Kingdom have from 1906 to 1980 been remarkably free to control their internal affairs, discipline their members, and use the power they had. For much of that time, from 1906 to about 1950, even the courts refrained from trying to make inroads upon that freedom. Whether those unions made the best use of such freedom is another story. Unlike some American unions, they have not noticeably abused their freedom in relation to their members, though many would say they have abused the converse freedom of the individual not to organise. Unlike American unions, they failed to develop collective bargaining to cover wide classes of terms and conditions of employment and failed to establish central control over local insularity. The courts began to attack their freedom again with the judgment in *Bonsor* v. *The Musicians' Union* ([1956] A.C. 104); the legislature (ineffectually), in 1971. There is little reason to suppose that the attack from either quarter will be permanently reversed, although from time to time it may pause. Doubtless from 1975 to 1979 the British public asked the question whether the trade unions were ungovernable, or even were in a position to prevent the operation of government, and were not comforted by the answer.

What, then, is the future for British trade unions ? The answer must be that it is one of increasing government intervention, on one side or the other, into their affairs and actions.

British trade unions currently retain wide freedoms. The closed shop probably involves six million people. The right primarily to picket or take industrial action is established and limitations on secondary action are relatively narrow, their effect unpredictable. Yet the present attack is unprecedented in the past one hundred years. Those leaders who, five years ago, openly thought that only their own restraint prevented them assuming the functions or even the mantle of government now face an immediate future in which they are unlikely to preserve their present freedoms unrestrained.

It seems very likely, possibly as a result of the decision of the European Court of Human Rights in an application by a number of former employees of British Railways dismissed for refusal to join the appropriate trade union (Applications No. 7601/76 and 7806/77 *Young, James and Webster* v. *The United Kingdom*) that the employer will lose his immunity from the normal consequences for dismissal on the grounds of non-unionism. It seems unlikely, however, that the non-unionist will obtain a reliable right to reinstatement in his job. The greatest effect, therefore, might be a massive increase in pre-entry closed shops, either formally or in practice. The foreign observer must face the fact that, incomprehensible as he may find it, the closed shop is now too deeply rooted in the folklore of British trade unionism to be shifted. However this may be, there seems little doubt that the considerable increase in numbers of closed shop agreements between 1974 and 1977 (itself a delayed effect of negotiations in the late 1960s interrupted by the 1971 legislation) will not recur while the 80% ballot provision remains in force. (There was a temporary rush of agreements in late 1979 to anticipate this prohibition.)

It also seems likely that the prohibitions on secondary action will not result in any significant number of civil actions for injunctions. The significance of such actions as may be brought will be to emphasise the inhibition on secondary industrial action in practice. Traditionally,

British trade unions have not applied their minds to the location of loopholes in the law, probably because they have, save for brief periods of judicial activity, had little need to do so. Nevertheless, in much the same way as a union may enhance its bargaining position by threatening to refer a dispute through some official system of arbitration, despite its well known aversion to such a step, so the fact that industrial activity is actionable will deter employees of an employer who, it is well understood, would be most reluctant to seek an injunction.

Whatever happens, there can be no doubt that the power of British trade unions which reached a peak in the mid-1970s has been restricted. The critical question is what use employers and government will make of their relatively stronger position. Resort to the attitudes of the 1930s will produce the same brooding resentment as then, which another swing of political power may allow to break out.

THE SPECIFIC LEGAL REGULATION OF INTERNATIONAL CONTRACTS IN POLISH LAW

J. Jakubowski

During the present century, the scope of international economic relations has been subject to such considerable growth and its contractual forms differentiated so widely that the legal aspects of these relations have gained an extraordinary importance.

The international exchange of goods has been increasing from decade to decade. This exchange is expressed mostly in the form of contracts of sale. As sales grow, so also do services attached thereto (agency, forwarding, bank services, etc.). New contractual relationships appear, such as contracts of distribution, of goods inspection, of factoring, and so forth. Of great practical importance are securities: documentary credits, bank guarantees, and other forms.

International co-operation in industrial development has brought an established practice of virtually self-regulatory contracts for the erection of complete industrial plants. To undertake large investment ventures of this kind, associations of a specific type (consortium) are created. The so-called transfer of technology has become one of the main sectors of international economic relations. Here also, besides the classical type of licensing agreement, new contractual forms have emerged, such as the know-how contract. International economic co-operation also entered the field of production, where the most important phenomenon is international industrial co-operation.

The above examples of new contractual forms in international commercial relations are not exhaustive. Other forms of comparable importance might be mentioned as, for example, leasing.

Some new types of contracts mentioned above were created in international trade for the purposes thereof. The practice of this trade enriched the instruments of the contemporary law of contracts. This enrichment takes place, however, also within traditional forms of relationships, *e.g.*, sales. It is sufficient to mention the price revision clause, protective monetary clauses, so-called hardship clauses, and others.

The practice of international trade is also the source of new forms of contractual relations, for example, the frame-contract (in German: Rahmenvertrag, Generalvertrag, or Mantelvertrag; in French: contrat-cadre) and new ways of entering contractual relations, for example, the letter of intent. Rajski rightly points out that the process described above enriched considerably the law of obligations, thus encouraging theoretical reflections.[1]

Many of the new legal relationships are subject to non-state regulation and form the so-called autonomous law merchant (*lex mercatoria*).[2] Some problems have been taken over by international legislation. These new legal phenomena of international economic relations do, nevertheless, constitute a task for internal legislation too. In the literature of many countries opinions appear more and more frequently that domestic regulation of such legal phenomena is needed. Many authors point to inadequacy of contemporary municipal law for the requirements of international commercial relations.[3]

---

1 J. Rajski, "Wpływ rozwoju handlu miedzynarodowego na teorie prawa zobowiazań," in *Studia z prawa zobowiazań* (Poznań, 1979), p. 161.

2 On this notion, see J. Jakubowski, *Umowa sprzedazy w handlu miedzynarodowym. Metody i formy regulacji* (Warsaw, 1966), p. 51ff.

3 For example, H.K. Leistritz, *Die definierten Leiferklauseln des internationalen Warenhandels* (4th ed.; Cologne, 1954), p. 6, and J.C. Honnold, "The Influence of the Law of International Trade on the Development and Character of English and American Law," in C.M. Schmitthoff, *The Sources of the Law of International Trade, with Special Reference to East-West Trade*

The need for municipal regulation is particularly strong in socialist countries. The reason is, above all, the introduction into the civil law of these countries of the trends implied by the socio-economic doctrine of socialism. These tendencies are incompatible with the liberalist attitude prevailing in respect of civil law relations in international trade.

The need for the civil law to take into account the specific nature of international transactions has been dealt with in different ways by particular socialist countries. For example, in Soviet and Polish law there are only a few provisions which take into account their specific nature, for example, Articles 124-126 of the Fundamental Principles of Civil Legislation of the USSR and Union Republics, or Article VI of the Law introducing the Polish Civil Code. The scope of such regulation in Hungarian law is wider, the regulations being correlated with the Hungarian economic model.[4] Czechoslovakia and the German Democratic Republic moved further in this direction by introducing compendious laws: in Czechoslovakia, the 1963 Code of International Trade; in the GDR, the 1976 Law on International Economic Contracts.[5]

(London, 1964), p. 74. According to Leistritz, the lack of adaptation follows from the fact that municipal commercial laws arose, in the first place, in the context of domestic trade.

4 Z. Stalev proposes that these questions be widely dealt with in the future Bulgarian Civil Code. See Z. Stalev, *Grazhdanskiyat kodeks, mezhdunarodnite graz danski otnosenya i socyalisticeskata ikonomiceska integracya*, in *Problemi na kodifikacyata na grazhdansko pravo v N.R. Bulgaria* (Sofia, 1975), p. 35.

5 On the Czechoslovak Code, see Rajski, "Kodyfikacja prawa handlu miedzynarodowego w Czechosłowacji," *Prawo w Handlu Zagranicznym*, IX (1965), pp. 81-88, and on GDR law, A.W. Wisniewski, "Ustawa NRD o miedzynarodowych kontraktach gospodarczych," *Przeglad Ustawodawstwa Gospodarczego*, no. 5 (1976), p. 135; also F. Zacharia-

The Polish Civil Code and International Trade Relations

The place of international transactions within the system of municipal law has also been discussed in Poland. The discussion was initiated by the present author in 1960 during the debate on the codification of the civil law.[6] Although maintaining that the regulation of overseas transactions in the draft 1960 Civil Code is very general and therefore inadequate, I did not propose, at that time, a separate regulation. That regulation I recommended in 1965[7] and, once more, in 1966.[8]

The failure of the Civil Code to accommodate foreign trade has been pointed out many times by Cz.P. Przymusiński.[9] J. Skapski, previously rather critical of the idea of separately regulating the problems of international economic trans-

---

siewicz, "Ustawa o miedzynarodowych kontraktach gospodarczych w NRD," *Problemy Prawne Handlu Zagranicznego*, I (1977), p. 186ff. According to information obtained by the present author from Rumanian lawyers, a draft act of similar kind already has been prepared.

6 Jakubowski, "Kodyfikacja prawa cywilnego a handel zagraniczny," *Handel Zagraniczny*, no. 7 (1960), pp. 305-308.

7 Jakubowski, "Zagadnienia kodyfikacyjne w zakresie handlu zagranicznego," *Prawo w Handlu Zagranicznym*, IX, (1965), pp. 11-20.

8 Jakubowski, note 2 above, pp. 270-271.

9 Cz.P. Przymusinski, "Kodeks cywilny a miedzynarodowy obrót handlowy," *Przeglad Ustawodawstwa Gospodarczego*, no. 2 (1965), pp. 33-36, no. 3, pp. 64-69; *id.*, "O pewnych trudnościach stosowania prawa wewnetrznego w stosunkach handlu miedzynarodowego (na przykładzie orzecznictwa Sadu Najwyzszego)," *Palestra*, no. 7-8 (1972), pp. 42-50; *id.*, "Problematyka stosowania prawa cywilnego w obrocie uspołecznionym," *Przoglad Ustawodawstwa Gospodarczego*, no. 4 (1973), p. 110.

actions,[10] now considers such regulation as advisable on condition of subordinating it to the Civil Code.

The proposal for integrated regulation of private law relations in international trade was raised for the first time in a wider forum during the debate on the state of Polish law (the Conference at Popowo, 15-17 December 1971). The "Report on the State of the Law", resulting from this debate and later also the "Programme for the Improvement of Law in 1974-1980" (decision No. 46 of the Council of Ministers of 8 February 1974), provided for the commencement of respective preparations.

This proposal has been widely discussed among lawyers upon the initiative of the Minister of Foreign Trade and Shipping. The first discussion, by academic lawyers, was held in Sopot on 8-10 October 1975. It was followed by two discussions organised by the Federation of Polish lawyers in Warsaw on 27 February 1976 and 29 June 1978.

During this debate, the vast majority of the participants, both law professors and practitioners, came to the conclusion that in order to properly regulate private law relations in international trade the introduction of a special law which takes into account the particular nature of these relations is necessary. This conclusion was in principle approved by the Legislative Council attached to the Prime Minister during the discussion on the "Report on the State of Law in the Field of Foreign Trade" (28 June 1978).

Thus began the discussion of such a law. The author of the present paper conceived it as a separate law, and not a revision of the Civil Code, but without prejudice to the principle of the unity of civil law, which he deems to be correct. The law in question would, therefore, not be independent

10 J. Skapski, "Kodeks cywilny a miedzynarodowy obrót handlowy," *Państwo i prawo*, no. 5 (1972), pp. 48-61; *id.*, "Application of the Civil Code in International Legal Cases," *Polish Yearbook of International Law*, IV (1971), pp. 19-36.

from, or parallel to, the Civil Code remaining the *lex generalis* of the whole of civil law. The law on international economic transactions should constitute a *lex specialis* in respect of the Civil Code. In the author's opinion, such a hierarchy of the sources of civil law is the consequence of the specific method of private law regulation.[11]

A. Tynel also spoke in favour of a respective special law.[12]

By order of 12 May 1977, the Minister of Foreign Trade and Shipping Created an Expert Commission for the elaboration of a draft law under a working name of the Code of International Trade.[13] In the work of the Expert Commission, besides the persons nominated as members thereof, many other specialists took part, both professors and practitioners.[14]

The introductory debate in the Commission, with the participation of other specialists attached thereto, has been confined to a final clarification of the question of whether separate private law regulation of international economic relations is needed. The answer to this question has been wholly positive. The same answer has

---

11 Jakubowski, "W sprawie koncepcji kodeksu handlu miedzynarodowego," *Przeglad Ustawodawstwa Gospodarczego,* no. 2 (1976), p. 44.

12 A. Tynel, "Uwagi w sprawie zakrosu kodeksu handlu miedzynarodowego," *Przeglad Ustawodawstwa Gospodarczego,* no. 7 (1976), pp. 207-209.

13 Members of the Commission are: Professor J. Jakubowski (Chairman), Dr. T. Opalski (Vice-chairman), Dr. A. Burzyński, Professor A. Całus, Judge M. Gintowt, Professor W. Górski, Professor J. Jodłowski, Mr. Z. Karkuoiński, Professor M. Pazdan, Mr. C.P. Przymusiński, advocate, Professor J. Rajski, Professor J. Skapski, Professor S. Sołtysiński, Professor M. Sośniak, Dr. M. Tomaszewski, Dr. A. Tynel, Dr. A. Wiśniewski (Secretary), and Mr. K. Borzyszkowski (Secretary).

14 Por. A.W. Wiśniewski, "Prace nad kodeksem handlu miedzynarodowego," *Prawo i Życie,* no. 23 (1979).

been given in the course of research conducted from 1976-79 by the Group for Legal Problems of International Economic Co-operation at the Faculty of Law and Administration of Warsaw University. The results of this research, in which many scholars and practitioners took part, have been incorporated in a "Report on the Basic Principles of a Polish Code of International Trade". The report, made at the request of the Institute of State and Law of the Polish Academy of Sciences, is rather complex and voluminous (291 pages).

In 1976, M.H. Koziński,[15] followed by W. Ludwiczak (1978),[16] J. Jodłowski (1979),[17] and J. Rajski (1979)[18] urged the separate regulation of civil law relations with overseas.

Two basic arguments can be mentioned in favour of separate regulation of the private law aspect of international trade relations:

(1) international trade is subject to fundamental principles and general clauses different from that of the socialist civil law. Special regulation of the institutions particular to international trade law in the Civil Code can not, therefore, give a satisfactory solution: the regulation of international trade calls for its own "hat" of fundamental principles and general clauses;

(2) the practice of international economic relations created numerous specific and elaborated institutions which are not appropriate for insertion

---

15 M.H. Koziński, "Prawo zatrzymania w zagranicznym obrocie handlowym," *Państwo i prawo,* no. 12 (1976), p. 111.

16 W. Ludwiczak, "Potrzeba kodyfikacji miedzynarodowego prawa handlowego w Polsce a założenia ogólne ustawy NRD o miedzynarodowych kontraktach gospodarczych," *Polska i Swiat* (Poznań, 1978), p. 237ff.

17 Jodłowski, "Problemy odrebnego unormowania postepowania cywilnego w sprawach z zakresu handlu miedzynarodowego," *Przeglad Ustawodawstwa Gospodarczego,* no. 3 (1979), p. 64.

18 Rajski, note 1 above, pp. 167-168.

into the framework of the Civil Code.

The above arguments require more detailed explanation.

Argument 1

The "philosophy" of private law relations in international trade is still a liberalist attitude. The expression thereof is, above all, the principles of *formal* equality in law, of the autonomy of the parties' will, and of the sanctity of contracts, and whether these contracts are balanced in view of the parties' interests. This "free-play" has, obviously, its limits resulting, for example, from the commonly accepted principle of good faith. These boundaries are, nevertheless, rather wide and flexible. Many factors influence this situation, for example, the formation of the philosophy of trade in the nineteenth century, an age of liberalism; the intersystemic character of international relations; participation in those relations of large companies which, it is commonly accepted, do not require protection as natural persons (moreover, as the practice of so-called transnational corporations has shown, which feel comfortable in this position). The developing countries are endeavouring to modify the situation described above (the idea and policy of a new international economic order), but so far with modest effect.

In light of the above, a civil code of a socialist state founded upon the principles of social justice and protection of the weaker party would require, by the very nature of things, a different basis in the sphere of the fundamental principles and general clauses than the law of international trade. Equally incompatible with international trade law are bureaucratic intrusions into socialist ideology which may be found in the civil codes of socialist countries, such as privileges of state property, treating state enterprises as some kind of state agencies, and so forth.

Such intrusions can and should be removed

from the Polish Civil Code. In the opinion of the author of this paper, however, provisions shaped for the protection of citizens and of a weaker party should not be removed from the Code. On the contrary, our Code should strengthen and develop such protection as consumer protection,[19] product liability,[20] protection against unjust rules and general conditions,[21] and so forth.

Taking into consideration that only the liberalisation and commercialisation of the Civil Code could make it adequate in its basic principles and general clauses to the needs and requirements of private law relations in international trade and that such a tendency would be contrary to the expectations of society, the reform of civil law can not be expected to eliminate the contradiction between the civil law of domestic relations and the civil law of international relations.

There is a unanimous view in the Polish literature that the fundamental principles and general clauses of the Polish Civil Code are incompatible with the needs and demands of international rela-

---

19 The rules providing for consumers' protection are not applied in international trade not merely because, normally, transactions in this trade are made between large producers and traders.

20 There have been efforts to introduce these questions in the programme of the UN Commission on International Trade Law (UNCITRAL), but without success, because only some countries, mostly developing countries, backed this idea. The representatives of industrialised countries were against the application of the concept of "product liability" in international relations.

21 Laws relating to general conditions of contract, tending to protect the weaker party, exclude, as a rule, their application to international transactions. See W. Marschall von Bieberstein, "La nouvelle réglementation allemande des conditions générales de contrat," *Droit et pratique du commerce international*, no. 3 (1977), p. 332.

tions.[22]

Argument 2

In the practice of international economic relations many specific and complex institutions emerged which could not be within the Civil Code. This relates both to particular types or variations of types of contracts, for example, contract of know-how, contract leasing, contract of goods inspection, contract of industrial co-operation, contract for the erection of a plant, documentary credit, etc., and particular clauses of various contracts (price revision clause, monetary clauses, hardship clause, etc.), and, moreover, new methods of arranging private law relationships (letter of intent, frame-contract, clauses providing for the filling of gaps by arbitration, etc.). Some of these regulations are so broad that their introduction into the Civil Code would be embarrassing from the standpoint of the principles or proportion and symmetry in legislation.

In light of both arguments, it is justified to attempt to regulate private law problems of international economic relations in a separate law. The solution of enacting a separate book in the Civil Code is difficult to achieve and less justified.

The Concept of the Draft Law on Civil Law Relationships in International Trade

As already mentioned, the work on this subject has been undertaken by the Expert Commission created for this purpose.

In 1978-80, the Expert Commission discussed more than forty introductory papers and worked out,

22 It is stressed by almost all the authors who have written on this subject (J. Jakubowski, J. Jodłowski, C.P. Przymusiński, A. Tynel). It also has been generally pointed out during all the conferences devoted to legislative problems on foreign economic relations.

on the basis of partial drafts by the authors thereof, a draft Law. This draft Law has been subject to threefold revision to take into account consultations with enterprises engaged in international trade and of the discussion among legal advisors working in the field of international trade which took place on 9-10 September 1980 at the Polish Chamber of Foreign Trade in Warsaw.

In the present section, we outline the Draft Law on Civil Law Relationships in International Trade which was produced as a result of the efforts mentioned above.

First, the concept of the law was considered. Some members of the Expert Commission and participants in the discussions and consultations initially favoured an integrated regulation in the form of a code of international trade, as in Czechoslovakia and the GDR. Others, among them the author of the present paper, spoke in favour of not such an ambitious conception, but for a separate law which would be *lex specialis* in respect of the Civil Code.[23] The debates on this matter continued for a long time. Eventually, the majority of the Commission backed the moderate conception of *lex specialis*. Following the suggestion made by C.P. Przymusiński, the present name of the law has been adopted as being more appropriate to this conception: the Law on Civil Law Relationships in International Trade.

The Draft Law is a lengthy instrument, containing 409 articles. Of this number, however, seventy-seven articles pertain to partnerships and companies, which by their very nature require detailed regulation.

The Draft is composed of a General Part (Articles 1-120); Special Part (Articles 121-402); and Final Provisions (Articles 403-409).

The structure of the General Part is as follows:

---

23 As already mentioned, I have held this opinion for a longer time. See Jakubowski, note 11 above, p. 44.

Title I.	Introductory Provisions		
Title II.	Polish Juridical Persons		
Title III.	Contracts and Other Legal Acts		
		Chapter 1.	Legal Acts
		Chapter 2.	Form of Legal Acts
		Chapter 3.	Conclusion of Contract
		Chapter 4.	Tender
		Chapter 5.	Interpretation of Contracts and Filling Gaps
		Chapter 6.	Expiry of Contracts Concluded for Unlimited Time and of Long-term Contracts
Title IV.	Performance and Consequences of Non-performance of Obligations		
		Chapter 1.	Principles of Performance of Obligations
		Chapter 2.	Right to Withhold and [Commercial] Lien
		Chapter 3.	Security by Cession of Right
		Chapter 4.	Consequences of Non-performance of Obligations
Title V.	Prescription (Limitation of Action)		

The most general provisions are in Title I of the General Part.

Articles 1 and 2 define the scope of the Law. The Law is intended to govern civil law relationships in international trade insofar as, under the respective private international law, Polish law applies (Article 1.1). We have, therefore, a civil law, as well as the Czechoslovak Code of International Commerce and the GDR Law of International Economic Contracts. The Expert Commission, taking into consideration comparative legal sources and doctrine, after many discussions came to the conclusion that it was neither possible nor desirable to define the notion of "civil law relationships in international trade," expecting it to be elaborated by judicial and arbitration practice and commentary. The term "international trade" is to be broadly understood, meaning international economic, scientific, and technical exchange and not only the exchange of goods and services.

It must be stressed that, following the Czechoslovak Code of International Commerce and the GDR Law on International Economic Contracts, the Draft Law provides it shall apply when Polish law, according to the respective private international law (conflict of laws), is applicable.

The place of the Law within the Polish legal system is laid down in Article 1.2: In questions not covered by the provisions of the Law and pertaining to legal relationships defined in the preceding paragraph, the provisions of the Civil Code and other laws are applicable insofar as these provisions are not contrary to general principles of the present Law, in particular set forth in Articles 3-6, 43-46, 50, 51, and 54. This provision determines the character of the Law as *lex specialis* and not a parallel act in relation to the Civil Code. The Expert Commission found, however, that the application of the Civil Code and other civil laws must be subject to basic principles and general clauses of the Law. In particular, the priority of principles accepted in international trade must be secured, above all the principle of equal treatment of the parties (Article 3), the specific principle of the abuse of rights (Article 4), the principle of the autonomy of parties' will (Article 5), the clause applying commercial usages (Article 6), principles related to interpretation of contracts and filling gaps in them (Articles 43-46), the principle of the parties' co-operation (Article 50), specific principles for the performance of obligations in international trade (Article 51), and principles relating to currency problems in international trade (Article 54). Thus, basic principles and general clauses of the Law would apply also in instances when the provisions of the ordinary civil law apply to private law relationships in international trade.

In accordance with a general principle prevailing in Poland, the provisions of the Law do not apply to civil law relationships in international trade insofar as those relationships are regulated by international treaties to which Poland is a party (Article 2).

Under Article 3, the provisions of Polish civil law pertaining to private law relationships in international trade (not only provisions of the Law here discussed) are to be interpreted and applied in correspondence with the principles accepted in this trade, in particular the principle of equal treatment of parties.

The provision relating to the abuse of rights (Article 4) reads as follows: "It is forbidden to make such use of one's right that would be contrary to the principle of fair trade. Such an act or omission of the person entitled is not deemed to constitute a performance of the right and is precluded from the protection of law." The principle of fair trade is one of the most important basic principles of the Draft.

It is obvious that the Law must proclaim the principle of autonomy of the parties' will. Pursuant to Article 5, the parties are allowed to shape their relationships in international trade according to their wish, unless the law provides otherwise. It must be added that there are few exceptions from this rule, *i.e.*, imperative provisions of law, in the Draft.

Article 6 explains the meaning of usages and practice. The consequences of the parties' conduct should be determined by taking into account the practice established between them and of the usages prevailing in the respective branch of international trade. The practice and usages have priority over the provisions of the Law except for the provisions which are mandatory for the parties (Article 5). The parties' will is, however, of the first priority: the usages of international trade do not apply when something else results from the will of the parties; the same principle pertains to the previous practice of the parties (Article 6.3).[24]

Title II: Polish Juridical Persons has been introduced into the draft in order to reiterate, for the purpose of international relations, the principles of the status of Polish state enterprises as legal entities separate from the Polish State. In accordance with Article 11.1, Polish state juridical persons authorised to conduct activity in international trade are separate from the state in the economic and legal sense. Such persons are liable for their obligations with their assets (Article 11.2). The State Treasury is not liable for obligations of such persons, and such persons are not liable for obligations of the State Treasury or of other state juridical persons (Article 11.3).

The legal status of state enterprises precludes them from claiming the protection of sovereign immunity (Article 11.4).[25] As a consequence, they should be also deemed exempt from liability in the event of decisions of Polish state organs acting *iure imperii*.[26]

The above regulation of the legal status of state enterprises is in accord with previous

---

24 Jakubowski, "Rola zwyczaju handlowego w polskim handlu zagranicznym," *Ruch Prawniczy, Ekonomiczny i Socjologiczny*, no. 2 (1963), pp. 43-63.

25 Jakubowski, "Zagadnienie immunitetu przedsiebiorstw państwowych," *Studia Prawnicze*, XVII (1967), pp. 108-123.

26 Jakubowski, *Przedsiebiorstwa w handlu miedzynarodowym. Problematyka prawna* (Warsaw, 1970), pp. 60-62; *id.*, "Les enterprises d'Etat polonaises dans le commerce international," in: *Problemi giuridici dell'impresa* (Rome, 1976), p. 90ff.; Wiśniewski, *Zwolnienie od odpowiedzialności kontraktowej na podstawie ogólnych warunków RWPG* (Warsaw, 1979), pp. 80-102.

principles and practice.

Title III reads: Contracts and Other Legal Acts. I would like to draw attention only to several most characteristic provisions of the Title.

Article 31 of the Draft, founded upon the rich practice and doctrine of the twentieth century, is noteworthy. Under this provision, general conditions of contracts, model contracts, and contractual regulations invoked by one party in his offer or at the acceptance of an offer are deemed to constitute a part of the contract, provided that the other party knew or easily could have known of them and has not informed the first party immediately that he rejects them (Article 31.1). If each party would invoke a document such as described in the preceding paragraph, the document most recently sent and not rejected has the effect described. If the most recently sent document was rejected, or both parties mutually reject the documnets invoked by them, the contract is effective within the agreed provisions, unless one of the parties immediately states that he deems the contract not concluded (Article 31.3). In any event, the provisions of the contract itself have priority over the provisions of such documents (Article 31.4).

Article 32, regulating frame-contracts, an increasingly important factor in contemporary international relations, especially scientific and technical co-operation and industrial co-operation, is a pioneering provision. According to this Article, insofar as the parties are bound by an agreement concerning conditions under which future individual contracts between them are to be concluded (frame-contract), the provisions of this agreement, in the event of doubt, have priority over general conditions, model contracts, or contractual regulations pertaining to individual contracts.

When, in order to conclude a contract, the approval of a state organ is required, a contract concluded before obtaining such approval is deemed to be concluded under a condition (Article 35.1).

The party obliged to obtain the approval is expected to exert due diligence in this respect and to inform the other party about obtaining or denial of the approval. In the event of doubt, the duty to obtain an approval falls upon the party having a place of business in the country in question, and when an approval of an organ of a third state is required, the party with whose obligations the duty to obtain approval is connected (Article 35.1). If an approval has not been granted within a year from the date of the conclusion of contract, either party is allowed to void the contract (Article 35.3).

Pursuant to Article 43.1, the consequences of a contract are to be read from the common intention of the parties and from the purpose of the contract rather than from the literal wording thereof. An interpretation of declarations should take into account the circumstances under which the declarations were made, subsequent conduct of the parties, the practice established between them, and usages prevailing in the respective branch of international trade (Article 43.2).

The parties may entrust a third party with completion of the contract in respect of particular clauses thereof (Article 44.1). A state court or an arbitration court may undertake such completion of a contract, change the conditions thereof, or rescind it only when this follows from the parties' will or from a provision of the present Law (Article 46). Thus, the Draft regulates the problem of filling gaps in international commercial contracts, so widely discussed today in the world's legal literature.

The provisions of Articles 47-49 are pioneering not only in Poland, regulating some problems following from contracts concluded for time unlimited or for a long period of time (long-term contracts).

Title IV of the General Part deals with performance and the consequences of non-performance of obligations. Some provisions of this Title ar discussed below.

Parties are obliged to co-operate during the performance of the contract to the extent required by the object and purpose of the contract (Article 50). The debtor should perform the obligation in accordance with the content thereof and with usages prevailing in the respective branch of international trade, being obliged to observe the diligence required in international trade for obligations of this kind (Article 51.1). In the same way, the creditor is required to co-operate in performance (Article 51.2). Both parties are expected to take steps in order to prevent damage that might follow from non-performance or improper performance or to mitigate such damage (Article 51.3).

As an exception from the principle of nominalism generally adopted in the Draft, valuation clauses are admissible (Article 54).

The provisions of Article 76 pertain to problems of great importance in the practice of international trade, the obtaining by parties of government licences required for the performance of contracts. Article 77 deals with repartition of taxes and similar charges.

The consequences of non-performance are dealt with in Articles 88-109. Only some provisions can be discussed here. The principle is that the debtor is not liable if non-performance or improper performance of his obligation has been caused by events which he could not, acting diligently, fore-e at the conclusion of contract and the conse-nces of which he could not prevent nor avoid ·icle 90). Besides the question of impossibi- of performance, in Article 107 the problem of ıfluence of changed circumstances upon obli-s has been resolved (hardship).

e problems of prescription (limitation of are dealt with in Title V of the General he Code. Naturally, the suspension of a on period is taken into account only ebtor's motion. Following the 1974 New tion relating to prescription of claims resulting from the international sale of goods,[27] the problem of the beginning of the prescription period in the case of ad hoc arbitration has been decided.

The Special Part is structured as follows:

Title I.	Sale
Title II.	Assembly
Title III.	Erection of Plants
Title IV.	Leasing
Title V.	Licensing Contracts
Title VI.	Know-how
Title VII.	Commission Agency
Title VIII.	Agency
Title IX.	Storage
Title X.	Inspection of Goods
Title XI.	Contract of Guarantee
Title XII.	Letter of Credit
Title XIII.	Co-operation
Title XIV.	Partnership
Title XV.	Company

The Draft provides for two types of association: partnership and company. Partnership constitutes an intermediary variation between a civil partnership and a company; this form is provided for partnerships with at least one partner having his place of business or domicile abroad. The regulation of companies became necessary because of the most decidedly inadequate regulation of this question by the resolution of the Council of Ministers, No. 24, of 7 February 1979, concerning the creation and activities in Poland of enter-

---

27 Jakubowski, "Konwencja ONZ dotyczaca przedawnienia roszczeń z miedzynarodowej sprzedazy towarów," *Państwo i prawo*, no. 1 (1975), pp. 17-29.

prises with participation of foreign capital.[28] Companies situated in Poland with at least one partner having his place of business or domicile abroad closely resemble in their legal structure a company with limited liability (German: Gesellschaft mit beschränkter Haftung; French: société à responsabilité limitée). Under Article 404.1 of the Draft, it remains possible to found mixed companies also in the forms prescribed in the 1934 Commercial Code.

---

28 A. Burzyński, "Bezposrednia działalnosć gospodarcza w Polsce zagranicznych esób prawnych i fizycznych," *Przeglad ustawodawstwa gospodarczego*, no. 6 (1979), pp. 153-160; no. 7, pp. 196-204.

COMMON ECONOMIC ENTITIES OF COMECON MEMBER COUNTRIES

E. Piontek

In general, integration may be defined as a process by which separate systems develop a common framework which allows for the common pursuit of certain goals and the common implementation of certain policies.

This paper dwells on some institutional legal aspects of socialist economic integration, namely on the common economic entities of the COMECON member countries. The very emergence of these entities, the pattern of their development, and their functions are deeply rooted in the conceptual model of integration accepted within COMECON. In a way they embody an essence of what should be the true work-shop of socialist integration, for integration is to be furthered mainly through the co-ordination of national economic plans, common sectoral planning, production specialisation, as well as through the development of common research programmes whose results are to be employed to the benefit of all COMECON member countries. These activities are considered to be the heart of the socialist integration process, whereas trade as such, for all its importance, plays a secondary role. These factors determine, at least potentially, the leading position of the common economic entities in the process of socialist integration.

Four types of common economic entities of COMECON member countries may be identified. They are:

- international economic organisations (IEO) [международная экономическая организация]
- transnational economic associations (TEA) [международное хозяйственное обьединение]
- transnational joint enterprises (TJE) [международное совместное предприятие], and

- transnational economic societies (TES) [международное хозяйственное товарищество].

International economic organisations are within the realm of public international law and may reasonably be regarded as having a limited legal personality under this law, whereas the remaining entities, under the common name of transnational economic organisations, should properly be classified as operating on the basis of municipal or "private law." Two of them, but not the last, possess legal personality under municipal law.

The 1971 Comprehensive Programme for the Intensification and Improvement of Co-operation and the Development of Socialist Integration of COMECON Member Countries listed two main types of such organisations, namely: international economic organisations and transnational economic organisations.[1] It provided for the possibility of establishing transnational enterprises which were not to be subordinate to any specific type of transnational organisation. On the other hand, the so-called "Model Provisions on the Conditions for Founding and for the Activity of Transnational Economic Organisations" introduce names for types of transnational economic organisations. These are: transnational economic associations, transnational economic societies, and transnational joint enterprises. International economic organisations have been excluded from the classification comprising transnational economic organisations, whereas, on the other hand, the transnational joint enterprises have been included and a new form of organisation, the transnational economic society, has appeared. These are the transnational economic units which presently constitute the prevailing type of the transnational economic organisations.

---

1 See Sect. 8, §3, pt. 3.1 and 3.2, 1971 Comprehensive Programme, transl. in W.E. Butler, *A Source Book on Socialist International Organizations* (Alphen aan den Rijn, 1978), pp. 77-80.

International Economic Organisations

International economic organisations are established on the basis of inter-governmental agreements. The states which are the members of such organisations may be represented by specific ministries, state committees, central offices, associations, and so on. The activity of international economic organisations is financed from common funds contributed by the member countries.

The inner structure of international economic organisations and the procedure for taking decisions are adapted to the types of tasks these organisations are to perform. Managing boards of international economic organisations exist on two levels. They consist of representative steering organs and executive bodies of an administrative character. The former have the power to decide upon the programme of action which ought to be performed, and decisions in this respect are taken by unanimous vote. Nevertheless, each member country may declare its non-interest in a particular issue, which does not prevent the other countries from adopting and implementing a recommendation. The recommendations have no binding force for the countries which declared no interest in them. Any such country may however, on certain agreed conditions, be able to join at any moment during the realisation of a recommendation. The aforesaid principles of adopting recommendations in the Comprehensive Programme do not prevent the members of international economic organisations from using different procedures.

In the framework of COMECON we may distinguish permanent and temporary forms of organisations set up to co-ordinate inter-governmental economic problems regarded as the objectives of international co-operation in the process of integration of socialist countries. International economic organisations are specific forms of completing the previously mentioned framework. Their tasks consist of co-ordinating and organising co-operation in more narrow and explicitly defined fields, such as a line of trade, branch, product, or a specific problem, such as the standardisation of norms for a certain product, or quality certification. The establishment of an international economic organisation may be connected with the existence of problems which, on one hand, require long-range activities, such as the co-ordination of investments, and on the other hand, which concern short-range activities, such as the standardisation of norms for a certain product, utilisation of temporary over-stocks of certain products, or of seasonal unused productive capacities of economic enterprises.

Generally speaking, we may characterise the functions of the international economic organisations as:

- co-ordinative;
- organising;
- informative;
- and in some instances, the performance of scientific research.

For some time, proposals to expand the functions of international economic organisations and to change the rules for fulfilling their tasks have been put forward. Thus, a transition from a budgetary to a self-sustaining economic system for international economic organisations is being proposed, and that they engage in direct production activity and create common international property of the means of production. Developments in this direction are proposed in particular for the Common Freight Car Pool.

Improvement of the Common Freight Car Pool would consist, first, of a change from budget financing to a self-sustaining economic system (that is, economic accountability). Later, when funds had accumulated, the organisation would create a pool of trucks based on the principle of common international property. The organisation also would have the possibility of implementing a homogeneous line of technological and utilisation policy and of creating its own repair shops.[2]

Such proposals could be brought into effect in two ways:

- existing international economic organisations might be dissolved and a new appropriate international organisation established; or

- an already existing organisation would be functionally transformed to fulfill the new tasks.

However, in practice there exist hybrid entities such as "Interkhim." Its mixed character arose from its original constitutive act. Thus direct authorisation for the performance of trade functions (Article 5(11), Agreement) is included in the range of activities allowed to this organisation. The Charter of "Interkhim" foresees the gradual transition of this organisation from a budgetary into a self-sustaining economic system (economic accountability) as does Article 12(3).[3]

Originally, and until the mid-1960s, there were very few organised contacts between an IEO and COMECON. Moreover, the establishment of institutional links between an existing IEO and the Council was considered to be of a voluntary nature, and actually was very loose. Important changes in this respect began only a decade ago. However, thereafter the institutional co-ordination of IEO activities with COMECON has evolved into quite an impressive system. Generally speaking, it is based upon special agreements concluded by each IEO with COMECON. It should be noted, however, that besides these agreements, some organs of the Council or even its subsidiary bodies conclude agreements of their own with an IEO. Agreements between the Institute for Economic Problems of the World Socialist System (IEPWSS) and the International Bank for Economic Co-operation (IBEC) or with the International Investment Bank (IIB) illustrate the practice.

---

2 See *Problemy sotsialisticheskoi ekonomicheskoi integratsii* (M., 1974), pp. 283-290.

3 Butler, note 1 above, pp. 411, 414.

The main emphasis in these agreements is on co-ordinating the activities of the respective organisations and on the mutual exchange of information between them. In most cases, such agreements provide for working collaboration of the parties in elaborating particular programmes and in their implementation. Usually the right to participate on an advisory basis in matters of mutual interest, and to submit in this regard proposals by the representatives of the parties to the agreement at the meetings or sessions of the other co-operating organisation organs, is also secured.

On the other hand, the parties used to be obliged to exchange protocols of the respective meetings and, on the basis of mutual understanding, to publish certain materials periodically.

The principle of maintaining continuous contacts between co-operating organisations has been generally accepted as well. On behalf of COMECON it is, first, one of the substantive "permanent commissions" of the Council and the Council's Secretariat itself which are competent to maintain the liaison or working contacts, and on the other side, the main or executive and administrative organs of the IEO in question.[4]

For some time, however, there was no specific clause in the agreements which would preserve a leading position, or an upper hand, for COMECON. Nonetheless, the Council actually has always enjoyed such a position within the system. It resulted from some objective facts. In the absence of horizontal links between the IEOs themselves, it was COMECON which, through the whole network of its vertical system of institutionalised contacts with IEOs, placed itself in the centre of the system. On the other hand, this dominant position of the Council resulted from the range of matters covered by its powers, of which every IEO

---

4 See Comprehensive Programme, Sect. 16, the Charter of COMECON, and provisions of the constitutive acts of most IEOs, as well as their Agreements with COMECON.

possesses only some. Hence, COMECON is the organisation that is tracing out the general patterns and directions of economic integration for its member countries, being their only members in most IEOs, and in others, constituting their majority. In effect, these organisations have always been, so to say, "condemned" to follow Council actions.

The dominant legal position of the Council in its relations with an IEO was formally sanctioned at the XXV Session of COMECON under the terms provided in the Comprehensive Programme. The Comprehensive Programme imposed upon member states of the Council an obligation to further the co-ordination of activities undertaken under the auspices of COMECON in general, and within the framework of their mutual economic entities in particular. To this end, a leading role and the dominant legal position of the Council should be preserved in constitutive documents of both existing and newly created IEOs, directly or through proper reference to the respective provisions of the Comprehensive Programme. This, with few exceptions, notably those of the IBEC and IIB, because of the specific character of their functions, includes an obligation to follow recommendations adopted by the Council.[5] At the same time, IEOs received the status of specialised institutions of COMECON, not so very different from the legal position of the United Nations specialised agencies.[6] So far,

---

5 Comprehensive Programme, Sect. VIII, pt. 1.1, 1.3 and the provisions of respective agreements, protocols, and other resolutions concluded between IEOs and COMECON. As far as the special position of international financial organisations is concerned, see the Preambles of the agreements of IIB and IBEC.

6 It should be noted that there was a discussion regarding the conception of "specialised organisations" of COMECON, as this notion is only used and not clarified by the Comprehensive Programme. Some authors are of the opinion that it should be understood as a definition of socialist countries' organisations having not universal but limited competence with regard to the given economic or technical area, which means the

however, unlike the United Nations or the Organisation of American States, COMECON has not worked out a linear or horizontal co-ordination of activities among IEOs themselves.[7] It would seem to be practical and useful to create such a system of co-ordination in the future. When this will transpire remains, however, to be seen.

Apart from what was said above about the co-ordination machinery of the IEOs and the Council, it should be noted that so far as transnational economic organisations, or at least transnational associations are concerned, co-ordination processes with COMECON and its organs are well advanced and intense. One, however, may wonder how this could happen with very few formal agreements to

---

organisations having specialised competences. Taking into consideration the membership of the organisations there, according to this view, specialised organisations of COMECON member countries and of socialist countries in general or socialist and other countries could be identified. See A.B. Altshuler, *Sotrudnichestvo sotsialisticheskih gosudarstv* (M., 1973), p. 90.

According to the other views, it is not the scope of competences of these organisations, but rather the nature of their specific relationship with COMECON which are the essence of the definition. Thus, the definition of the specialised organisations of COMECON is not technical, but juridical in character. See P.A. Tokareva, "Pravovoi status spetsializirovannykh organizatsii SEV," *Sovetskoe gosudarstvo i pravo*, no. 8 (1973), p. 128. The author of this paper shares the latter interpretation. It may be worth mentioning that such an interpretation has also been accepted within the United Nations system in regard to its specialised agencies.

7 In most cases, however, it would not be a very difficult task to establish such co-ordination since the constitutive acts of the majority of IEOs provide for the maintenance of relations with other international organisations.

this end.[8]

One explanation may be that, in principle, they all were established as a result of direct COMECON initiatives, are to implement selected economic or scientific programmes, and in one way or another are supervised by the Council. It should also be mentioned that the charters of transnational economic entities authorise them to enter into co-operation and other respective agreements between themselves.

Transnational Economic Associations

Transnational economic associations constitute one of the forms of co-operation among members of COMECON. The Comprehensive Programme emphasises their role in creating direct links among economic entities of COMECON member countries. The establishment of direct economic and organisational relations among economic units and enterprises of member countries has in view the further development of specialisation and co-operation in production, as well as intensification of the flow of information on inventions and technology. The Comprehensive Programme points out that "the contract is the most feasible form for formalising the mutual obligations of parties implementing direct ties," and further it says that "contracts are concluded within the framework of those rights and powers which the parties have

---

8 There would be a basis for this created on the one hand by the Comprehensive Programme and, on the other, by the agreements setting up these organisations. It is difficult to say whether such a system has been set-up by the terms of the agreements concluded between the respective COMECON organs and TEOs. The practice up to the present allows one to suggest that such a system with regard to TEOs will be created on the basis of the agreements concluded between the respective organs of COMECON (or with COMECON as a whole) and the foregoing organisations. Some agreements have already been concluded.

in accordance with the system of management of the national economy in a particular country, as well as on the basis of individual special decisions within the country."[9]

The Programme also states that transnational economic organisations are to be established in order to develop real co-ordinating activity in co-operation and mutual economic activity in defined fields. The "Model Provisions" for the founding and activity of transnational economic organisations and their general functions concerning all types of such organisations are defined in a similar way. These are: "... co-ordinating the activities of their participants relating to collaboration, conducting their own economic activity, and effectuating joint economic activity by participants."[10] As far as economic units are concerned, the Comprehensive Programme reads as follows: "... [they fulfil the functions of] co-ordinating activity on collaboration and co-operation and for joint economic activity in scientific research and design work, in production, in the realm of services, and in foreign trade ..."[11]

The common feature of international economic organisations and transnational economic organisations consists in their role as the institutionalised forms of planned integration processes within an overall scheme of socialist integration. The object of the activity comprising the economic, scientific, and technical relations is also common to both types of organisation.

The Comprehensive Programme mentions the following types of transnational economic organisations as the examples: transnational economic associations, institutes, centres, joint enter-

---

9 See Comprehensive Programme, Butler, note 1 above, p. 77.

10 See "Model Provisions" (1976 edition), Sect. 1, para. 2, pt. 1.

11 See Comprehensive Programme, Sect. 8, para. 3.2, 3.3, note 1 above.

prises, trade or design-agencies, and so on.

The above characteristics of transnational economic organisation refer, first, to transnational economic associations. If the IEOs are generally established on the basis of the inter-governmental agreements, the TEAs are, in principle, established by subjects of municipal law of the member countries.

M. Lachs-Knothe and W. Morawiecki rightly point out, however, that "... as practice shows, there is not always direct dependence, close connection, and accord between the type of constitutive act and the character of the organisation (which has been created by it). It also happens that the parties to the agreement are not the members of the organisation."[12] Such organisations as: The Common Freight Car Pool, "Intermetall," and the International Bank for Economic Co-operation were established on the basis of international agreements, and thus they are international economic organisations (IEO). On the other hand, "Interatominstrument" was established on the basis of an inter-governmental agreement and thus is a transnational economic organisation and a subject of municipal law in the respective member countries. It must be pointed out that certain differences between transnational economic organisations and international economic organisations refer not so much to their functions as to ways of fulfilling them. The former complete the organisational structure of COMECON, fulfilling primarily co-ordinating functions, whereas the latter unify the co-ordinating functions with the organisation and the carrying out of joint economic activity. The range of tasks marks the ways of bringing them into effect.[13]

---

12 M. Lachs-Knothe and W. Morawiecki, "Organizacje Wyspecjalizowane Krajów RWPG w Dziedzinie Przemysłu (Wybrane Zagadnienia Prawno-Ekonomiczne)," *Państwo i prawo,* no. 1 (1974), p. 58.

13 Appendix 9 to the Protocol of the 53d Meeting of the Executive Committee. Moscow, June 1971, pp. 2-3.

The co-ordinating functions of international economic organisations embrace, first, the existing productive potential. This form of co-ordination may be defined as passive, for the object or the field of co-ordination already exists. On the other hand, the sort of co-ordination performed by transnational economic organisations may be defined as active. The active co-operation carried out through organising and performing joint economic activity allows the creation of new productive powers and on this basis an intended division of labour and specialisation of production.

The partners of transnational economic organisations which comprise legal subjects of COMECON member countries enter into direct intercourse on the basis of the agreement. The relation between the partners of the organisation is based on an economic interest, which is linked with economic profits or gains, as well as with the risk of loss for which they are entirely responsible. This way of regulating the relations between the partners of the organisation strengthens the principle of economic efficiency and stimulates the formation of them according to economic criteria while committing the partners to certain obligations and to undertaking joint economic activities. A specific characteristic of a TEA is that the range of co-operation undertaken by these entities may include all production processes such as: research, design, production, and sales. It creates the possibility of concentrating production on the basis of concerted resources and other means. This in turn enables the use of the most recent achievements of technology which are in the possession of the member countries or the joint purchase of advanced foreign licences and the improvement of production organisation. The optimum should be set not according to the country's internal production conditions but according to international standards. Production for the needs of markets of certain countries rather than for any single market is preferred on the principle that mass production produces greater economic profits.

Of course, if the transnational economic

organisations are to fulfil their creative role effectively, they have, on one hand, to possess a certain independence and, on the other, to have proper relations with the countries in which their economic units and enterprises operate. The autonomy of the TEA may to a great extent be derived from the scope of autonomy which economic units and enterprises enjoy in their own countries. It is one more evidence of mutual interdependence and assimilation between the system of management and administration of the national economy in the respective countries and the system of multilateral co-operation in the process of socialist integration.

As a consequence of recent economic reforms, economic units and enterprises enjoy a wider scope of independence in foreign trade, in international co-operation, and in specialisation of production. Their active role in working out their own medium and long-term plans for production development is emphasised. In such conditions, the contract is a convenient and adequate way for partners to enter into economic intercourse and, at the same time, it serves the purpose of stabilisation and long-term development of the organisation itself. A TEA might function in this way when its activities result from the general plans of co-ordination of social and economic development agreed within COMECON at an inter-governmental level, and from the integration activities envisaged in national economic plans of the respective countries.

The problem of independence also embraces the inner structure and management methods of the economic units. In principle, this structure is two-tiered and consists of managing and executive organs. The essential decisions are taken by the former, which consists of the plenipotentiaries of the member countries. Thus, as in general within COMECON, in these organs the decisions are taken unanimously. On the other hand, in the executive committees which are set up to secure effective and competent implementation of the operational activity of the organisation, the majority principle is accepted. Transnational economic associations are formed on the basis of existing technical, productive, economic, and organisational links, and their participants retain property ownership, organisational, and legal independence.

Transnational Joint Enterprises

Transnational joint enterprises are included in the category of transnational economic organisations. We have to consider certain issues arising out of this classification, the topic being somewhat controversial. Doctrine does not accept homogeneous classification criteria and, moreover, several authors express them in vague terms. It is stated, for example, that two types of transnational economic organisation are distinguished in the Comprehensive Programme. These are: transnational economic associations and transnational enterprises. But the text of the Comprehensive Programme does not confirm this view, apart from a mere mention of the transnational enterprises in a separate passage of the chapter relating to transnational organisations in COMECON. A similar view is expressed in a report on the investigation of the legal and organisational aspects of transnational organisations. The document says that: "... on the basis of basic functions carried out and on the principal objects of activities, two types of transnational economic organisations can be distinguished. They are: transnational economic associations, hereinafter just associations, and transnational enterprises." Production, transport, science, technology, and so on may be either the objects of activity of TEA or TJE.

Although each object of activity has some specific characteristic, such as technological, it nevertheless would influence in a similar way both the transnational economic associations and transnational joint enterprises. Thus, it cannot serve as an adequate classification criterion and does not allow us to include a certain economic entity on the above basis within one type of organisation or the other. There is also another view. It says that: "Transnational joint enterprises do not have the character of transnational organisations. These are rather national enterprises brought into existence on the basis of relevant agreements between foreign partners for production activity in a country of their choice."[14] This reasoning points at least to the importance of the specific way of creation, and of carrying out activities, the character of property relationships, as well as internal structure and ways of management of TJE as crucial factors which deserve careful examination in any attempt to classify and define what transnational joint enterprises really are.

The Comprehensive Programme provides for the possibility of the establishment of transnational joint enterprises by the transnational economic organisations of the countries which declare an interest. The rules and regulations of transnational economic associations provide for the creating of their branches on the territories of COMECON member countries. Such branches have been created by "Interatominstrument" in a few countries. Because of the establishment of a Technical Service Work-Shop as a branch, new rules for the organisation of this enterprise have been formulated.[15] The Model Provisions for the founding of transnational economic organisations worked out pursuant to the Comprehensive Programme meet the demands of practice in a section devoted to the establishment of branches of transnational economic associations. It is assumed that their own economic activity may be realised through the activities of the transnational enterprises acting

---

14 See *Problemy sozdaniia i funktsionirovaniia mezhdunarodnykh ekonomicheskikh i khoziaistvennykh organizatsii* (Prague, 1974), p. 61.

15 See the *Polozhenie o predpriiatii po tekhnicheskomu obsluzhivaniiu mezhdunarodnogo khoziaistvennogo ob"edineniia po iadernomu priborostroeniiu "Interatominstrument," v dalneishem "predpriiatii," s mestonakhozhdeniem v zelenei gori* (Warsaw, 1975). Also see note 10 above, para. 55, second sentence, in connection with paras. 40 and 41.

within the limits set by the transnational associations. The Model Provisions open to transnational associations and joint enterprises the possibility of establishing their own branches on the basis of their own assets and economic activity. They may or may not possess legal personality. The branches of transnational associations and joint enterprises, after having obtained the consent of the respective organs of the country of their seat, carry out their economic activity according to the laws passed by the headquarters country.

The problem of transnational joint enterprises was discussed for the first time in the 1971 Comprehensive Programme. It reads that: "... In the course of realising the Comprehensive Programme, it may become advisable to form [transnational joint enterprises] ... that have their own property, that are subjects of civil law, that operate on the basis of economic accountability, and that are fully answerable with their property for their obligations assumed."

Transnational joint enterprises may be created by the respective countries, their organs, or the transnational economic organisations of COMECON member countries which have declared an interest. The above view expressed in the Comprehensive Programme arises from the fact that the legal systems of the majority of COMECON member countries do not provide uniform ways for organising transnational joint enterprises. A treaty or any other sort of inter-governmental agreement comprises a constitutive act which refers to the specific initiative of creating a certain transnational joint enterprise. It is already a long time since economic circles within COMECON started to express the view that there was both the necessity and the possibility of working out model legal rules for all member countries in order to solve that problem. The idea of establishing transnational joint enterprises is connected with the fact that the Comprehensive Programme particularly emphasised the need to develop direct economic relationships, bilateral and multilateral, between economic entities of COMECON member countries on the plane of their horizontal links.

A characteristic of the legal status of the transnational joint enterprise consists in the fact that they are the subjects of civil law. Legalisation of a transnational enterprise may be carried out only in the headquarters country and in accordance with the legal procedure in force in that country.[16]

In economic writings, the notion of transnational joint enterprise is defined either from the standpoint of economic theory or from the more interesting standpoint of international integration. In the first instance, the formulated definitions would be the general ones expressing certain essential features of transnational joint enterprises or broad ones expressing many characteristic features. In the second case, the definitions refer to the specific function of transnational joint enterprises in co-operation among COMECON member countries.

Thus, T. Kiss is interested in common economic entities seen in the light of bi- and multilateral investments carried out in the socialist community. The author treats the common economic entities as one of the forms of this type of undertaking in the field of investment. He gives the following characterisation of a transnational enterprise: "The property rights in a transnational enterprise are divided among the investing countries or the enterprises. Transnational enterprises in principle act according to the jurisdiction of the country they are in. The division of profit and loss, as well as the suitable forms of delivery of goods or the exchange of currency, are carried out according to the laws of the country the enterprise acts in."[17]

---

16 See Note 10 above, para. 9; compare J. Jakubowski, *Miedzynarodowe Organizacje Gospodarcze Krajów RWPG - Zagadnienia Prawne* (Warsaw, 1980), pp. 141-169.

17 T. Kiss, *Problemy sotsialisticheskoi integratsii stran* (M., 1971), p. 81.

Z. Ario, on the basis of an economic analysis of the categories of property relationships existing in a transnational enterprise, gives a sort of general definition of the TJE. He says that: "Transnational enterprises are in fact nothing more than the specific form of international, socialist relations in a sphere of production, which distinguishes them to a great extent from international economic organisations."[18]

According to J. Jakubowski, "We may take for transnational enterprises such types of enterprise in which the capital, the managing staff, or both come from at least two different countries."[19] Thus, by transnational joint enterprises of socialist countries, we understand a form of international economic co-operation wherein the transnational economic organisations belonging to different countries jointly create economically and legally independent complexes in the field of production, trade, and transport, scientific research, services, and so on, or jointly produce or plan their activity and run the whole enterprise.[20] The above definition comprises three basic elements which typify the transnational enterprises:

(1) TJE constitute a form of international economic co-operation;

(2) they are economically and legally independent;

(3) they cover a wide range of fields where they can develop their economic activity.

The treatment of the transnational enterprises as forms of co-operation in production (with joint investment undertakings as one of the forms of their activity) is reasonably justified, but it ought to be considered a means linked with their

---

18 See note 14 above, p. 86.

19 Jakubowski, "Przedsiebiorstwa miedzynarodowe. Pojecie i klasyfikacja," *Państwo i prawo*, no. 7 (1968), p. 115.

20 See the definition by E. Fraudie, note 14 above, pp. 93-94.

economic activity rather than an objective.

The problem is not one of looking for a universal definition. We are interested rather in transnational enterprises as economic entities having specific production conditions because this is dispositive of its nature. All other features are derivative. In this approach to the TJE, the elements expressing the heart of the matter are the economic relationships in the enterprise and the objective economic rules defining the functioning of recently integrated complexes.

Thus we would regard the transnational joint enterprises as an economic body, formed on the basis of collective (in the international sense) ownership of the means of production (in order to achieve their most efficient employment) and whose functioning is subordinated to the legal and economic system of the country they have their seat in.

The property relationships in transnational enterprises are another issue under discussion. Pursuant to the Model Provisions (especially Article 30), transnational economic associations and transnational enterprises have the right to possess, use, and dispose of their property. The problem of interpreting the notion of "the property of transnational enterprises" has evoked a lot of doctrinal controversies.[21] We dwell on the interpretation which seems to be, in my view, the most cogent one. Thus, Jakubowski rightly says that "the establishment of transnational enterprises as corporate bodies has its equivalent in the sphere of patrimony, because they are endowed with rights which suffice for regarding them as the owners of

---

21 Compare H. Spiller, "Rechtsprobleme Gemeinsamer Betriebe Sozialistischer Staaten," *Recht im Aussenhandel*, no. 7 (1963), pp. 4-8; L. Rüster, *Das system rechtlicher regelung der sozialistischer ökonomischer integration. Grundriss* (Berlin, 1976), pp. 3, 117; V.M. Senin, note 14 above, pp. 162-170; S. Szer, "Wspólne przedsiebiorstwa państw członkowskich RWPG," *Studia Prawnicze*, no. 9 (1965), pp. 216 and seq.

their estate."[22] A similar interpretation has been advanced by Professor A. Wasilkowski of the Polish Academy of Sciences. He supports the idea of so-called "trusteeship." Wasilkowski proves that "such a solution would be extremely useful in the process of internationalising property."[23] The trustee is responsible for his actions to those who entrusted him, but in the relationships with other subjects he acts as a rightful owner. Such a solution would fully suit the requirements discussed above: the international economic entity as a trustee would not be a formal owner, and the demands of economic exchange. Also other detailed features of this economic organism should be considered from the point of view of these two elements of the definition; that is:

(1) the ways of joining the shares or contributions into the single common property of a transnational enterprise; and

(2) as far as its inner relationships are concerned, from the point of view of independence and self-sufficiency in the participation of the benefits, and so on.

Similar consequences in respect of external relationships arise out of the fact that transnational enterprises are constituents of the entire national economic complex of the host countries they have their seats in. That very fact will also determine how the activity of an economic society would be included in the national plan for socio-economic development, foreign trade, and so on.

The objectives of transnational enterprises are defined in their constitutive acts and result from the goals of economic policy of the countries

---

22 Note 16 above, p. 199.

23 A. Wasilkowski, "Problemy internacjonalizacji własności w obrebie RWPG," *Państwo i prawo,* no. 12 (1969), p. 979.

which established them, which in turn are included in the socio-economic plans of these countries. The plans and their co-ordination are the principal sources inspiring integration undertakings, which include the detailed tasks of the particular enterprises. Regulatory mechanisms for the functioning of a transnational enterprise (such as its financial-economic system or indicators of its activity) are derived from economic policy, which shapes them, particularly in the country where the enterprise has a seat. Thus defining the detailed tasks or mechanisms which make possible the existence of an enterprise does not seem necessary in a general definition. Only the question of the place assumed by a transnational enterprise in the national economy of the COMECON member countries is worth considering. The Comprehensive Programme gives only one general indication: "... all the other issues connected with their establishment and activity [of transnational enterprises] shall be regulated by the interested parties."

The actions undertaken by the countries which create the transnational enterprises are objectively determined by the following factors:

(1) the stage of development of their productive forces;

(2) the level of maturity of production relations in these countries and characteristics of their legal systems.

Theoretically speaking, different solutions determining the ways in which transnational enterprises function in a socialist system are possible. Three of them are specially worth considering. They are as follows:

(1) a transnational enterprise has the character of a "limited enclave," which means that it is managed directly by the plenipotentiaries of the promoting countries. Its activity is only indirectly linked with the economy of the country it

has its seat in;

(2) a transnational enterprise has the character of a "full enclave," which means that its activity consists in the fact that all the relationships with the outside are regulated in terms of foreign trade, including the country it has its seat in;

(3) a transnational enterprise develops activity to satisfy common and national interests of the promoting countries and is a constituent of the national economy at the country it has its seat in.

At the core of the first two concepts of transnational enterprise lies the idea of the supranational character of transnational enterprises. They differ only in the degree of isolation from the national economy of the country they have their seat in. But neither the idea of the "limited enclave" nor the "full enclave" finds justification in the political and economic relationships prevailing presently in COMECON member countries.

During the process of economic integration of COMECON member countries, the principle of showing respect for national forms of ownership and of their preservation is observed. It also appertains to transnational economic organisations, including the transnational economic societies. The former include national economic entities. They play the role of "joint management" in the broad sense of the word. Management so understood may consist of the co-ordinating function exercised in respect of the national economic entities which belong to the given organisation or in the management of their own enterprises, which denotes the action of management in the strict sense of the word.

As far as transnational enterprises are concerned, we have to deal not only with joint management in international economic organisations, but also in the transnational economic units because the transnational enterprises have their own property.

The property of the transnational enterprise originates from the contributions of funds, or of other assets, and later on from results of the productive activity of the enterprise. The property of the respective members of the enterprise does not lose its particular national features, but unites them in a specific way. The method used to create this property and the principle of proportional division of profits induces us to call it "international socialist collective property."

The transnational enterprise operates on the basis of economic accountability and is entirely responsible for its obligations. Thus in a great many respects it has a similar status to any state enterprise in the country it has its seat in. The expenses for current production and reinvestment are covered from the floating capital of the transnational enterprise and its development fund. Different local levies, such as municipal taxes and other similar burdens, are paid in the locally accepted way. The basic difference in the status of a transnational enterprise and a state enterprise lies in the mode of creating and distributing the net income. Transnational enterprises do not give priority in their activity to the principle of obtaining the maximum possible profit, but to the principle of satisfying the needs of member countries for a given product. Thus, net income is frequently allocated to development funds which are to increase in future the production of the enterprise.

If the production of a transnational enterprise is to be received by the countries which are its co-owners (as it is up to now), the benefits of the countries need not be expressed in their share of the net income. They might be expressed by a means of different proportions of social outlays or in differences in prices in the respective countries. The differences in approach to the problem of the size of profits and to their division might appear particularly between the country the transnational enterprise has its seat in and its other co-members.

It happens thus because the transnational enterprise, in accordance with the general principles of its organisation and functioning, is a part of the economic system of the country it performs its activity in. It goes without saying that each of these countries would tend to increase the economic potential, the stability of the labour conditions of a transnational enterprise, and to secure favourable prospects for the future activity of the enterprise.

If the production of goods in order to satisfy the needs of the member countries appears to be the basic aim of a transnational enterprise, its financial-economic system should serve the efficiency of reproduction processes and the fulfillment of production plans of the enterprise. On the other hand, if we assume that the export of goods to third countries and in particular to non-members constitutes the basic aim of a transnational enterprise, then the financial outcomes of its activity shall play the leading role. In either of the above instances, the financial-economic system of a transnational enterprise should be adapted and even subordinated to the objectives of the enterprise's activity. Thus, a clear definition of the objectives of the transnational enterprise's activity is the most important matter.

Transnational Economic Societies

Here we have a new organisational form invented to co-ordinate economic activity. For the first time it was explicitly defined in "The Model Provisions on the Founding and the Activity of International Economic Organisations." They provide for the co-ordinating functions of such societies in co-operation between its members or, on the other hand, they allow for joint economic activity to be carried out by transnational economic societies. It should be emphasised that the word "joint" was not used in this sense at random, but that it distinguishes the type of activity of the TES from the activity of any other organisation. Transnational economic societies are to operate on the basis of joint control exercised by members, one of them managing current affairs on behalf of the others. They are not a legal corporate body. Societies may be endowed with property necessary for their activity on the basis of "general joint-stock property" or "the right of disposition."

From the definition of the functions of transnational economic societies and from the ways of fulfilling them arises the conclusion that TES should be regarded as more loose than any other (TEA or IEO) form of institutionalised co-operation within the framework of COMECON. Apart from it, there is also a difference between the transnational economic societies and the other economic organisations, for the TES are to fulfil definite purposes and thus their existence is only temporary.

INDEX